Cultural Critique

100

Summer 2018

Special Issue: Pornocracy

Guest Editors: Karyn Ball and Stefan Mattessich

EDITORIAL STATEMENT

Cultural Critique provides a forum for creative and provocative scholarship in the theoretical humanities and humanistic social sciences. Transnational in scope and transdisciplinary in orientation, the journal strives to spark and galvanize intellectual debates as well as to attract and foster critical investigations regarding any aspect of culture as it expresses itself in words, images, and sounds, across both time and space. The journal is especially keen to support scholarship that engages the ways in which cultural production, cultural practices, and cultural forms constitute and manifest the nexus between the aesthetic, the psychic, the economic, the political, and the ethical intended in their widest senses. While informed by the diverse traditions of historical materialism as well as by the numerous critiques of such traditions from various parts of the globe, the journal welcomes contributions based on a variety of theoretical-methodological paradigms.

Cultural Critique appears four times a year. General issues, including essays, book reviews, and thematic sections, as well as entire issues devoted to special topics, are regularly published. The editors welcome the submission of freestanding essays, special issue proposals on topics of interest to the journal, and reviews of relevant, new, and not-so-new books.

Cultural Critique Books is the companion series of the journal. It seeks to attract work by those scholars across the humanities and social sciences who continue to draw inspiration from, and seek to contribute to, the theoretical movements and debates so long nurtured at Minnesota. Book proposals should be addressed to one of the three editors at: *Cultural Critique,* Department of Cultural Studies and Comparative Literature, 235 Nicholson Hall, 216 Pillsbury Drive S.E., University of Minnesota, Minneapolis, MN 55455-0229, U.S.A., or via email to cultcrit@umn.edu.

PLEASURE FOR PLEASURE'S SAKE?
ON PIERRE-JOSEPH PROUDHON'S "PORNOCRACY" TODAY

Karyn Ball

In *Pornocracy, or Women in Modern Times*, the nineteenth-century father of mutualism, Pierre-Joseph Proudhon, defines an ideal marriage as "the union of force and beauty," which embraces "an absolute pact of devotion" that allegedly "immunizes" men and women "against all crime and felony."[1] In contrast, a concubinage "formed solely in view of pleasure . . . is the habitual resort of parasites, of thieves, of forgers and assassins." While fulminating a neotraditional view of marriage may seem hypocritical for the author of *What Is Property?*, Proudhon's *Pornocracy* pamphlet is worth revisiting insofar as it dramatizes a fantasy that aligns female circulation and the authority granted magistrates to arrange marriages (a governmental intrusion that Proudhon compares, predictably, to pimping) with the bankers' power to commoditize debt and profit through financial speculation and thus promote a "promiscuity" of value that he lambasts under the rubric of *bankocracy*. Keeping in mind how his atavistic moralism lives on today, the contributors to this special issue employ Proudhon's anxious pornocracy fantasy as a lens for amplifying the contradictions in contemporary situations where sexual economies reflect, threaten, or resist prevailing political–economic rationalities.

PLEASURE FOR PLEASURE'S SAKE

Writing during the Second Empire of Napoleon III, Proudhon vehemently responds in *Pornocracy* to Jenny D'Hericourt's and Juliette Lambert's criticism of his moral philosophy by proclaiming his commitment to women's truest contentment in the household where they sit across from their husbands as equals. "Marriage in the purity of its idea is," for Proudhon, "an absolute pact of devotion. Pleasure figures only as secondary: all exchange of wealth that produces the man against the joys that procure the woman, all voluptuous commerce, is combined, in order not to be mutual prostitution. It is thus," as Proudhon insists, "that marriage becomes for spouses a cult of conscience, and for society the very organ of justice." The implications of this claim extend well beyond matrimonial harmony, since Proudhon depicts traditional marriage as a mise-en-scène of social stability. Mutual devotion between man and woman, in accordance with their different virtues, force and beauty, founds a society that promotes reciprocal respect and thereby defends itself against individual, civil, and economic decadence.

Proudhon scorns "pleasure for pleasure's sake" as a bohemian and libertine exercise that "subordinate[s] law to the ideal, in the decadent manner of idolatrous polytheists"; and in this way, as he says, presumably addressing his feminist critics, "you accord perfectly with the modern bohemian, for whom the maxim is, as you know, *art for art's sake,*" with its corollaries, "which enter naturally into your catechism: power for power, war for war, money for money, love for love, jouissance for jouissance."

While *Pornocracy* preeminently showcases Proudhon's preoccupation with pleasure unmoored from marital devotion, he also directs his ire at Barthelemy Proper Enfantin, social reformer and a founder of Saint-Simonianism, who, as Stefan Mattessich notes, influenced Proudhon's feminist critics as well as Second Empire reforms. In his introduction to the translation of selections from the unfinished *Pornocracy* pamphlet, Mattessich highlights the intensity of Proudhon's indignation regarding the "technocratic bent in Enfantin's conviction that magistrates should arrange, and not simply ratify, marriages"—in other words, to assess "the aptitude of the spouses [and] their mutual *suitability* . . . according to a science . . . [of] their sympathies and their antipathies" (85, cited by Mattessich in this volume). Such a science reifies "more intimate aspects and values of personhood," thereby facilitating what Proudhon calls a form of "national prostitution" or "amorous democracy" that transforms people into "producers of their own pleasures and agents of their own oppression."

Another prominent symptom of Saint-Simonian decadence, in Proudhon's view, was the so-called law of the Triad, which, as its label suggests, assumes the necessity of a third term in credit operations that "will come from the Bank of France, authorized by the State, from joint stock banks, equally authorized, from privileged stockbrokers, etc." The danger is that providers of credit services assume a "right to *discounts,* to *charges,* to *commissions,* or to *interest,*" words that, for Proudhon, "express nuances of one and the same thing: the right of intervention." In configuring promiscuity and prostitution with bankocracy, Proudhon's fantasy betrays his anxiety, not just about the role of circulation but also *mediation* as corroding both mutualism and civic life. Setting aside his retrograde sexual politics, what left-leaning cultural critics might share with Proudhon are his concerns about liberal state interventions that instrumentalize marriage at the expense of mutual devotion. In excoriating reification under the rubric of "pornocracy," Proudhon invites us to consider how political–economic rationalities warp intimate domains.

The antiliberal motifs in Proudhon's sexual politics recall an earlier confrontation with the political stakes of pleasure from the history of French letters. In "Kant with Sade," Jacques Lacan illuminates the political subtext of Proudhon's antipathy toward "pleasure for its own sake" in proposing to show how the Marquis de Sade's *Philosophy in the Bedroom* "gives the truth" of Immanuel Kant's *Critique of Practical Reason,* thereby "completing" it. Originally intended as a preface to Sade's pamphlet, Lacan's "Kant with Sade" focuses on the superegoic surplus troubling Kant's categorical imperative as a "voice in the conscience," which, "in articulating itself as a maxim, proposes the order of a purely practical reason or of a will" (56–57). "Sade" serves Lacan's agenda by inverting this imperative into a jouissance maxim: "I have the right of enjoyment *[le droit de jouir de]* over your body, anyone can say to me, and I will exercise this right, without any limit stopping me in the capriciousness of the exactions that I might have the taste to satiate" (58).

In Lacan's formulation, the "truth" of Sade's "rule for jouissance" abides in its paradigmatic negation of dispassionate reason's universal purview. By stipulating the moral law's identity with reason and its nonpurposiveness, Kant, in Lacan's interpretation, liberates "the field of moral law" from the pathological but also from "any concern for a good, for a passion, even for a compassion" (59). Kant herewith institutes a split between the subject of an enunciation and the subject of a statement that replays itself, through Lacan's famous auditory motif, as a "voice in the conscience" in and beyond Kantian voluntarism (59). Lacan therefore views Sade's jouissance maxim as unmasking the "bipolarity by which a moral Law institutes itself" (59) in keeping with Kant's scheme, and through which "the law and repressed desire are one and the same thing" (68).

On an historical level, Sade's jouissance maxim deals more than one blow to the French revolutionary ideal of equality, contradicted early on by the bourgeois prioritization of property rights as a guarantor of individual freedom. In his maxim, Lacan hears Sade's respect for the Rights of Man doctrine that "no man can be the property of another man" expressed as the premise that the other who cannot be owned also "cannot make this the pretext to suspend the right to enjoyment over him" (59). As Lacan underscores, this premise overtly dispenses with the "problem" of the object of desire's consent; hence the law that incorporates citizens as hysterical vehicles of its desire is the same law that legitimizes itself by dangling consent before its addressees' noses, all the while coercing it.

In his annotations to his translation of "Kant with Sade," James Swenson comments on the legal valence of jouissance, which "designates the benefit gained from the possession or use of a thing; it refers to a relation to these benefits and not the ownership of the thing itself" (80). In Sade's words, "the act of a possession can only be exercised upon a chattel or an animal, never an individual who resembles us." Thus, while men bear the right to express their wishes to all women, a corresponding right "to compel their submission" is temporary rather than exclusive: "I have no real right of possession over such-and-such a woman," Sade emphasizes, "but I have incontestable rights to the enjoyment of her; I have the right to force from her this enjoyment, if she refuses me it for whatever the cause may be" (Swenson, 82, citing Sade, 318–19). Even as this qualification augments the potential for sexual circulation, it does not alter the fundamental condition and aim of libertinage: a "community of brother predators" and a corresponding model of society based, as Élisabeth Roudinesco characterizes it, on generalized perversion (35).

A couple of centuries before Lacanian psychoanalysis reckons with love as a fantasy that all but fails to cover over the nonexistence of a sexual relation, Sade formalizes a renunciation of self-sacrifice as love's proper expression in a Catholic milieu. As Kenneth Reinhardt has observed, Sade's devotion to an asymmetrical jouissance also overturns the commandment to love one's neighbor. Translated into a liberal ratio, this commandment enjoins the sacrifice of narcissistic desires in the name of mutual devotion as the only guarantee of a lawful and egalitarian living with over and against Hobbes's paternalist sovereign state. The Sadean jouissance maxim thus counters the Christian infrastructure of liberalism's investment in mutual recognition as a foundation for the democratic good life, and Sade kills two birds with one stone when he subtends "love thy neighbor" along with its attendant values: reciprocity and equality before the law.

Roudinesco foregrounds the history of libertinage in her depiction of Sade's early years. According to Roudinesco, it was thanks to the debauched circle of Philippe d'Orléans, who became regent after Louis the XV's death, that libertinage "found its ultimate political form, left its mark on the whole century and became one of the causes of the French Revolution" (29–30); hence, "Orgies, acts of blasphemy, economic speculation, a love of prostitution, luxury, extravagance and caprices, a taste for the whip and transgression: all these practices helped to challenge the values of tradition, which were contrasted with a desire for fleeing pleasures" (29–30). Given this characterization, it is hardly surprising that the "libertine ideal" that emerged in 1595–1600 as "a reaction against the wars of religion" became a formative element in the Marquis de Sade's upbringing" (30). Born in 1749 "into a France that was being torn apart by new political upheavals and . . . surrounded from birth by unscrupulous predators descended from an arrogant nobility that brooked no restrictions on its pleasures and that lived in the secrecy of its chateaux," Sade, as Roudinesco writes, "very quickly began to believe that he was better than anyone else and authorized to use others as he saw fit, and to act and speak as a master who had no need to be censured by either his conscience or humanity" (30, citing Lever, 60).

Revisiting Lacan's "Sade" with Roudinesco's account in mind summons the image of a Marquis wistfully hearing the ascendant rhetoric of French Republican equality in a historical moment that would enshrine the incipient liberal–democratic ideal of mutual recognition between citizens and government, so distinctively lacking in the ancien régime (and now, in a different way, under the conditions of advanced capitalism). From this perspective, Sade's fiction appears to perform the nobleman's not-quite-yet nostalgia for his ruling-class prerogative to disregard the other's consent, not merely in matters of desire but in various legal and extralegal realms. For if, as Lacan argues, the Sadean paradigm proclaims transgressive pleasure an absolute end and, indeed, an aim of ethics and an "unconditional practice of reason" as such, then it derails the very reciprocity with respect to the moral law that champions its universality, since the unrestricted right to enjoy another's body will be asymmetrical in practice, if it does not, in fact, depend on this asymmetry.

AMOROUS DEMOCRACY

In the first section, I suggested that both Proudhon's "pornocracy" and Lacan's "Sade" deliver fantasies about sexual circulation that react to changing structures of governance and their attendant sociomoralisms. In supposing with Lacan that Kant's categorical imperative formalizes a hysterical internalization of the liberal ideal of equality before the law, which respects a reciprocity between state and popular sovereignty, Sade's jouissance maxim, I want to propose, aligns with neoliberalism in staging liberal–democratic capitalism's sadomasochistic "truth."

To elucidate this libidinal logic, I will turn now to Susanne Soederberg's and Wendy Brown's respective discussions of neoliberalism's disciplinary matrix.

In *Debtfare States and the Poverty Industry: Money, Discipline and the Surplus Population*, Soederberg diagnoses the market-led rhetorical and regulative means through which capitalist governments naturalize debt as the fulcrum of material, disciplinary, and ideological abjection. Her analysis connects the national and global valences of "debtfarism" in demystifying the rhetoric of "financial inclusion" that bolsters the credit card, student loan, and payday loan industries as well as the microfinance and housing industries. In Soederberg's perspective, the neoliberal insistence "that there is no alternative to market-based growth" depends on the instauration of a poverty industry whereby workers rely increasingly "on credit to augment and/or replace the living wage or government benefit cheque" (3). Instead of promoting decent pay or regulations that protect workers, neoliberal policies and debtfarism as such uphold "market freedoms and equality in order to ensure that all consumers—regardless of their income or lack thereof—may benefit from standards of fairness, competition, transparency and accountability." These policies promulgate the illusion that Marx called "the community of money," a trope that configures "capitalist society as based on 'individualism and concepts of liberty, freedom and equality backed by laws of private property, rights to appropriation and freedom of contract" (3, citing Harvey, 168). The supposed neutrality of the legal obligation that debt entails hereby dovetails with the language of "consumer protection" to install this illusion as both a grammar of interpellation and an object of desire; for if the business of lending to the poor has metamorphosed into a profitable integral of mainstream financial institutions, this is because it not only exacerbates but also securitizes the very need it purports to deflect as debt becomes less of a consensual undertaking and more of a "last hope" for the vulnerable to avoid falling through the cracks (1).[2] Credit floats the poorly paid, underemployed, or unemployed workers who cannot subsist without it as the mounting cost of living and medical expenses outpace most budgets.[3] The financial industry hereby benefits from policies that culminate in the working poor's "increased reliance on credit cards," a harsh fate compounded by the "vicious cycle in which high fees and interest payments are paid monthly as opposed to paying off the balance" (78).[4]

In *Undoing the Demos: Neoliberalism's Stealth Revolution,* Brown borrows from Michel Foucault to elucidate how "neoliberalism comes to govern as a form of normative reason" (115–16). As Brown explains, neoliberalism transforms the conditions of political possibility by replacing the liberal as-ifs, albeit unfulfilled, of liberty as consent without coercion and equality as recognition before the law by compelling "the subject to become a responsible self-investor and self-provider." So defined, *responsibilization* "reconfigures the correct comportment of the subject from one naturally driven by satisfying interests to one forced to engage in a particular form of self-sustenance that meshes with the morality of the state and the health of the economy." By extension, businesses are no longer tasked with generating collective benefit by pursuing their own interests; instead, job seekers construed as "human capital" are tethered to "the project of macroeconomic growth and credit enhancement," which compels them to operate "in a context replete with risk, contingency, and potentially violent changes, from burst bubbles and capital or currency meltdowns to wholesale industry dissolution" (84). By hypostasizing social–contractual consent, neoliberal responsibilization rhetoric occults the interests that benefit from wage stagnation, labor fungibilization, and a stripped down safety net. The result is an always-striving, never-secure job seeker whose survival enjoins flexibly self-capitalizing entrepreneurial "choices."

Soederberg's and Brown's respective outlines of neoliberalism invite speculations about how the poverty industry, fungibilization, and responsibilization implant themselves on an imaginary level as a *fantasy,* or even as a *libidinal economy*. For if *sadocapitalism* names the power to maximize plutocratic jouissance by squeezing bare life from the working poor, students, and the under- or unemployed (or blood from stones), how does consent beyond coercion emerge on the other side of the ledger?

Soederberg and Brown foreground what I would like to call neoliberalism's "sadocapitalist" injunction to workers: accept their lack of protection from exploitation and interchangeability as the disciplinary condition of a deregulated labor market. Yet to view pornocracy as a sexual as well as a political–economic fantasy is to speculate about how a *sadocapitalist* dramaturgy seduces a *masocapitalist* underclass. This is a class whose members might adapt to insecure labor conditions by learning to enjoy their own abjection, their own learned helplessness as indebtedness inclines toward indentured servitude. From a Lacanian point of view, the masocapitalist subject might be understood as identifying with the locus of sadocapitalist jouissance—idealizing and internalizing the other's desire as a will-to-dispossess. These masocapitalists would also be market-disciplined subjects who might find themselves increasingly disposed to retreat into recalcitrant passivity in response to relentless "responsible choice" rhetoric.

We might be grateful to Sade for inaugurating a transversal critique of liberal consent fetishism in matters of sex and governance that a post-liberal, post-Marxist, and post-psychoanalytic Foucault dynamically extended. In the face of a declining Gaullism and an ascendant neoliberal technocracy, Foucault comments in a 1974 interview on a preponderance of porn shops selling Nazi insignia as a sign of a "pathetic," "ridiculous," and "extreme" re-eroticization of power that compensates for the impossibility of attaching erotically to a Brezhnev, a Pompidou, or a Nixon (127).[5] To take Foucault at his word (about the porn shops) is to contemplate the sexual symptomatology of liberal ideals in decline as society, the one-time moral bulwark against government overreach, coalesces into neoliberal rationality, or what amounts to possessive individualism's more instrumental evil twin. By extension, a 1970s fascination with Nazi erotica might be read as refracting a sociohistorical shift from liberal to neoliberal values as a regression of consent into a matrix of sovereign-master and passive-victim identifications.

Foucault's 1974 observations about American porn shops theoretically amplify the sadomasochistic fantasy structure that cements identification with a neoliberal rationality. The Hugo Boss–outfitted SS appeal at once to *sado*-identifications with the perversely masculinist authoritarian who followed through on his genocidal bloodlust without apology or, alternatively, to *maso*-identifications with SS victims—those *who could not possibly consent* to their own brutalization. It is important to underscore that both identifications effectively renounce a preconscious consent to be governed that no longer comes with the same level of government protection and thus renders individual survival competitive at all levels. From this standpoint, resurgent longings for authoritarian leadership potentially reveal a sadomasocapitalist fantasy in which the pressures of neoliberal "responsibilization" are disavowed through a visceral embrace of an apparently decisive strength.

As his lectures amply demonstrate, Foucault was prescient in marking the signs that liberal–democratic ideals were, in his day, ceding ground to neoliberal policies that, in our current moment, conscript a masocapitalist precariat looking for love in all the wrong places (*Fifty Shades of Grey*, Brexit, and Trump). This masocapitalist conscription, as I am calling it, has shaped and been shaped by the history of progressive causes, including feminist praxis. In "Top Girls? Young Women and the Post-Feminist Sexual Contract," Angela McRobbie responds to a shift in the feminist legacy since the 1960s, evinced in a transformed private/public divide, as the endeavor to mobilize a formerly disavowed female desire to speak on its own behalf against power broadened the boundaries of politics. This shift has shaped a new sexual contract that conflates sexual with economic autonomy in a cult of appearance subservient to male desire. While a politically engaged feminism advocated for resistance against phallocracy, the postfeminist counterrevolution prioritizes an entrepreneurial style of managing phallic enjoyment and the sexual market that serves it. In keeping with this new contract, female sexuality appears, now, not as leverage against the powers that subordinate women while excluding them from public life but as a by-product of "market discipline" with its exacting beauty standards and its inducements to relegate other modes of fulfillment to a self-sexualizing feminine performativity.[6] Without requisite gains in political, economic, and sociocultural equality for women and girls, the notion of sexual liberation that has normalized transactional sex (without feeling) has mainly benefited men hanging on to the last vestiges of their presumed sovereignty.

In recent years, Nancy Jo Sales has published articles in *Vanity Fair* attesting to the influence of postfeminist ideas on explicitly instrumental sexual economies that promote the sale of self as a rational pursuit in a "free market." In "Daddies, 'Dates,' and the Girlfriend Experience: Welcome to the New Prostitution Economy,"[7] Sales investigates the "growing number of young people [who] are selling their bodies online to pay student loans, make the rent, or afford designer labels" (2016). The gloss for the article poses the issue in stark terms: "Is it just an unorthodox way to make ends meet or a new kind of exploitation?" What follows is a sketch of exchanges made through "Seeking Arrangement, the website and app that match 'sugar daddies' with 'sugar babies,' whose company the daddies pay for with 'allowances.'" Sales gives her readers a glimpse of an extensive online community composed of websites, blogs, and private pages on Facebook for "sugar babies," including one where "members proudly call themselves 'hos' (sometimes 'heaux') and post coquettish photographs of themselves, dressed up for 'dates.'" More tellingly, posters also "offer information on how to avoid law enforcement and what they carry to protect themselves (knives, box cutters, pepper spray). They give advice on how to alleviate the pain of bruises from overzealous spanking and what to do when 'scammers' refuse to pay."

Selling the "girlfriend experience" might provide a meal ticket or debt relief, but "daddies" can also pay their "babies" through items on an Amazon wish list, which might specify luxury goods, among other things. Referring to one of the babies she interviewed, Sales remarks that "the most surprising thing about Miranda's story is how unsurprising it is to many of her peers. 'Almost all of my friends do some sort of sex work,' says Katie, 23, a visual artist in New York. 'It's supercommon. It's almost trendy to say you do it—or that you would.'" This is a transactional sex economy, where autonomy coded as "sexual liberation" coalesces with entrepreneurial self-invention and self-commodification as such.[8] Yet in the aftermath of the 2007–8 crisis, when severely diminished job prospects set back a generation of American college graduates weighed down by student loans, the transactional sex economy seems less "liberated" than coercive as young people have faced rising rents. The potentially coercive aspects of the "girlfriend experience" reveal a dark side of the sex positive feminist affirmation of women's sexual pleasure without shame beyond reproduction. In the age of internet-facilitated transactional sex, a recoding of sex work as entrepreneurial self-empowerment seemingly fleshes out a postfeminist sexual contract that subscribes to neoliberal "market discipline."

In "Tinder and the Dawn of the Dating Apocalypse," Sales quotes a trio of roommates working as "budding investment bankers" for a financial firm. Though he falls short of his roommate who hooked up with five girls in one week, the interviewee she calls "Marty" is, as she says, "no slouch at 'racking up girls.' He says he's slept with 30 to 40 women in the last year: 'I sort of play that I could be a boyfriend kind of guy,' in order to win them over, 'but then they start wanting me to *care* more . . . and I just don't'" (2015).

Tinder's alleged hookup culture, as Sales portrays it, becomes "pornocratic" in Proudhon's sense as some users fetishize no-strings-attached sexual circulation (see Singal). If anyone finds this economy frustrating or hurtful, it is because they make the mistake of hoping for intimacy and reciprocity beyond sex—that is, hoping for potentially lasting attachments and solidarities. Sales believes that the upper hand seemingly belongs to those who successfully harden themselves against emotional connections in order to strategically maximize the quality and quantity of their sexual partners, not just for pleasure, but to attain sovereignty in their peers' eyes.

Sales discovers a mirror for her anxiety in the judgments of David Buss, a professor of psychology at the University of Texas at Austin who "specializes in the evolution of human sexuality." Buss contends that "it is the very abundance of options provided by online dating which may be making men less inclined to treat any particular woman as a 'priority'" (Sales 2015). In his estimation, "Apps like Tinder and OkCupid give people the impression that there are thousands or millions of potential mates out there." One problematic "dimension of this," Buss speculates, "is the impact it has on men's psychology." Buss assumes that "when there is a surplus of women, or a perceived surplus of women, the whole mating system tends to shift towards short-term dating. Marriages become unstable. Divorces increase. Men don't have to commit, so they pursue a short-term mating strategy. Men are making that shift, and women are forced to go along with it in order to mate at all."

Writing for *New York Magazine*, Jesse Singal rightly criticizes Sales's reliance on anecdotal evidence and her capitulation to confirmation bias.[9] For my purposes, however, the value of Sales's hookup-culture exposé lies not in its scientific validity but rather in its illustration of two sides of a transactional economy in which pleasure without emotional baggage can be exchanged as a supposedly mutual benefit. On one side, Sales's cherry-picked male interviewees confess their entrepreneurial management of the sex market: gaming affective ambiguities in the system to boost sexual capital. On the other side, a female Tinder user hints that what she refers to as "third wave feminism" has shaped her participation in the reified sexual economy Sales depicts. Here, the "third wave feminism" signifier seemingly buttresses a libertine lifestyle fantasy misrecognized as the apex of autonomy. Sales overtly worries that young women's translation of "sex-positive feminism" into a contemporary form of libertinage continues to be overshadowed by a double standard that corroborates men's sexual sovereignty as a freedom to circulate ruthlessly at the expense of females who lose the battle of the sexes by failing to shed their "retrograde" liberal desire for mutual recognition. Where Proudhon's specter haunts Sales's dystopic portrait of twenty-first-century hookup culture is in her presentiment that women pay the steeper price for sexual liberation at the expense of commitment.

Read together, Sales's 2015 and 2016 *Vanity Fair* interventions indicate her investment in narratives about how the nonduped err as she discerns the possibly self-defeating repercussions of a sex-positive feminism that has promoted sexual pleasure without shame beyond heteronormativity, marriage, and reproduction. Her angle at times echoes Proudhon's premise that circulation will ultimately degrade women in rendering them dispensable from the man's point of view, even as her illustration of the girlfriend experience shows us that women can be as instrumental as hookup culture's "fuck boys." Ultimately, however, from the standpoint of a Frankfurt School lament about ubiquitous reification, she might be justified in her concerns about the networked proliferation of nonintimate intimacies. For if the mandarins of the German sociological tradition taught us anything, it is that the seepage of a self-hardening and compartmentalizing mindset into other domains is uncontainable.

THE ENJOYMENT OF THE EMPEROR

For a dramatization of Proudhon's pornocracy fantasy, we might remember the ritualized orgy scene from Stanley Kubrick's last film, *Eyes Wide Shut,* released in the summer of 1999, four months after the director's death. This cinematic adaptation of Arthur Schnitzler's 1926 *Traumnovelle (Dream Story)* anchors its depiction of class-conscious castration anxiety in 1990s New York in the perspective of Bill Harford, a wealthy doctor played by Tom Cruise, who makes discrete house calls for the superrich. The heretofore complacent Bill feels threatened when his wife, Alice (played by Nicole Kidman, Tom Cruise's offscreen wife at the time), intentionally derails him with a confession about lusting after a naval officer staying in the hotel on the Cape where the couple was vacationing. The film's climax transpires as Bill infiltrates a masquerade organized by a secret society at a palatial mansion. As Cruise walks from room to room, the camera establishes his gaze touching on women and men clustered in eerily de-eroticized sex acts that hyperrealize intercourse to the point of boredom, a scene rendered ominous through Jocelyn Pook's quasi-religious scoring, which incorporates Romanian liturgical elements, along with a Tamil song, "Migrations," sung by Manickam Yogeswaram.

With *Eyes Wide Shut,* Kubrick availed himself of a Sadean literary tradition that self-consciously visualizes limitless access to a sexual underclass as the imprimatur of aristocratic enjoyment. The film theatricalizes this tradition by overtly staging pornocracy as masquerade, conspiracy, and paranoia: Kubrick's mise-en-scéne of pornocratic influence lays bare a societal-wide nexus of sex workers servicing a plutocratic Elect that not only exercises a sovereign prerogative to lease anyone to fulfill its members' libertine predilections but also menaces the well-off protagonist with its seemingly omnipresent surveillance and retribution powers.

If Proudhon could survey the contemporary scene, he would no doubt sympathize with Harford's paranoia about the sexual and financial omnipotence of rentiers. What Silvio Berlusconi's wife Veronica Lario once referred to as "the enjoyment of the emperor" while characterizing her husband's sex parties (cited by Edemariam) is a conspicuously paraded privilege that distinguishes members of a pornocratic class, a "community of brother predators," as Roudinesco phrased it, whose exploitative excesses prove they are above the law. To follow the fortunes of Dominique Strauss-Kahn and Donald Trump is to discover that Sade never died: his self-proclaimed inheritors convert his antiliberal fictions into virility clichés—the stock imagery of an obscene political unconscious.

On May 14th, 2011, the sixty-two-year-old IMF director was removed from a first-class cabin on an Air France plane two minutes before it was scheduled to take off for Paris from John F. Kennedy International Airport and charged with sexually assaulting a thirty-two-year-old maid, Nafissatou Diallo, in his $3,000-a-night hotel suite at the Sofitel Hotel in Times Square (see Reuters). Diallo told detectives that her attacker "came out of the bathroom naked, ran down a hallway to the foyer where she was, pulled her into a bedroom and began to sexually assault her" (Chrisafis, Willsher, and Rush).

Naturally, the maid herself came under hyperintensive scrutiny as rumors linked her to a conspiracy to take down a powerful politician, while others surmised she was maneuvering the accused for financial gain. Meanwhile, research unveiled that she lied about the violence she faced in Guinea in order to bolster her application for asylum.[10] As evidence undermining her shifting story turned up, the New York District Attorney's office eventually dropped its case against Strauss-Kahn. The latter returned to France somewhat sullied by her accusations, though a few years passed after the incidents in question before the man known as DSK succumbed irrevocably to scandal.

Following his arrest in New York, Tristane Banon came forward to testify again about his proclivity for sexual aggression (see Willsher). The evidence for debauchery mounted with the news of his participation in orgies staffed with prostitutes who attested to their less-than-consensual subjection to sodomy and sadomasochistic acts (see Chrisafis). Pigeon-holed as the long-suffering wife, the television journalist and heiress Anne Sinclair, who had stood by her man during his house arrest in New York, finally divorced him as multiplying accusations doomed him ineluctably to ignominy.

In the aftermath of DSK's arrest, reporters questioned the accuser's testimony but ultimately conceded that Strauss-Kahn's sperm on the bathroom wall made plain that "something" of a consensual or non-consensual sexual nature had transpired.[11] What this evidence also indicates is that one of the most powerful members of the global elite had apparently perceived a darker-skinned maid as someone who could or must temporarily cater to his sexual needs. Whether or not she lied on her asylum application, Diallo hails from the IMF-disciplined hemisphere of the globe, a circumstance that did not trouble the highly privileged white director of that agency when he pursued his "emperor's enjoyment."

The French initially registered their contempt for an American scene in which the accused are treated as guilty before being proven innocent; for a police force that parades the accused, regardless of status, in cuffs; and for Americans' déclassé puritanism, so hypocritical in their eyes. Defending Strauss-Kahn, Bernard-Henri Lévy denounced DSK's "pornographic" and "obscene" treatment by the American judicial system and tabloid press, and called for DSK's full exoneration (Graham Holm). Pascal Bruckner cautioned French travelers to the United States "to get an official document from [Americans you want to flirt with] stipulating that you can enjoy their body." Scolding Americans from on high, Bruckner rehashed the French premise about the United States' Protestant "problem with sex," a legacy that "also has it giving the whole world lessons in morality" even as Americans uphold a "double-faced" and "prurient" puritanism that "uses the vocabulary of freedom and coexists with a thriving porn industry."

While there is no denying Bruckner's point about American hypocrisy,[12] he confuses "maturity" with approval of a Sadean-spirited old-order sexual prerogative that Strauss-Kahn reactivated at the Sofitel hotel in New York, among other places. Yet the exercise of this prerogative is neither proof of "enlightenment" nor exclusively European; the United States can also boast of a rich tradition of glorifying sexual aggression as a sign of ruling-class election.

An icon of conspicuous self-enjoyment, our reality-television star president has circulated promiscuously as an omnipresent brand name for skyscrapers, steaks, cologne, casinos, mattresses, suspect real estate ventures, and a fraudulent university, while continually reactivating a salient principle of the nineteenth-century Proudhon's functionally differentiated sex-gender economy: *it is women's job to be beautiful*. In keeping with the premise that any woman failing in her prime directive deserves his scorn, he has rated Halle Berry's body parts; bemoaned Heidi Klum's "decline"; called women "pigs" and "dogs"; branded the 1996 Miss Universe winner, Alicia Machado, "Miss Piggy" and "Miss Housekeeping" when she gained weight; and demeaned both former presidential candidates Carly Fiorina's and Hillary Clinton's looks. Brandishing his macho prerogative to judge women on the basis of their beauty alone, Trump exhilarates his thralls with vulgar comments about women, including his own daughter, Ivanka. His election to the presidency following the release of the Access Hollywood tape in which the thrice-married real estate mogul bragged about groping women who, as he proclaimed, let him get away with it because of his fame, seemingly fulfills Foucault's premise that people crave a sadomasochistic erotics of power; hence, the man who lowered the bar in presidential candidate debates to penis level[13] comes out ahead if he not only brags about past affairs and flaunts his former bathing suit model wife but also insinuates that women should be punished for seeking abortions and that those accusing him of assault are not attractive enough for him to have been bothered with.

His egomaniacal boasting about his financial and sexual conquests has goaded the *New York Times'* Frank Bruni to refer to the "priapic twins," Trump and Berlusconi, who are "identical in their insistence on being seen as paragons of irresistible lust.[14] If hideously sexist utterances ensue, so be it. Loins before decency. Pheromones over good sense." Bruni hails *Trumpusconi* as "a study in the peril and pitfalls of unchecked testosterone and tumescent avarice. It's a commentary on wealth in the Western world: how ardently certain blowhards pursue it, how much the rest of us forgive in those who attain it, how thoroughly we equate money and accomplishment."[15]

LIBIDINOUS STATECRAFT

To reconceptualize pornocracy as a paranoid fantasy about sexual circulation is to acknowledge an intellectual debt to Lauren Berlant and Michael Warner's 1998 "Sex in Public" essay deconstructing the relegation of sex to the private sphere. As they argue, this compartmentalization obscures the heteronormative contract's public valences as furthered by the family metaphor, which deflects attention from "systemic racism and other structural inequalities" while buttressing welfare-state governmentality (313–14).

Berlant and Warner enunciate the historical baggage of a sex act "shielded by the zone of privacy," which, as they stress, represents "the affectional nimbus that heterosexual culture protects and from which it abstracts its model of ethics." This zone is, to a certain extent, nominally "private," since it frames the currency of "social belonging supported and extended by acts less commonly recognized as part of sexual culture."[16] Paying taxes, carrying wallet photos, and buying economy-size among other everyday practices dovetail with a notion of intimate life as "the endlessly cited elsewhere of political public discourse, a promised haven that distracts citizens from the unequal conditions of their political economic lives, consoles them for the damaged humanity of mass society, and shames them for any divergence between their lives and the intimate sphere that is alleged to be simple personhood" (317).

In 1998, Berlant and Warner called for critical attention to federal- and state-level subsumptions of sexual life that would now prominently feature the June 2014 Hobby Lobby decision. In allowing "'closely held' for-profit corporations run on religious principles" to exempt themselves from covering contraception, Hobby Lobby empowered dogmatic skinflints to curtail women's reproductive freedom and, by extension, their sexual pleasure in and beyond marriage, and to save money by adjudicating "morally acceptable" female health expenses.[17]

Rush Limbaugh's attacks on President Obama's contraception mandate are worth remembering in this connection as an instance of pornographic machoism couched as anti-pornocratic libertarianism. While deriding Georgetown law student Sandra Fluke's 2012 campaign for federally mandated contraception insurance coverage, Limbaugh claimed a voyeur's prerogative when his tax dollars abet women's alleged libertinage: "So Miss Fluke, and the rest of you Feminazis, here's the deal. If we are going to pay for your contraceptives, and thus pay for you to have sex, we want something for it. We want you to post the videos online so we can all watch" (cited by Keyes).

Limbaugh's pornographic moralism crassly couched as a tax-paying citizen's voyeuristic entitlement coincided with other conservative endeavors to regulate women's sexual activity. In the same year, Republican legislators of Virginia proposed to force women seeking abortions to undergo vaginal ultrasounds. To forge this punitive policy, which, they subsequently commuted to "jelly on the belly" ultrasounds in response to protests, these male legislators had to *co-imagine* the scene of vaginal penetration in which a medical gaze would *specularize* and *survey* women's intimate parts, which is why Janet D. Howell (D-Fairfax) aptly characterized the original bill as "state rape."[18] The lesson to draw here is that the interests preoccupied with women's sexual circulation must *visualize* what they would control.

The "Republican war on women" as waged by Limbaugh and the Virginia legislature in 2012 evinces the historical entanglement of pornography and democracy that Lynn Hunt traces in *The Invention of Pornography*, cited by Natasha Hurley in her contribution to this issue. Hunt examines the intensified "feminization of both the aristocracy and monarchy" after 1789 in the vicious attacks against the queen, which fostered a "fraternal bond" that the "circulation of images of women's bodies" and the visualizations prompted by pornographic writing and print media helped to cement. This history implies that women were "essential to the development of democracy and, in the end, excluded from it" (Hurley, citing Hunt, 329); it thus illuminates the myriad and sometimes contradictory roles that porno-visualization continues to play in conservative, religious, or otherwise patriarchal attacks on a quasi-liberated sexual economy.

In the current centrifuge of Republican hatreds, evangelicals play Proudhon's "third term" in marriage and sexual reproduction matters, seeking to punish women's and queers' nonreproductive pleasures while ignoring a deregulated financial industry that spins subprime-mortgages into gold for its operatives and crisis for everyone else. In the tricky Republican amalgam of evangelical and libertarian values, the circulation of sexual pleasure without marital devotion is "improper," while the circulation of fictitious capital without regulation is sacrosanct; accordingly, Planned Parenthood, queer marriage, and Rent-Boy demand extraordinary governmental scrutiny, yet Dodd-Frank must go so that oligarchs may maximize their potential to appropriate financial and erotic assets while their legislative minions punish specters of biblically defined promiscuity.[19]

Given this hypocritical admixture, no one should have been surprised at Trump's pick for vice president. Trump and Mike Pence are two sides of American neoliberalism's pornocratic coin, with the former playing caddish maverick to Pence's punitive theocrat. As senator, Pence mobilized the GOP crusade to defund Planned Parenthood and, with Ted Cruz hot on his heels, instigated threats to shut down the government to coerce his colleagues into decimating the agency. As governor, Pence successfully defunded Planned Parenthood, thereby undermining one of Indiana's few providers of HIV testing, with deleterious results; he also "[supported] one of the nation's toughest so-called 'Religious Freedom' laws," effectively legalizing the ostracism of LGBT consumers and backing down "only when big businesses from Apple to SalesForce to Angie's List said they'd curtail commerce in his state" (Walsh).

Yet theocrat is not only as theocrat does but also what he (or she) does not do. During Pence's tenure as governor, the Indiana Criminal Justice Institute subtracted 1.18 million dollars without Pence's interference from funding that supported victims of domestic violence.[20] Pence also refused to comply with the Prison Rape Elimination Act because it "would require the redirection of millions of tax dollars currently supporting other critical needs for Indiana" (Tuohy).[21] While it appears that criminals "deserve" to be raped in Pence's worldview, not all rape is "legitimate" when women are the accusers. As Joan Walsh reports, Senator Pence co-sponsored a bill in Congress "that would have redefined rape and limited federal funding for abortion to women who suffered 'forcible rape'—what [Todd] Akin famously described as 'legitimate rape' when he doomed his 2012 Senate bill." In this and other endeavours, Pence's malignant ignorance aligns with Trump's misogynist solipsism, manifest not just in the latter's crass objectifications of women but in a history of sexual harassment and rape charges (including his ex-wife Ivana's that was settled).

In the months leading up to the 2016 presidential election, one might speculate about the mainstream press's reluctance to remind us about Trump's friendship with Jeffrey Epstein—a Democratic Party contributor, former Mar-a-Lago member, and Level 3 registered sex offender—in the months leading up to the 2016 presidential election. To follow this chain of links is to track Epstein's history as a procurer of young, even adolescent, women for his own and others' uses. As reported by Brandy Zadrozny in the *Daily Beast*: "For the alleged systematic victimization of young girls—most of whom were plucked by Epstein's assistants from Palm Beach's poorer neighborhoods and groomed to adore or acquiesce to him—he was slapped with a 2008 conviction on a single charge of soliciting a minor; and sentenced to an 18-month stay in a Palm Beach county jail—of which he served only 13 months and was allowed to leave six days out of every week for 'work release.'"[22]

Trump's friendship with Epstein, whose parties the former attended, received little or no attention in newspapers such as the *New York Times,* which explicitly endorsed Hillary Clinton's presidential bid. Perhaps the newspaper's board wished to avoid calling attention to her husband's multifarious connections to the "billionaire pedophile," who donated millions to the Clinton Foundation after his conviction for soliciting a minor (Zadrozny). Flight logs indicate that Bill Clinton was a passenger at least twenty-six times on Epstein's private 727, dubbed the "Lolita Express" because it supposedly featured a bed for passengers to enjoy group sex with the young women Epstein obtained from modeling agencies, such as M2 (Prestigiacomo; Zadrozny). In addition, Clinton is "widely reported to have visited Little St. James, Epstein's private island in the US Virgin Islands," unofficially known as "sex slave island" or "orgy island," where, "according to attorneys for Epstein's victims, many of the worst crimes against minors were committed by Epstein and friends who traveled with him" (Silverstein).

As the revelations about the people who facilitated, took part in, or were complicit with Epstein's sex schemes involving underage women have multiplied (a list that includes Alan Dershowitz who, along with Gerald Lefcourt, defended the financier), Kubrick's *Eyes Wide Shut* dramatization of pornocracy becomes all too literal. Yet insofar as Trump was elected shortly after the Access Hollywood tape was publicized, it might be assumed that, if known, Epstein's connection with the misogynist-in-chief would not have made a difference to the latter's supporters, who cherish their candidate's "winner's" prerogative to take what he wants when he wants—by force if necessary. Writing about an Epstein-linked rape accusation against Trump, Lisa Bloom encapsulates the outlook precisely: "We live in a world where wealthy, powerful men often use and abuse women and girls. . . . What do you call a nation that refuses to even look at sexual assault claims against a man seeking to lead the free world? Rape culture."

"RELAX AND ENJOY IT"

In "Trump Deals the Woman Card," Gail Collins mentions the candidate's proud anticipation that he would imminently receive "an endorsement from 'the great Bobby Knight,'" a former basketball coach (nicknamed "the General") who, according to Collins, "once told an NBC interviewer that his theory on handling stress was, 'I think that if rape is inevitable, relax and enjoy it.'" Knight's comment encapsulates the to-the-victor-go-the-spoils sense of entitlement associated with "rape culture," which demotes women's bodily sovereignty to men's sexual prerogative. References to rape culture have intensified in recent years' news coverage about universities failing to respond effectively to campus rape accusations or provide redress for victims. To be sure, rape culture in the United States extends beyond a "boys will be boys" attitude about fraternity brothers and college athletes to the availability and use of rape drugs; it also comprises the ressentiment-curdled masculinity clichés that foster tolerance for or even admiring acceptance of sexual aggression. In this context, the North American press's attentiveness to "honor killings" and "backward cultures" narratives sometimes serves an ulterior purpose: to distract us from the history, magnitude, and racial undercurrents of sexual violence perpetrated here.

Hortense Spillers's conceptualization of "pornotropes" offers crucial material for an examination of the pornocratic fantasies that overdetermine race relations. In her canonical 1987 essay, "Mama's Maybe and Papa's Baby: An American Grammar Book," Spillers famously counters Daniel Patrick Moynihan's celebrated report of the late sixties blaming mothers for "Negro family" dissipation in the absence of fathers. Very briefly, Spillers accentuates the blind spots of family-sentimentalizing frameworks that overlook the situation of enslaved women whose status as property emptied out kinship claims while vesting their white masters with what amounted to rape rights. Because slave women did not legally possess their own bodies, they could not be registered in law as victims of violence perpetrated by their masters; nor could slave mothers and fathers claim their children. Indeed, black patrilineage was doubly crossed out when white slave-owners disavowed the children that resulted from raping female slaves.

Maintaining that master–slave sexual relations throw the "customary lexis of sexuality" into crisis,[23] Spillers coins the term "pornotrope" to accentuate "meanings imposed on the fungible body of the black slave, whose corporeality becomes the 'source of irresistible, destructive sexuality' while it is, at the same time, reduced to 'a thing, becoming *being* for the captor.'" Since the Moynihan report, slavery's figurative legacy continues to shadow contemporary racial tensions through pornotropes constructing black men as "potential rapists" and black women as "sites of 'unrestrained sexuality'" (Frost in this volume, citing Spillers, 67).

Adrienne D. Davis details the background for Spillers's pornotropology in analyzing slavery as a "sexual political economy" in which "sexual and racial subordination converged around the bodies of enslaved black women" (457). By spotlighting the tripartite role of black women who were forced "to labor in three markets—productive, reproductive, and sexual" (458), Davis seeks "to cast the institution of slavery in a new light: as an early and particularly virulent strain of institutionalized sexual harassment" (457). Not only did enslaved women "give birth to enslaved children," regardless of who the father was, as Davis emphasizes, they also "found themselves coerced, blackmailed, induced, seduced, ordered and, of course, violently forced to have sexual relations with men" (459). While the "law of rape and access to patriarchal protection" supposedly applied to white women, albeit ineffectually, "these protections were completely unavailable to enslaved women" (459). In short, slaveholders retained absolute license to sexually exploit their female property "for profit, pleasure, and punishment—simultaneously and without contradiction" (462).

One of Davis's crucial claims is that "slavery illustrates what feminists have argued since the earliest conceptions of sexual harassment: sexual subordination in the workplace is a central tool of labour, sexual, *and* racial control" that targeted both individuals and the larger black community. According to Davis, slavery is, thus, paradigmatic for its "widespread, institutionalized, state-sanctioned sexual harassment implemented in perhaps its most corrupt form" (464).

If "slavery puts the sex back in sexual harassment," as Davis contends, it is because such fantasies stemming back to the sexual terrorism perpetrated against female slaves that entrenched white plantation owners' control over black men and all women constitute the racial–patriarchal unconscious of a society that disenfranchises and jails people of color disproportionately. My contention is that the disavowal of these conjoined fantasies unleashes what we might now understand as a form of pornocratic paranoia that would immobilize black men (through police shootings, mass imprisonment, and disenfranchisement) along with women of color to shore up a white male droit du seigneur.[24]

A racial pornotropology beginning with literal master–slave relations partially illuminates the abiding force of the "dangerous black man" specter that holds sway in the United States, as the alarming frequency of police shootings of unarmed blacks seemingly proves. Such shootings are not new, of course; Americans are mainly witnessing the compounding intelligibility of a long-standing injustice that intensifies as the police subject blacks to inordinately higher degrees of scrutiny and aggression, thereby increasing the chances of lethal interactions (see Bui and Cox). It nevertheless bears reiterating that racial pornotropology assumes more explanatory value in the face of a mounting toll of black deaths at police hands, which should remind us of a history of extrajudicial lynchings in which white mobs ritualistically castrated, executed, and burned black men. Behind the "phobic imago" construing black men as primitive conveyors of a bestial sexual aggression "lurks a dark intruder," as David Marriott contends, an image rendered all the more threatening since it routes rage against the specter of a putatively monstrous black penis that shames the white men who covet it.

In the first chapter of *On Black Men,* Marriott sets out to disinter the vicious desire that permeates photographs of lynchings, in which jubilant white adults and children are juxtaposed with the "bitter fruit" they have harvested through ritualized torture and dismemberment. Produced at the same "technological moment which gives us the Kodak, the first turn-of-the-century-mass-produced roll-film camera," these pictures confirm the sometimes "carnavalesque" atmosphere that entered into "grotesque family album[s]" as keepsake "toes, fingers, or—most highly prized—a black penis, a black scrotum" (9).

Spillers, Davis, and Marriott disclose a not-so-latent racial pornocracy in the United States, where blacks attract more scrutiny and more punishment while receiving fewer protections under the law. The racial–pornocratic unconscious that conjures a "monstrous" black penis and black female "availability" has in the past led to the lynching and castration of black men and the rape of black women along with other women of color. We might speculate that this unconscious presently underwrites the continuing legality of white nationalist groups, including the historically murderous Ku Klux Klan, as well as state-sanctioned violence. Without a conception of the contents of this unconscious, how else can we understand the contemporary resurgence of unabashed racism among Trump-supporting Fox News viewers, evangelicals, and the alt-right if not as poorly constrained longing to enjoy cruelty—openly and without consequences—and a confirmation of a white nationalist birthright?

PROUDHON'S "PORNOCRACY" TODAY

I have been characterizing pornocracy as a paranoid fantasy about the political–economic implications of Proudhon's parallel between sexual and financial circulation as authorized in his mind by the feminists of his day and technocratic Second Empire reforms. Reading Proudhon alongside Lacan's "Kant with Sade" conjures another avatar: the aristocrat (or "bankocrat," in Proudhon's terms) whose jouissance-in-domination dispenses with the liberal framework of mutual recognition and consent where his own sexual pleasure is concerned and enjoins the creation of a "masocapitalist" underclass whose precarity neoliberal policies (and "sadocapitalism" as such) exacerbate. Sales's

Vanity Fair articles about transactional sex economies seem to play out another Proudhonian fear about reification displacing devotion in collusion with a postfeminist self-actualization narrative that provides cis-gendered women with a rationalization for taking pleasure in their entrepreneurial embrace of the beauty regime and encourages some to emulate porn star standards (lip injections, Brazilians, breast implants, and vaginoplasty) in the name of sexual liberation. Ultimately, then, I have been employing the term *pornocracy* to evoke the obscenity of a law that underwrites libertinage and bankocracy among the Berlusconis, Strauss-Kahn's, Trumps, and Epsteins of the world, while restricting the circulation of women along with ethnic, racial, and sexual minorities.

My derivation of these valences of pornocracy is indebted to conversations beginning in 2011 with my coeditor, Stefan Mattessich, and to the contributors to this special issue, who spotlight on an international scale the issues I have raised mainly about the American context. In "Pornocratic Fantasy and the Contractarian Framing of Prostitution," Amy Swiffen takes up the problem of consent fetishism in her examination of the Supreme Court of Canada's recent moves to reconsider legislation constricting the locations for negotiating and practicing sex work. To determine how the advocacy for legalizing prostitution founders on the question of women's subordination, Swiffen revisits Carole Pateman's feminist challenge in *The Sexual Contract* to the formally neutral but substantively gendered language of contracts for "property in the person"—that is, "for services that are inseparable from the materiality of the body, such as sexual and surrogacy services," and that also, therefore, ineluctably impinge on the self (Swiffen in this volume). In reading Pateman's "essentialist" opposition to social–contractual defenses of sex work with and against Proudhon's defense of marital devotion as a means of protecting the "weaker sex" and upholding civil society, Swiffen exposes the underside of the "property in persons" contract language that hypostasizes sex workers' autonomy by occulting the actual socioeconomic conditions of their work. To speculate with Swiffen that this language implicitly authorizes the pornocrat's fantasy of a permanent "class of individuals whose bodies are available for exchange" is to pose a concomitant question about how an underclass is conscripted to service the plutocrat's entitlement.

In problematizing the hypostatization of consent in the legal treatment of sex workers, Swiffen's essay also stresses the potentially dangerous repercussions of presuming the reality of sexual autonomy without considering the power asymmetries that perpetuate the contemporary denigration of women and girls. At stake here is how the "liberation" promoted by sex-positive feminism has been both intensified and undermined on a political level by pseudo-existentialist and entrepreneurial self-actualization narratives that rationalize the pleasures of embracing a sexually objectifying beauty regime.

How this embrace undercuts feminist praxis is one of the problems that Dina Al-Kassim illuminates in her contribution to this issue. In "Feminist Pornocracy? Femen and the Politics of Resistant Nudity," Al-Kassim focuses on the image politics of the Ukrainian protest group who emerged in 2006–9 just as Ukraine was losing its notoriety as a major source of sex traffic, which moved to neighboring countries rather than disappearing. Drawing from a history of "feminist art practice and especially from activist body art and its strategies of self-exposure," Al-Kassim maintains that the Femen breast is intended as defiant "speech and weapon" against a pornocratic state that both profits from and controls women's sexual circulation; however, the group's resolute allegiance to beauty system standards alongside its exuberant reliance on mass media spectacle and entrepreneurial self-promotion (including the sale of autographed "boob-prints") are "firmly anchored in a patriarchal logic of public and private decorum characteristic of a prior age." In circulating a "spectacular body unwilling to relinquish the mystifications of beauty," Femen sextremism, Al-Kassim contends, capitalizes on both a Proudhonian demonization of women-in-public as whores and a postfeminist sexual contract that solicits a liberated woman's enjoyment in objectified display for a male gaze as an act of sovereign self-authorization. Coupled with Femen's denunciation of the "learned feminism of social justice movements and university scholars," the group's carefully painted breasts, salon-dyed hair, and garlanded heads glamorized by professional photographers and documentarians flesh out the script of a new postfeminist sexual contract that, as McRobbie explains it, reauthorizes gender inequity by interpellating "young women as subjects of capacity . . . endlessly working on a perfectible self" while donning "a mask of womanliness to avert anxiety and the retribution feared from men'" (Al-Kassim in this volume, citing McRobbie, 726).

While Al-Kassim problematizes Femen's entrepreneurial mobilization of public nudity as spectacle, Eyal Amiran reflects on the fantasmic repercussions of a technologically produced scopic regime that infiltrates the sexual lives of the powerful and the ordinary alike. In "The Pornocratic Body in the Age of Networked Paranoia," Amiran borrows Proudhon's "pornocracy" to "[designate] the way the sexual exhibition of the body is understood to secure political power." In the "networked age," as Amiran writes, "Radar, sonar, and spy satellites" enhance "perceivability, detection, and exposure" by extending "the capacity of the apparatus to spy anything anywhere." Paranoia arises as the "systemic vision" promised by these overlapping technologies seems to operate as an imaginary world government that increasingly exerts its power autonomously without human intervention. Though its aim is total visibility, this indifferent mechanical gaze neutralizes the aura of intimate exposure in drone shots of couples "on rooftops or on hillsides"; it also engulfs the anonymously released telephone conversations of sexually bantering royals. With their banal secrets revealed, Prince Charles with Camilla Parker Bowles and Princess Diana with James Gilbey seemed to "become unworthy of spectacle," as if the royal body caught in the networked regime could no longer serve as a public body and so, subsumed by the surveillance apparatus that reveals it, disappears from political efficacy. At the same time, the presumed sophistication of the recording technologies involved and the anonymity of the leaking agencies occasioned paranoia about government or even military espionage, thus highlighting "contradictions built-in to the public body." As Amiran contends, "They help guarantee the exceptionality of that body" while rendering it common on a formal level.

In "Pornocracy's Queer Circulations," Natasha Hurley identifies the catachrestic reversibility of the paranoia that adrenalizes "Proudhon's cautionary tale about a coming pornocracy" in order to ask what this phantasm "animates for a contemporary politics of gender and sexuality as matters of sexual circulation." Her essay excavates the queer forms Proudhon's fantasy "takes and conceals within itself," including a potentially subversive and even "world-making capacity" for redistributing sex and gender roles (as Proudhon feared) in projecting a sexual sociability "outside of heteronormative contracts."

In August 2015 the Department of Homeland Security and New York police raided Rentboy.com's offices and arrested seven employees. In its nineteen years as an extensive male escort site, Rentboy made a profitable business out of "creating the conditions under which sex workers can make their own economic arrangements." Even if the site's activities were liminally legal, Hurley is right to question the impetus to conjure brothels where there are none and to deploy a federal agency "charged with protecting America from terrorists" to take down an enterprise that operated "according to the standards of business available to it under conditions of American democracy."

Intersecting with Amiran's contribution, Hurley's reflections about the Rentboy raid make a strong case for viewing pornocracy as a paranoid fantasy that underwrites "the interests of conservative and sexist forms of political rule" that uphold certain sexual circulations at the expense of others. The hypocritical misrecognition that Hurley distinguishes as a "central, even constitutive feature" of the pornocracy fantasy registers as a gap between its phantasmatic content "and the norms of speech, gender, and political economy that it enacts through . . . naming"—that is, between the disavowed desire at its heart and a normative deployment that formally exceeds its putative content. We might speculate that Omar Mateen was caught in this gap when he shot forty-nine people at the Pulse nightclub in Orlando in June 2016.[25] The mass shooting gives cultural critics still more urgent reason to confront paranoia fantasies about sexual circulation that plot the licentious other's immobilization.

In "'There's Plenty of Rapists Here': 'Rape Culture' and the Representation of Anene Booysen's Rape in the International and South African Press," Helen Frost compares news treatments of two particularly gruesome gang rapes in India and South Africa respectively: that of twenty-three-year-old Jyoti Singh Pandey on a bus in Delhi and that of seventeen-year-old Anene Booysen, whose body was discovered in a construction site in Bredasdorp. What comes to the fore in Frost's analysis is how the international press's deployment of the term "rape culture" to signify "a complex of beliefs that encourages male sexual aggression and supports violence against women" (Frost, citing Buchwald) allows Western whites to sympathetically appropriate rape scenes, thereby translating at a fantasy level intraracial into interracial violence.

Frost's essay goes on to detail the situation in postapartheid South Africa, "where a woman is more likely to be raped than to be literate, and where one in three women will be raped in her lifetime." In this connection, Frost cites Franco Barchiesi's assessment linking intraracial violence against women to "disenchantment with precarious employment," which is then "transposed 'into a revanchist image of order and purity'" (Frost, citing Barchiesi, 232). For Frost, the specificities of this situation call on feminists to take distance from rape narratives that override the contexts and conditions of intraracial violence in serving as ciphers "for national anxieties." What South Africa and the United States hold in common, according to Frost, are "rape narratives that catalogued racist anxieties [and] effectively criminalized black men, [obscuring] the history of violence of white men against women of color, and [justifying] the necessity of white dominance." Yet even when they are meant to register solidarity with the victims, such narratives displace the women in South Africa and India who are actually affected by rape while shoring up the Western subject's moral authority. In circulating these narratives, the Western media can dispose of sexual violence onto "inherently uncivilized" black and brown men, thus stereotyping the latter as the progeny of barbaric "cultures that rape."

THE DUTY OF THE TYRANT

"One can erect as a duty the maxim of countering the desire of the tyrant, if," as Lacan says, "the tyrant is the one who arrogates to himself the power to enslave the desire of the Other" (70). Lacan's sally about Sade's "treatise on education" aptly describes Proudhon's insistence that domesticity constrains women for their own good. In the contemporary moment, it also applies to the ongoing war against sexual–reproductive rights and queer marriage advanced by evangelicals and Republicans in the United States, who punish sex that does not further a patriarchal plot. In Lacan's words: "The sermon is excruciating for the victim, self-infatuated on the part of the instructor" (72).

Since I began drafting this introduction in the months prior to Trump's election in November 2016, exposés published in the *New*

York Times and the *New Yorker* in the fall of 2017 about Harvey Weinstein's decades-long serial harassment of women in "the industry" (Kantor and Twohey; Farrow) have precipitated the #MeToo campaign uncovering a succession of once mighty chief executives, politicians, directors, producers, actors, comedians, newscasters, journalists, writers, artists, and chefs among others who have been falling one by one on their swords, so to speak. The ever-growing list currently includes James Toback, Louis C.K., Kevin Spacey, Ben Affleck, Brett Ratner, Chris Savino, Russell Simmons, John Besh, Ken Baker, Roy Price, R. Kelly, Mark Halperin, Michael Orekes, Lockhart Steele, Leon Wieseltier, James Levine, Robert Scoble, David Blaine, Matt Lauer, Garrison Keillor, Gianni Versace, Dustin Hoffman, Rick Najèra, Jeremy Piven, Steven Segal, Alex Kozinski, Ed Westwick, Roy Moore, Al Franken, John Conyers, George H.W. Bush, Blake Farenthold, Ruben Kihuen, and Morgan Freeman.[26] Despite their widely divergent fates, the cases of Weinstein and Trump are paradigmatic in attesting to a systemic exchange between sex, power, and capital that defies the false appearance of eruption when politicians' and celebrities' sex lives become public matters. For what becomes clear, if anything, from the exposures of Dennis Hastert, Eliot Spitzer, Anthony Weiner, Arnold Schwarzenneger, Mark Sanford, John Edwards, Larry Craig, Newt Gingrich, Bill Clinton, Tim Murphy, Scott DesJarlais, David Vitter, and, in prior eras, Clarence Thomas and Gary Hart, is that these men are sometimes, though not always, ruined by their sexcapades. In these situations, the government faces a stark choice: either "deny it or prosecute itself," as Amiran puts it, referring to a different context, or wait and hope that an outraged public moves on to new scandals.[27]

Yet even as corporations assume more rights, privileges, and protections than citizens (as officiated by Citizens United), the internet-enhanced scopic regime has simultaneously increased the average person's ability to watch, make, or star in a porno while affirming platitudes about self-inventive agency. In this vein, media exposés of sexual transgression weave a voyeuristic public sphere where prurient visualizations of the secret lives of sex-addicted politicians, royals, and celebrities distort our judgments about the ulterior reality of power. Meanwhile, revanchist *ressentiment* against "politically correct elites" congeals into increasingly brazen racism and misogyny—between Gamergate, the alt-right, and "lock her up"; between gerrymandered

red state voting booths and a Republican-controlled House and Senate. While many of us not long ago too readily dismissed Trump's presidential candidacy as a joke, this white supremacist, fat-shaming, egomaniacal reality-TV bully who stands plausibly accused by multiple women of unwanted touching and even sexual assault currently holds the highest office in the land, the crowning boil of a long-simmering toxic-masculinist backlash.[28]

It has been a dizzying (and impossible) task to keep up with this cruelly pornocratic regime that does everything in its power—with its environmental, health, immigration, sexual, labor, and tax agenda—to enrich the 1 percent[29] while undermining public education as well as union membership and intensifying the beck-and-call readiness of a survival-anxious and heavily-indebted underclass. As Michelle Goldberg notes, the president who once made a cameo in a soft-porn film signed "a new, souped-up version of the global gag rule three days after he was sworn in." Hence, while it may have been "inevitable," as Goldberg acknowledges, that "a Republican president would reinstate this policy, first enacted by Ronald Reagan, prohibiting foreign aid organizations receiving family planning funding from making abortion referrals or lobbying for abortion law reform," our pornocratic leader "dramatically expanded the gag rule's scope, so that it now applies to all foreign health assistance programs—affecting more than $8.8 billion in funding, instead of just $600 million" (2017b).[30] Despite their failure to pass a health-care bill that would neutralize the benefits of the Affordable Care Act and leave millions with pre-existing conditions uninsured, Paul Ryan and his sadocapitalist ilk continue to set their sights on Medicaid cuts that could, along with the fierce campaign against Planned Parenthood, deprive poor women of prenatal and postnatal care (see Cauterrucci). And there is apparently no limit to the Republicans' machinations to force families to shoulder the costs associated with childbirth and compel women not only to bear children but also stay home.[31] While cynically invoking the First Amendment on behalf of religious business owners who eschew the ACA's provision of insurance coverage for birth control for their female employees, Republican legislators at the federal and state level have also systematically chipped away at the constitutional right to abortion and balked at shoring up maternity leave. Women who cannot afford birth control or access abortion might, if the Republicans have their way, be obliged to give birth without either access to medical attention or legal protections that ensure their ability to hold down jobs while caring for newborn infants.

In this political climate, it can no longer surprise anyone that both Trump and the RNC endorsed the virulently homophobic, Islamophobic, and racist Roy Moore to replace Jeff Sessions as an Alabama senator. As a new adaptation of Margaret Atwood's *The Handmaid's Tale* filled our screens with scarlet, Republican Proudhons who consistently advance restrictions on women's sexual–reproductive freedom ultimately backed a sexual predator who is rumored to have been banned from the Gadsden, Alabama, mall for stalking teenagers (see Palma). A majority of white voters in Alabama preferred a gun-toting pedophile who locates family values and the good old days in the antebellum South because of his antiabortion credentials to the Democrat Doug Jones, a former state district attorney famous for prosecuting the remaining Ku Klux Klan perpetrators of the Sixteenth Street Baptist Church bombing in 1963. Jones won the senate seat despite white Alabama voters who, on behalf of the unborn, condoned a master's right to dispense with the thorny issue of underaged girls' consent.

Finally, though Proudhon presumably believed his own polemics, our historical distance from Second Empire France generates an occasion to reflect on how his paranoid "rule by harlots" fantasy not only incites today's theocrats but also inspires those identifying with the rich and powerful who, along with their fans, venerate a Sadean above-the-law sexual sovereignty. Resurrecting Proudhon casts a critical light on how sexual liberation narratives have not only "freed" bodies and pleasures but also supplemented cultural scripts that groom the susceptible into believing that servicing sadists sexually and/or economically is an act of self-empowerment or, indeed, self-care. The danger, as Swiffen intimates, is when the masocapitalist subject position becomes the only viable "choice" for expanding national and global majorities. In her critique of Femen, Al-Kassim raises concerns about the impact of a postfeminist contract that affirms the pleasures of performing femininity for an objectifying gaze as a vehicle of personal fulfillment and economic autonomy over and against prior feminist waves' déclassé stridency about equality. Amiran, Hurley, and Frost have reflected on the implications of asymmetrical surveillance on a national and global scale as they sketch the psychosocial contours of an everyday scopic regime in which women, queers, people of color, Muslims, and emigrants exceedingly bear the compounding strain of ubiquitous scrutiny and lethal threats restricting their ability to circulate. Among the many questions these contributors raise is how members of the targeted groups manage the sense of betrayal that accrues as state representatives either model or implicitly authorize the paranoia that incites hate speech, rape, police brutality, and lethal violence against those perceived as corrupting, subverting, or "stealing" the emperor's enjoyment. It is a matter of navigating a systemic double bind: either internalize and perform surrender, which nevertheless does not guarantee survival, or refuse the command and face the hate. Woe, then, to those who do not masochistically enjoy their abject lot and therefore fail to honor a contract not of their making, or, as Hurley indicates, whose threat cannot be contained because it does not exist.

Swiffen warns that if an underclass does not already exist to service self-styled pornocrats, then they will create it, and what more optimal method than neoliberal policies underwriting less-than-subsistence wages, flexibilization, predatory loans, for-profit schools, coerced childbirth, inadequate health insurance, and unraveled safety nets that wear down the increasingly precarious into acceding to oligarchical whims? To wrestle with the moralism that a critique of contemporary pornocracy risks is to confront a perverse imaginary that misrecognizes Sade's tyrannical dispatch of consent as the secret and proof of success.

Karyn Ball is professor of English and film studies specializing in critical theory at the University of Alberta. Her articles have appeared in *Cultural Critique, Women in German Yearbook, Research in Political Economy, Differences, English Studies in Canada, New Literary History, Alif,* the open-access journal *Humanities, Holocaust Studies: A Journal of Culture and History, Law and Critique,* and *Angelaki.*

Notes

1. Cited from the translation included in this volume.

2. From a Marxian standpoint, fictitious capital consists of "a claim over a share of future surplus value (profit), as opposed to existing commodities." According to Harvey, it is implied "whenever credit is extended in advance, in expectation of future labour as counter-value; that is, the extraction of surplus

value through primary forms of exploitation" (Soederberg, 36, citing Harvey, 269). Insofar as fictitious capital has increasingly eclipsed capital accumulation in recent decades, it threatens "the quality of real money upon which credit money rests" while reinforcing the erroneous appearance of accumulated debt as accumulated capital. Recent crises transpire as credit systems "register the height of distortion to the degree that the accumulation of future claims of labour as counter-value outruns real production" (36, citing Harvey, 269).

3. The trope Soederberg designates the "democracy of money" promotes the myth that "all individuals—despite different resource endowments and different assets—can become good market citizens" (74). "Good market citizens" are ostensibly equal before the law: when they enter into exchanges as lenders or borrowers, they are depicted as operating on a level playing field, which "also implies that the poor will be held accountable to meet their payment obligations" (74–75). At the state-policy level, the emphasis thus falls on "access, fairness, and transparency" rather than on "guaranteeing a living wage, social protection and the subsidization of basic social services" (75).

4. Soederberg demonstrates how the collusion between neoliberal policies and debt securitization has transformed the credit card industry into a highly lucrative sector run by "a handful of Wall Street banks," an oligopoly in effect by VISA, which controls half of the market share; by MasterCard at a quarter; and American Express, Discover, along with other smaller companies absorbing the remaining 25 percent (78–79).

5. In this connection, Foucault quotes Giscard d'Estaing as saying, "I'm going to march down the streets in a lounge suit, shaking hands with ordinary people and kids on half-day holidays" (127).

6. Ida Dominijanni traces the implications of a postfeminist sexual contract in her critical examination of the Italian media's depictions of young women potentially seeking jobs in the TV stations Italian prime minister Berlusconi owned, who staffed "orgy-like parties" at his residences in Rome and Milan. The pornocratic underside of sexual autonomy fetishism manifested itself in the media's investment in affirming the young women's "freedom" to profit from the use of their bodies. After Italy's president, Giorgio Napolitano, pressured Berlusconi to resign and thereafter installed a technocratic government, an austerity-oriented "debt and guilt" rhetoric displaced the Berlusconi-gate discourse of sex, consumption, and pleasure.

7. The so-called "girlfriend experience" has been dramatized in a series created, written, and directed by Lodge Kerrigan and Amy Seimetz, based on a 2009 film by Steven Soederberg, who is also the show's executive producer.

8. One "baby" Sales interviewed characterized her situation in this way: "'While in college,' she goes on, 'I've had the ability to focus on developing myself because I'm not slaving away at a minimum-wage job. I reject it when people say I'm oppressed by the patriarchy. People who make seven dollars an hour are oppressed by the patriarchy.' 'She's in control of the male gaze,' says another woman at the table, Erin, 22" (Sales 2016).

9. Jesse Singal's interrogation of Sales's moral panic rhetoric is worth heeding. As Singal writes, Sales is "hardly the first journalist to raise this alarm: Over the last few years, reports on 'hookup culture'—some focusing on alcohol and campus culture, some on technology, and some on both—have become a thriving genre." In his editorial for *New York Magazine,* Singal questions Sales's reliance on anecdotal evidence. The problem with Sales's analysis, according to Singal, is that "we hear almost exclusively from young, single people who are active (sometimes overactive) Tinder users, and almost entirely from men who are constantly looking for casual sex." To the extent that Sales "is talking to exactly the sorts of people you'd expect to use dating apps in a way that will help them find more people to sleep with," Sales inevitably ascertains "that these promiscuous people use a promiscuity-enabling app to find other promiscuous people to have promiscuous sex with." Sales then compounds this error by "reporting back to us that we're in the midst of a promiscuity-fueled dating 'revolution' in how people deal with romance and sex." As Singal declares, "This is known as *confirmation bias.*" While "Tinder super-users are an important slice of the population to study," as Singal acknowledges, "they can't be used as a stand-in for 'millennials' or 'society' or any other such broad categories."

10. As reported by Andrew Longstreth in the *World Post* on July 7, 2011: "Prosecutors said [Strauss-Kahn's accuser] told them her 2004 application for asylum was filled with false information about her experiences in Guinea, including that she was gang-raped. She stated that she and her husband were beaten by police and soldiers of the country's ruling party, which they opposed. She also stated that after her husband was arrested and tortured to death, she fled the country in fear for her life. But in interviews with prosecutors, she said a man gave her a cassette recording to coach her on what to say on the application."

11. Diallo ultimately settled a civil case against Strauss-Kahn in December 2012 and opened the Chez Amina restaurant in New York in May 2015. See Buettner; Hu.

12. Bruckner writes: "What was the real point of the Dominique Strauss-Kahn and Clinton cases? They were a perfect vehicle to condemn eroticism in order to be able to talk more about sex. For weeks, even months, American people licked their lips over every intimate detail: about fellatio, sperm, genital organs—always with a false indignation. The fact that the alleged victim's lawyer Kenneth Thompson talked about the 'assaulted' vagina of his client Nafissatou Diallo with obscene jubilation is a telltale sign of this phenomenon."

13. See Krieg; Peyser. See also Berenson.

14. "When asked if they would like to have sex with me," Silvio Berlusconi reportedly boasted, "30 percent of women said, 'Yes,' while the other 70 percent replied, 'What, again?'" (quoted by Bruni). In her *Vanity Fair* story, "La Dolce Viagra," Evgenia Peretz writes: "Imagine a President Donald Trump with the media holdings of Rupert Murdoch and the sexual tastes of an aging Charlie Sheen, and you're approaching the idea of Berlusconi" (quoted by Bruni). As Bruni quips, "Trump is Berlusconi in waiting, with less cosmetic surgery. Berlusconi is Trump

in senescence, with even higher alimony payments." "It's even a porn flick—or close to one," Bruni opines: "Trumpusconi stars overlapping cads who cultivate dovetailing images as epic playboys: 'Best Sex I Ever Had' blared a front-page headline in the New York Post in 1990. It ostensibly quoted Marla Maples, the second of Trump's three wives, but a skeptical reader wondered who really planted that story, especially as the years went by and Trump's boasts flowered: 'All of the women on "The Apprentice" flirted with me, consciously or unconsciously. That's to be expected'; "Oftentimes when I was sleeping with one of the top women in the world I would say to myself, thinking about me as a boy from Queens, 'Can you believe what I'm getting?'" In "The Trump-Berlusconi Syndrome," Roger Cohen recalls how the "man known as 'The Knight' ended up convicted of tax fraud and paying for sex with an underage prostitute—but it took 17 years of intermittent scandal and incompetence, from 1994 to 2011, for Italy to rub the stardust from its eyes." According to Cohen, "What Berlusconi teaches is that Trump could go all the way in a nation thirsting for a new politics." Cohen quotes Alexander Stille on the deregulation of broadcast media in the United States and Italy, which, in contrast to Britain or France or Germany, where state media companies still "act as a kind of referee for civil discourse" and "commonly accepted facts," has fostered the fact-lite free-for-all of "alternate realities" that mire Trumpism.

15. Since the 2016 presidential election, we might take little solace in Jean Starobinski's observation that, in Sade's time, the aristocracy's fascination with "the most excessive pleasures" seemed secretly to connive "with the judgments that condemned it," thereby undermining it "from within by the imminence of its own demise" (cited by Roudinesco, 30).

16. According to Berlant and Warner, among the many forms this matrix of belonging assumed during Clinton's administration were "new welfare and tax 'reforms' passed under the cooperation between the Contract with America and Clintonian familialism [that] seek to increase the legal and economic privileges of married couples and parents" while "vouchers and privatization rezone education as the domain of parents rather than citizens." When Senators Jessie Helms and Ted Kennedy favored amendments targeting materials that explicitly depict or describe "sexual or excretory functions or organs," they attempted both to delegitimize and contain the public circulation of gay pleasures as the enemy of hetero-familial reproduction's devotion-based glory (314).

17. See Carroll. Justice Ginsburg voiced her concern that the decision, split along gender lines, had, for the first time, extended religious freedom protections to 'the commercial, profit-making world'" (see Liptak). From the standpoint of a critique of pornocracy, Hobby Lobby served Proudhonian interests in restricting women's mobility as sexual agents. In contrast, the 2010 Citizens United v. Federal Election Commission decision expanded "bankocracy" by ending limits on corporate contributions to super PACS, which were already operating beyond campaign parameters. In conjunction, the Citizens United and Hobby Lobby cases imply that corporations are supracitizens with more rights and protections than a citizen-individual.

18. Anita Kumar quotes Senator Janet D. Howell's elaboration on this point: "'Very rarely do I get angry, but I am angry about this bill,' she said. 'It reflects an attitude that is demeaning to women. It presumes the legislature—which as we look around is virtually all male—knows better what should happen to a woman's body than the woman herself and her physician."

19. Republicans renewed their 2016 platform's opposition to same-sex marriage, despite the Supreme Court's 2012 ruling (Peters).

20. Elle Roberts reports that, in fiscal year 2013, "nearly $350,000 in domestic violence funding was reverted back to the Indiana's general fund as directed by Pence's Office of Management and Budget (OMB)," even though, as Roberts emphasizes, "funds were already designated and approved at every level. The office has yet to answer why—other than to boost the bottom line."

21. A calculation was apparently made that the amount of federal funding withdrawn would be less than the amount needed to fulfill the Act's terms.

22. According to Zadrozny, Epstein "also agreed to a few dozen confidential, out-of-court payoffs to his accusers, the most recent of which was finalized in 2011."

23. Saidiya Hartman amplifies Spillers's 1987 intervention in attending to "seduction narratives" in representations of slavery that occult the female slave's inability to consent or resist, and who is therefore "presumed to be always willing" (81).

24. Davis intervenes in historiography of the feminist movement that locates its origins in white women's abolitionism (thus whitewashing feminism) when she outlines a history of feminist activism in which black women workers were among the first plaintiffs to bring Title VII harassment claims against white and black men (470). Davis lists Margaret Miller, Paulette Barnes, Diane Williams, and Maxine Munford "among the earliest women to litigate sexual harassment as prohibited sex discrimination" (470). In this connection, she quotes Nadine Taub, who conjectures that it was probably no accident "that many of the early cases were brought by black women because," as Taub surmises, "a lot of white women could be tricked into thinking that [something] could be worked out, whereas for black women, they knew. They'd been exploited since day one" (Davis 478, citing Marshall, 776). This history is crucial to remember when we examine the racial breakdown of the votes that cost Roy Moore a senate seat in Alabama, a state that implemented voter identification protocols and, at one point, shut down DMVs in predominantly black areas, though it has since reversed that action according to German Lopez writing for *Vox*.

25. See Shariatmadari. Though Trump was quick to congratulate himself for predicting trouble from Muslim immigrants (ignoring Mateen's U.S. citizenship), the mentally ill shooter's homophobic paranoia links him to a majority of evangelical voters whose loyalty Trump currently commands.

26. See Santiago; see also Almukhtar, Gold, and Buchanan.

27. For an alternative list of infamies, see Listal's "Politicians Who Cheated," compiled and published by astro_man23 in May 2011. The list features comments about each politician's hypocrisy and does not stop short of deriding married Founding Father Thomas Jefferson for "sticking [his] paw in the brown sugar jar."

Under the "omg" category, "Jefferson" brags: "I was the founding father of more than just America, bitches. Mocha babies!"

28. The idea of an interconnection between sadomasochism, authoritarianism, and "toxic masculinity" has been gaining currency in the media since Trump's election. See Ray Williams, "The Rebirth of Macho: Toxic Masculinity and Authoritarianism" and Michelle Goldberg, "Fifty Shades of Orange." Goldberg quotes Eric Fromm, "a German-Jewish psychoanalyst who fled Nazism [and] described authoritarian personalities as simultaneously craving power and submission. 'The authoritarian character loves those conditions that limit human freedom; he loves being submitted to fate,'" he wrote. Fate, in his formulation, can be the laws of the market, the will of God, or the whims of a leader. According to Fromm, authoritarians might make a show of valuing freedom and independence—watchwords of the American right—but long to be ruled by a stronger force. . . . Certainly, it's understandable that people on the right would try to get what they can out of this president. But the relationship between Trump and many Republicans increasingly looks less like a marriage of convenience than a sadomasochistic affair."

29. In December 2017, Trump signed the Republicans' $1.5 trillion tax bill that permanently slashes the corporate rate from 35 to 21 percent and conspicuously favors rentiers.

30. As Goldberg (2017b) reports: "On April 13, the president signed a law repealing an Obama-era rule protecting Planned Parenthood from state efforts to withhold money allocated by Title X, the only federal program expressly devoted to family planning. (Planned Parenthood cares for about a third of the four million Americans served by Title X.) Adding insult to injury, the official appointed by Mr. Trump to oversee Title X is an antiabortion activist named Teresa Manning, who has said that contraception 'doesn't work.'"

31. Writing for *CNN Money*, Julie Rovner reports that "the total price charged for pregnancy and newborn care ranges widely but averages about $30,000 for a vaginal delivery and $50,000 for a cesarean section, with commercial insurers paying out an average of $18,329 and $27,866." She also notes that, "Seema Verma, the consultant on private health insurance who was nominated to head the agency that oversees the health law, said at her Senate confirmation hearing last month that she does not necessarily support keeping maternity care as a requirement for insurance plans."

Works Cited

Almukhtar, Sarah, Michael Gold, and Larry Buchanan. 2017. "After Weinstein: 45 Men Accused of Sexual Misconduct and Their Fall from Power." *New York Times*, December 15. https://www.nytimes.com/interactive/2017/11/10/us/men-accused-sexual-misconduct-weinstein.html?_r=0.

Astro_man23. 2011. "Politicians Who Cheated." Listal, May 17. http://www.listal.com/list/did-not-have-sexual-relations.

Barchiesi, Franco. 2011. *Precarious Liberation: Workers, the State, and Contested Social Citizenship in Postapartheid South Africa*. Albany: State University of New York Press.

Berenson, Tessa. 2016. "Donald Trump Backs 'Punishment' for Women Who Get Abortions, Then Backtracks." *Time*, March 30. http://time.com/4276862/donald-trump-abortion-ban-punishment/.

Berlant, Lauren, and Michael Warner. 2000. "Sex in Public." In *Intimacy*. Ed. Lauren Berlant, 311–30. Chicago: University of Chicago Press.

Bloom, Lisa. 2017. "Why the New Child Rape Case Filed against Donald Trump Should Not Be Ignored." *Huffington Post*, June 29. http://www.huffingtonpost.com/lisa-bloom/why-the-new-child-rape-ca_b_10619944.html.

Brown, Wendy. 2015. *Undoing the Demos: Neoliberalism's Stealth Revolution*. Brooklyn, N.Y.: Zone Books.

Bruckner, Pascal. 2011. "Making War, Not Love: A French View on Sex in America—From AbuGhraib To DSK." *Worldcrunch*, August 25. http://www.worldcrunch.com/making-war-not-love-french-view-sex-america-abu-ghraib-dsk/eyes-on-the-u.s./making-war-not-love-a-french-view-on-sex-in-america-from-abu-ghraib-to-dsk-/c5s3642/. Originally published under the title "L'affaire DSK aura révélé une bien triste image de l'Amérique" in *Le Monde*, August 24. http://www.lemonde.fr/idees/article/2011/08/24/l-affaire-dsk-aura-revele-une-bien-triste-image-de-l-amerique_1562650_3232.html.

Bruni, Frank. 2015. "La Dolce Donald Trump." *New York Times*, July 18. http://www.nytimes.com/2015/07/19/opinion/sunday/frank-bruni-la-dolce-donald-trump.html.

Buchwald, Emile, Pamela R. Fletcher, and Martha Roth. 2005. "Introduction." In *Transforming a Rape Culture*. Rev. ed. Ed. Emile Buchwald, Pamela R. Fletcher, and Martha Roth, xii–xvii. Minneapolis: Milkweed Editions.

Buettner, Russ. 2012. "Hotel Worker Settles Claim Strauss-Kahn Forced Sex." *New York Times*, December 10. http://www.nytimes.com/2012/12/11/nyregion/strauss-kahn-and-hotel-maid-settle-suit-over-alleged-attack.html?rref=collection%252Ftimestopic%252FDiallo%252C%20Nafissatou&action=click&contentCollection=timestopics&region=stream&module=stream_unit&version=latest&contentPlacement=5&pgtype=collection.

Bui, Quoctrung, and Amanda Cox. 2016. "Surprising New Evidence Shows Bias in Use of Force But Not in Police Shootings." *New York Times*, July 11. http://www.nytimes.com/2016/07/12/upshot/surprising-new-evidence-shows-bias-in-police-use-of-force-but-not-in-shootings.html?_r=0.

Carroll, Aaron E. 2014. "How the Hobby Lobby Ruling Could Limit Access to Birth Control." *New York Times*, June 30. http://www.nytimes.com/2014/07/02/upshot/how-hobby-lobby-ruling-could-limit-access-to-birth-control.html?action=click&contentCollection=U.S.&region=Footer&module=MoreInSection&pgtype=article&_r=0.

Cauterrucci, Christina. 2017. "Trumpcare Is the Perfect Document of the GOP: Pro-birth, Anti-woman, Anti-child." *Slate*, June 26. http://www.slate.com/blogs/xx_factor/2017/06/26/trumpcare_is_a_war_on_women_s_health.html.

Chrisafis, Angelique. 2015. "Strauss-Kahn Subjected Me to Sex Acts against My Will, Woman Tells Court." *Guardian,* February 11. https://www.theguardian.com/world/2015/feb/11/dominique-strauss-kahn-sex-act-woman-french-court.

Chrisafis, Angelique, Kim Willsher, and Dominic Rush. 2011. "Dominique Strauss-Kahn Charged with Sex Attack on New York Hotel Maid." *Guardian,* May 15. https://www.theguardian.com/world/2011/may/15/dominique-strauss-kahn-imf-sex-charges.

Cohen, Roger. 2016. "The Trump-Berlusconi Syndrome." *New York Times,* March 14. http://www.nytimes.com/2016/03/15/opinion/the-trump-berlusconi-syndrome.html?src=me.

Collins, Gail. 2016. "Trump Deals the Woman Card." *New York Times,* April 28. http://www.nytimes.com/2016/04/28/opinion/trump-deals-the-woman card.html?action=click&contentCollection=Opinion&module=Trending&version=Full&region=Marginalia&pgtype=article.

Davis, Adrienne D. 2013. "Slavery and the Roots of Sexual Harassment." In *Directions in Sexual Harassment Law.* Ed. Catherine A. MacKinnon and Reva B. Siegel, 457–78. New Haven: Yale University Press.

"Dominique-Strauss-Kahn Accusation Details Emerge." 2011. *World Post,* May 16. http://www.huffingtonpost.com/2011/05/16/dominique-strauss-kahn-accusation_n_862728.html.

Dominijanni, Ida. 2014. *Il trucco. Sessualità e biopolitica nella fine di Berlusconi* [The Trick: sexuality and biopolitics in the end of Berlusconi]. Rome: Edièsse.

Edemariam, Aida. 2009. "Being Mrs. Berlusconi." *Guardian,* April 30. https://www.theguardian.com/world/2009/may/01/veronica-lario-silvio-berlusconi-marriage.

Farrow, Ronan. 2017. "Harvey Weinstein's Army of Spies." *New Yorker,* November 6. https://www.newyorker.com/news/news-desk/harvey-weinsteins-army-ofspies.

Foucault, Michel. 1996. "Film and Popular Memory." In *Foucault Live: Collected Interviews, 1961–1984.* Ed. Sylvère Lotringer, 122–32. New York: Semiotext(e).

Goldberg, Michelle. 2017a. "Fifty Shades of Orange." *New York Times,* December 22. https://www.nytimes.com/2017/12/22/opinion/fifty-shades-trump-republicans.html?_r=0.

Goldberg, Michelle. 2017b. "The Playboy President and Women's Health." *New York Times,* July 14. https://www.nytimes.com/2017/07/14/opinion/donald-trump-women-reproductive-rights.html.

Graham Holm, Nancy. 2011. "Civilization in Suite 2806." *Huffington Post,* July 11. http://www.huffingtonpost.com/nancy-graham-holm/dominique-strauss-kahn_b_891411.html.

Hartman, Saidiya V. 1997. *Scenes of Subjection: Terror, Slavery, and Self-Making in Nineteenth-Century America.* New York: Oxford University Press.

Harvey, David. *The Urban Experience.* Baltimore: Johns Hopkins University Press, 1989.

Hu, Winnie. 2015. "Accuser in Strauss-Kahn Case Builds Restaurant and a Refuge." *New York Times,* February 3. http://www.nytimes.com/2015/02/04/nyregion/accuser-in-strauss-kahn-case-builds-restaurant-and-a-refuge.html.

Hunt, Lynn. 1996. *The Invention of Pornography, 1500–1800: Obscenity and the Origins of Modernity.* Cambridge, Mass.: Zone Books.

Kantor, Jodi, and Megan Twohey. 2017. "Harvey Weinstein Paid Off Sexual Harassment Accusers for Decades." *New York Times,* October 5. https://www.nytimes.com/2017/10/05/us/harvey-weinstein-harassment-allegations.html.

Keyes, Alexa. 2012. "Rush Limbaugh Doubles Down on Sandra Fluke, Offering 'As Much Aspirin to Put between Her Knees as She Wants.'" *ABC News,* March 1. http://abcnews.go.com/blogs/politics/2012/03/rush-limbaugh-sandra-fluke-a-slut-and-prostitute/.

Krieg, Gregory. 2016. "Trump Defends Size of His Penis." *CNN Politics,* March 4. http://www.cnn.com/2016/03/03/politics/donald-trump-small-hands-marco-rubio/.

Kumar, Anita. 2012. "Virginia Senate Approves Contentious Ultrasound Bill." *Washington Post,* February 28. https://www.washingtonpost.com/local/dc-politics/va-senate-approves-contentious-ultrasound-bill/2012/02/27/gIQAvhiVgR_story.html?noredirect=on&utm_term=.8145cbcffe2b.

Lacan, Jacques. 1989. "Kant with Sade." Trans. James Swenson. *October* 51 (Winter): 55–75.

Lever, Maurice. 1991. *Sade*. Paris: Fayard.

Liptak, Adam. 2014. "Supreme Court Rejects Contraceptives Mandate for Some Corporations: Justices Rule in Favor of Hobby Lobby." *New York Times,* June 30. http://www.nytimes.com/2014/07/01/us/hobby-lobby-case-supreme-court-contraception.html.

Longstreth, Andrew. 2011. "Dominique Strauss-Kahn's Accuser Could become the Accused." *Worldpost,* July 7. http://www.huffingtonpost.com/2011/07/07/dominique-strauss-kahns accuser_n_892551.html.

Lopez, German. 2017. "Voter Suppression in Alabama: What's True and What's Not." *Vox,* December 12. https://www.vox.com/policy-and-politics/2017/12/12/16767426/alabama-voter-suppression-senate-moore-jones.

MacKinnon, Catherine A., and Reva B. Siegel. 2013. *Directions in Sexual Harassment Law*. New Haven: Yale University Press.

Marriott, David. 2000. *On Black Men*. New York: Columbia University Press.

Marshall, Anna-Maria. 1998. "Closing the Gaps: Plaintiffs in Pivotal Sexual Harassment Cases." *Law and Social Inquiry* 23: 775–82.

McRobbie, Angela. 2007. "Top Girls? Young Women and the Post-feminist Sexual Contract." *Cultural Studies* 21, 4–5 (July/September): 718–37.

Palma, Bethania. 2017. "Was Roy Moore Banned from a Shopping Mall for Harassing Teen Girls?" Snopes, November 22. https://www.snopes.com/2017/11/17/roy-moore-banned-mall-harassing-teen-girls/.

Pateman, Carole. 1988. *The Sexual Contract*. Stanford: Stanford University Press.

Peretz, Evgenia. 2011. "La Dolce Viagra." *Vanity Fair,* July. http://www.vanityfair.com/news/2011/07/silvio-berlusconi-201107.

Peters, Jeremy. 2016. "Emerging Republican Platform Goes Far to the Right." *New York Times,* July 12. http://mobile.nytimes.com/2016/07/13/us/politics/republican-convention-issues.html?partner=rss.

Peyser, Eve. 2016. "A History of Donald Trump's Penis." *New York Magazine,* March 4. http://nymag.com/thecut/2016/03/donald-trump-best-penis-moments.html.

Prestigiacomo, Amanda. 2016. "Both Trump and Clinton Went to Epstein's Sex Slave Island." *Daily Wire,* May 16. http://www.dailywire.com/news/5749/both-trump-and-clinton-went-jeffrey-epsteins-sex-amanda-prestigiacomo.

Reinhardt, Kenneth. 1995. "Kant with Sade, Lacan with Levinas." *MLN* 110, no. 4: 785–808.

Reuters. 2011. "Dominique Strauss-Kahn Accusation Details Emerge." *Huffington Post,* May 16. http://www.huffingtonpost.com/2011/05/16/dominique-strauss-kahn-accusation-_n_862728.html.

Roberts, Elle. 2014. "The Wrong Side of Domestic Violence." *Nuvo,* September 24. https://www.nuvo.net/news/news/the-wrong-side-of-domestic-violence/article_bb7660cd-61ad-5284-805c-36cd2355dcf0.html.

Roudinesco, Élisabeth. 2009. *Our Dark Side: A History of Perversion.* Trans. David Macey. Malden,Mass.: Polity.

Rovner, Julie. 2016. "Families to Pay the Price if Maternity Coverage Gets Cut in GOP's Healthcare Plan." *CNN Money,* March 13. http://money.cnn.com/2017/03/13/news/economy/maternity-obamacare-gop/index.html.

Sade, Marquis de. 1990. *The Complete Justine, Philosophy in the Bedroom, and Other Writings.* Trans. Richard Seaver and Austryn Wainhouse. New York: Grove Press.

Sales, Nancy Jo. 2015. "Tinder and the Dawn of the Dating Apocalypse." *Vanity Fair,* August. http://www.vanityfair.com/culture/2015/08/tinder-hook-up-culture-end-of-dating.

Sales, Nancy Jo. 2016. "Daddies, 'Dates,' and the Girlfriend Experience: Welcome to the New Prostitution Economy." *Vanity Fair,* August. http://www.vanityfair.com/style/2016/07/welcome-to-the-new-prostitution-economy.

Santiago, Amanda Luz Henning. 2017. "Thirty-Six Powerful Men Accused of Misconduct after Weinstein." *Business Insider,* November 29. http://www.businessinsider.com/powerful-men-accused-of-sexual-misconduct-after-harvey-weinstein-list-2017-10/#actor-ben-affleck-1.

Sarnoff, Conchita. 2010. "The Billionaire Pedophile's Sex Den." *Daily Beast,* July 22. http://www.thedailybeast.com/articles/2010/07/22/jeffrey-epstein-pedophile-billionaire-and-his-sex-den.html.

Shariatmadari, David. 2016. "Omar Mateen's Interest in Gay Men Makes This No Ordinary Act of Terrorism." *Guardian,* June 14. https://www.theguardian.com/commentisfree/2016/jun/14/omar-mateen-gay-men-terrorism-pulse-jackd-sexuality.

Silverstein, Ken. 2016. "The Salacious Ammo Even Donald Trump Won't Use in a Fight against Hillary Clinton." *Vice News,* January 29. https://news.vice.com/article/the-salacious-ammo-even-donald-trump-wont-use-in-a-fight-against-hillary-clinton-bill-clinton.

Singal, Jesse. 2015. "Has Tinder Really Sparked a Dating Apocalypse?" *New York Magazine,* August. http://nymag.com/scienceofus/2015/08/has-tinder-really-sparked-a-dating-apocalypse.html.

Soederberg, Susanne. 2014. *Debtfare States and the Poverty Industry: Money, Discipline and the Surplus Population*. Oxford: Routledge.

Spillers, Hortense. 1987. "Mama's Baby, Papa's Maybe: An American Grammar Book." *Diacritics* 17, no. 2: 64–81.

Starobinski, Jean. 1979. *Les emblèmes de la raison*. Paris: Flammarion.

Swenson, James. 1989. "Annotations on 'Kant with Sade.'" *October* 51:76–104.

Tuohy, John. 2014. "Indiana Won't Comply with Prison Rape Act, Will Lose Federal Funding." *Indystar,* June 2. http://www.indystar.com/story/news/politics/2014/05/30/indiana-comply-prison-rape-act-will-lose-federal-funding/9781479/.

Walsh, Joan. 2016. "Mike Pence Is a Smooth-Talking Todd Akin." *Nation,* July 15. https://www.thenation.com/article/mike-pence-is-a-smooth-talking-todd-akin/.

Williams, Ray. 2017. "The Rebirth of Macho: Toxic Masculinity and Authoritarianism." *Psychology Today,* August 17. https://www.psychologytoday.com/blog/wired-success/201708/the-rebirth-machotoxic-masculinity-and-authoritarianism.

Willsher, Kim. 2011. "DSK Accuser Tristane Banon Writes Book about Assault by 'Baboon.'" *Guardian,* October 13. https://www.theguardian.com/world/2011/oct/13/dominique-strauss-kahn-tristane-banon.

Zadrozny, Brandy. 2016. "The Billionaire Pedophile Who Could Bring Down Donald Trump and Hillary Clinton." *Daily Beast,* June 29. http://www.thedailybeast.com/articles/2016/06/30/the-billionaire-pedophile-who-could-bring-down-donald-trump-and-hillary-clinton.html.

PORNOCRACY, OR WOMEN IN MODERN TIMES

Selections translated by Stefan Mattessich

Pierre-Joseph Proudhon

What is marriage?—The union of force and beauty, a union as indissoluble as that between form and matter, in which divorce implies the destruction of both. It is precisely in this that marriage differs from an essentially atomizing civil and commercial society, in which the object is gain. Force and beauty unite in gratuitous title: between them there is no reciprocal payment, the first for services, the second for favors; there is no possible commensuration between the fruits of labor and the gifts of the ideal. Marriage, in the purity of its idea, is an absolute pact of devotion. Pleasure figures only as secondary: all exchange of wealth that produces the man against the joys that procure the woman, all voluptuous commerce, is combined, in order not to be mutual prostitution. It is thus that marriage becomes for spouses a cult of conscience, and for society the very organ of justice. A sacred marriage, if it doesn't put each spouse beyond reproach, nonetheless immunizes them, vis-à-vis others, against all crime and felony; while concubinage, a union of man and woman, secret and solemn, but formed solely in view of pleasure—however excusable this might be in certain cases—is the habitual resort of parasites, of thieves, of forgers and assassins.

Oh! Ladies, I know well how much this moral appears severe to you, who take pride in force and even more in beauty, and for whom pleasure and wealth are definitively the true social contract, the true religion.[1] Admit, however, that in the conditions of work and frugality that nature imposes on our species, if you want to make marriage solid, and society virtuous, this theory of devotion is worth more than your epicurean maxims. In any case, you can't mean that I do wrong to woman, the weaker being, in my opinion; it is as such, more or less, that I treat her.

As for the family, the economy of existence divides in two principal parts: *production* and *consumption*. The first is much ruder: I make it the attribute of man; the second is more facile, more joyous: I reserve it for woman. Man labors, sows, reaps, and grinds the wheat; the woman bakes bread and cakes. All her existence, in that which concerns work, comes down to this distinction: it is of little importance in what manner, in the future, work will be divided, organized, or picked up again; in the final analysis, all operations, whether virile or feminine, are respectively dependent on plow or stew. How can you tell me that this division is unjust? . . . The table made, and the dinner served, why should I tell the woman to sit in a corner; wait, before eating, for her lord and master to make her a sign, force her to make do with stale bread, while the bread he eats is white and fresh? Far from this, I instruct spouses that all that is best in a household must be always for the women and children, and that his pleasure, for him, should be composed of theirs. Without doubt, I omit many things; I don't deny, let it be understood, that I seem in this not very gracious or good-natured; but all the same you will admit that mine are not the ways of an egoist, an exploiter, a tyrant. If it's the happiness of women that you pretend to serve, count on me to number among your partisans.

I say, following Auguste Comte, and better than him, that woman, incarnation of the ideal, seems of a superior nature to man, who has nothing but force to offer; while he procures needs, she alone gives felicity; for this reason she must be, as much as possible, freed from all utilitarian work, especially rude and repugnant work. I make of monogamy the fundamental law of the androgynous couple; I prohibit divorce; I say that, in a truly dignified marriage, love must be subordinated to conscience, to the lesson that for genuine spouses good conscience can and should take the place of love: All this to whose benefit, you ask? Obviously to the benefit of woman, of those in marriage who rule above all by beauty, who, consequently, are the most at risk of degradation.

As for matters on the outside, I don't want, for the same reasons, war, since war suits beauty as little as servitude.

I don't want politics, because politics is war.

I don't want legal, police, or governmental functions, because this too is always war.

The place of woman is in the family; the sphere of her influence is the conjugal home; it is thus that man, in whom the woman must love not beauty but force, will develop his dignity, his individuality, his character, his heroism and his grace, and it is in order to make man more and more courageous and just, and his wife consequently more and more of a queen, that I attack centralization, bureaucratization, financial feudalism, exorbitant government, and the permanence of a state of war. For this I protested, from the month of October 1848 on, against the re-establishment of the Empire, which I considered a national prostitution, and for this I have not ceased to demand economic reforms that, in making pauperism, revolt, and crime less frequent and less intense, progressively reduce the number and the tenure of magistrates, and little by little return to social order a pure and simple liberty, which means the complete restoration of the family and the glorification of woman.

I criticized, with all the energy of which I was capable, seduction, adultery, incest, stupor, rape, prostitution, all the crimes and offenses against marriage and the family, which is to say against women. I denounced them as signs and instruments of despotism: and I dare flatter myself that my words will not appear to you suspect. If, in a certain measure, and before the gravest authorities, I have on occasion excused concubinage, it was again in the interest of women. I have no doubt that it hasn't been possible to speak better in this regard than I have; but in any event I spoke as best I could according to my feeble means, and if I look around me, if I look back into the past, I don't see another author, not one, who took equally to heart the cause of your sex.

~

There is no power without beauty, and, reciprocally, no beauty without power, no more than there exists matter without form, or form without matter; for this reason one speaks of a *male beauty* and a *female strength*; this is why woman has her place in domestic production, the same as man has his in the art of living well, which is nothing but housekeeping all over again.

But power and beauty, as intimately united as matter and form, are not the same thing; their nature is not identical, their action even less. No effort of thought can reduce them to a single expression. In organic sexuality, there exists a difference that everyone feels and that reason proclaims irreducible between man and woman.

But is this difference not illusory? Is it really, as you pretend, ladies, nothing but an effect of education and habit, to such a degree that one can hope, by a change of regime, to make it disappear and to leave between the sexes no difference but that constructed by social device? In other words, must the system of relations between men and women, which I sought to establish in the *equivalence* of their attributes, be grounded on the contrary in the EQUALITY and IDENTITY of these same attributes? The entire dispute is here.

Note that the law of the sexes depends on that of the family, and it extends also to the order of society, to the constitution of all humanity.

I said the facts reveal that which every individual of good faith glimpses and knows: That man is stronger, but less beautiful; woman more beautiful, but less vigorous. At this you laugh. You deny the facts, because, contrary to your own thesis, you imagine that I cite them with bad intent. You go so far as to say that I don't produce facts; even more, that the facts favor you. The woman surprised in adultery always denies; her husband still has an obligation to believe her. Remember then the facts, at least roughly, and the manner in which one passes over them in silence . . .

~

To speak only of sensual relations, it is a law of nature among all the animals, that the female, lured by the reproductive instinct, and employing many means, seeks out the male. Woman does not escape this law. She has naturally more of a penchant for lasciviousness than man; first because her ego is weaker, and liberty and intelligence struggle less in her against the inclinations of animality; then because love is the great, especially singular occupation of her life, and in love, the ideal always implies the physical . . .

~

From the point of view of intelligence and conscience, as from that of the body, man and woman form a complete unit, a being in two persons, a veritable organism. This couple, called by Plato *androgynous,* is the true human subject. Considered in isolation, each of the two halves that compose this organism appears mutilated. You cannot deny it, you, ladies, who prevail upon this pretty word *androgyne, man-woman,* to conclude in favor of what you call the equality of the senses. But recall that this androgyny doesn't exist, if the two people are equal in everything, if they are not each distinguished by the special qualities the combination of which precisely constitutes the organism . . .

Can one sell modesty? The modesty that is sold, you know what one calls that: prostitution.

Even beauty, the word by which I summarize all the prerogatives of the woman, can be neither sold nor discounted: it is outside commerce. This is why between husband and wife there is not, as one says and you imagine, association of goods and gains as between negotiators or landlords: there is the mutual and free gift, absolute devotion. The marriage contract is then of a completely different nature from that of the contract for sale, exchange, or payment: it is exactly the opposite.

Man, expression of force, is attracted by beauty. He wants to appropriate it, to unite with it in an indissoluble union. How will he attain it? What price will he offer for it? None. Nothing of what man possesses, of what he can create or acquire, can pay for beauty. Even the caresses of love are not a fit price for it: lovers who take for their cause mere voluptuousness are egoists, their union is not a marriage, universal conscience they call fornication, bawdiness, licentiousness. A dignified man, for whom the heart aspires to the possession of beauty, understands one thing straight off, that he cannot obtain it except by devotion. He who has force goes down on his knees before the woman, he consecrates to her his service and makes himself her servant. He who knows the woman to be weaker, drunk on love, becomes respectable, he moves away from all voluptuous speech and thought. His fortune, his ambition, he sacrifices for her pleasure; only his conscience he will not sacrifice, because his conscience is his force and it is only in the union of force and beauty that marriage consists. Absolute devotion, devotion of strong and stainless conscience, is in reality all that the groom offers his bride, the only thing that he can offer and that she, on her side, can accept.

The same movement [occurs] on the side of the woman. The more predominant beauty is in her, the more she inclines to force. This force, so desirable, she dreads at first; all weak creatures experience a certain fear of the strong creature. In order to tame this force, the offer of her beauty must be free or it is an act of prostitution. In order to conquer the man's force, the woman's beauty is as impotent as force itself is impotent to conquer beauty. Here, as before, there remains only one means: devotion.

Devotion for devotion, a call of attraction that proves for one and the other both force and beauty; this is then, definitively, the conjugal pact, of all pacts the most sublime, which older pacts of chivalry imitated. Can you see how for voluptuousness, for love, a more elevated sentiment is substituted, a sentiment that doesn't exclude voluptuousness and love, but commands them, dominates and effaces them, and even of necessity beseeches them? Ladies, here is the essence of marriage, which you appear to me not to understand. Without it, take note of my words, there is nothing for woman but shame and prostitution. The man and woman who are thus married know, you can take my word for it, what justice means: no felony will enter into their common conscience. For that it would be necessary that they become, in common, what they didn't want to be, what they swore to one another they never would be, impure cohabitators *[concubinaires]*. Their marriage is one more column added to the eternal temple of humanity that Christ wanted to build in our souls, and that I accuse you, you and your adherents, of destroying . . .

Once the household is formed, the husband is in charge of work, of production, of all exterior relations; the wife of the administration of the interior. This division is determined by the respective qualities of the spouses. To the stronger, action, struggle, movement; to she who shines and loves, but who must shine only for her husband, love only him, domestic cares, the peace and modesty of the home. Both are responsible, and yet free in their functions; always the husband will have the right of control over the wife, while the wife offers only that which aids, advises, and informs the husband. The reason for this is manifest: control over the household depends much more on virile production than vice versa, and as the man is charged with working, and since the superior power and responsibility incumbent on him is greater, he finds himself, by right and by power, MASTER of the community. And the right as much as the duty of the wife is to recognize this power, to demand its action, to provoke it, to serve it, to devote herself to it. Take this marital mastery away, remove the devotion to beauty and force, and you fall into concubinage, you destroy marriage . . .

Man, by his efforts alone, is at pains to provide for his proper needs; for even stronger reasons he is at pains to provide for the maintenance of his wife and children. It is necessary that he combine his industry with the industry of his equals. From this we get political society, of which the family is only the embryo. This society has its laws and its proper destiny, of which philosophy understands but little; one cannot doubt, however, that it has for its aim, on one side, the increase of dignity and virile liberty, on the other, the augmentation of the wealth and well-being of all. The relation of the family to the State, in a word the *Republic*, is, for the male sex, a problem to be resolved. Women intervene only in an indirect manner, with a secret and invisible influence. How could it be otherwise? Embryonic organ of justice, husband and wife make but one body, one soul, one will, one intelligence; they are devoted one to the other in life and in death; how could there be a different opinion or a different interest? On the other hand, the politics that bear on families have no other end than to constitute their solidarity, and to assure them all guarantees of liberty, of property, of labor, of commerce, of security, of education, of information, of circulation that they demand, all things that exalt the attributions of man. How could women be even nominally consulted? To suppose that the woman could express in the assembly of people a vote contrary to that of her husband is to suppose their discord and prepare their divorce. To suppose that the reason of the first could balance that of the second is to go against the wish of nature and degrade virility. To admit, finally, to the exercise of public functions a person that nature and the conjugal law have consecrated to purely domestic functions is to infringe familial modesty, to make the woman a *public* figure, to proclaim the confusion of the sexes, the community of lovers, the abolition of the family, the absolutism of the State, the servitude of people, and the feudalization of property.

This is how the subordination of wife to husband is set up in marriage. Such subordination has nothing arbitrary about it; it is neither a legal fiction nor a usurpation of force, nor a declaration of indignity for the weaker sex, nor an exception to her positive right as given by the necessities of domestic and social order; this subordination results from the patent and incontestable fact that virility embraces the great majority of both public and domestic affairs; it does not constitute, for man, and to the detriment of woman, the least prerogative of well-being or honor; to the contrary, in imposing on him the heaviest charge, it makes him the minister of feminine fidelity, for which alone it follows that he must hold on to his own.

Change, modify, or interfere with this relation between the sexes, in whatever fashion, and you destroy marriage in its essence; from a society where justice is predominant you make a society where love is predominant; you fall back again to concubinage and infidelity; you can still have fathers and mothers, as you still have lovers, but you no longer have the family; and without the family, your political constitution will no longer be a federation of men, of families and of free cities, it will be a theocratic and pornocratic communism, the worst of tyrannies.

To make this clearer, suppose that nature, which, on my account, has endowed the two sexes, constituted marriage, and the family, and civil society, in such a manner that we see, or at least it is easy for us to determine, the types—suppose, I say, that this same nature had wanted to establish human society in another mode. What would it have made? The plan would have to go against what we have here ruled out: it would have to distribute equally all the faculties between the sexes, give them both an equal force and beauty; make the woman vigorous, productive, warrior, philosopher, judge, like the man; the man, pretty, nice, adorable, agreeable, angelic and all that follows, like the woman; in a word, it would have to displace every difference between them except the genital . . .

In these conditions, it is clear that man and woman, having each the fullness of attributes that we find only in the couple, when equal and similar in all things would exist in relations completely different from those that should characterize marriage today. Man would not be devoted to the beauty he seeks to possess; woman would not be devoted to force, to which he had been equally devoted in sharing. The influence that man and woman exert on each other, in the present [i.e., egalitarian—TRANS] state of their constitution, would not be the same: there would be between them neither admiration nor worship, no devotional inclination; no need of praise, confidence, or encouragement, nothing more than protection, service, or support. Things would become between man and woman what we see between persons of the same sex: service for service, product for product, idea for idea. Without doubt there would be love, since we conserve, in this express aim, the sexual distinction. But men and women would be affected in another manner: their love would not transcend mere voluptuous excitation; they would have nothing in common with the conscience they prize; not being transformed by an absolute devotion, they would not hold to an indissociable monogamy. They would live in a zone of liberty and concubinage; not arousing jealousy,[2] not excluding any idea of infidelity, on the contrary, exalting themselves through emulation of those with vast wealth; ensuring that the general tendency would be to enclose a community of lovers, children, and households in the unique family that would be the State.

This organization, outside both monogamy and the family, has been dreamt of by all those who, like our modern emancipated women and their emancipators, have believed in the equality of power and beauty in the two sexes; mystics placed this distinction in heaven, where, they say, there will no longer be either male or female; nowadays, it seems to a great number of people, even well-informed people, the singular means to destroy antagonism, and consequently to extinguish crime and misery. But could such a society really exist? I dare to affirm it would be one hundred times worse than ours; to be more precise, I consider it radically impossible.

Society subsists in the subordination of all human forces and faculties, both individual and collective, to justice. In the system I've just sketched, the individual, having in himself the fullness of attributions that accords, as well as we have been able to convince ourselves, only with the couple, would be exorbitant in his personality; the idealist element would become in him predominant; conscience would be subordinated; justice reduced to a pure idea; love, synonym for voluptuousness, a simple *jouissance*. Thus is exposed, with an indomitable violence, the contradiction between the individual and society: this same individual, which one flattered oneself had been linked to public order by the community of lovers, women, children, families, households, would be all the more repugnant to social communism the more completely he was emancipated. It is even possible that one could not stand in defense of women, since, according to the egalitarian hypothesis, and with regard to the physical and moral constitution of the individual, there could be no jealousy [and so no interest in the opposite sex—TRANS]; but competition would be all the more intense for loot, for riches, for comfort and luxury, for all things the production of which, submitted to the same laws in a society drunk on love and the ideal, would be even more insufficient than it is today. Establish, with the community of lovers, a celibate universality, and, I fear to say, you will have a surfeit of consumption, less labor, less saving, more misery; in the final analysis, along with a police state, a society devoted to thievery or, otherwise, to the most degrading servitude. This result, for any man who reflects on the relations between the family, marriage, work, production, and the accumulation of wealth, as well as on the conditions for justice in Society, is as certain as the fact that two plus two equals four.

Thus we confirm, by the development of the contrary thesis, the theory of marriage. Society, that is, a union of forces, rests on justice. Justice has as an organic condition a dualism, outside which it reduces quickly to a pure and inefficacious notion. This dualism is marriage, the union of two complementary people, and in which the essence is devotion, the preparation love.

Thus we resolve this apparent contradiction, which says to the man: *command, to better serve*; to the woman: *obey, to better reign*, a contradiction that expresses with full force the matrimonial spiral, and contains all the law and mystery of the sacrament. The world is full of these oppositions; it neither lives nor progresses except this way. If the sense of the famous maxim *The king reigns and does not govern* is obscure only to demagogues who aspire to absolute power, all the more reason why these two propositions: *command, to better serve, obey; to better reign,* must appear clear to every man who has the sentiment of his duty and his right, to every woman who has a respect for her husband and his proper dignity.

Just as man, in his manifestations, is not always strong, or his virility sufficiently accentuated, woman is not always beautiful either: in morals, as in physical looks, she is subject to a thousand disfigurements.

Often she acts beneath herself: she is loose, slack, and beastly, as George Sand put it. One can say then that she abuses the permission of nature, which wishes her, not inept, but relatively weaker, and yet more beautiful than her companion. Sometimes even a contrary phenomenon presents itself. While man expands in plunging into the *delights of Capua,* one sees the woman emancipate herself; take, as it is said in the Bible, the vestments of man, affect his forms, his language, his virile allures, and aspire to the exercise of his functions.

Everywhere and in all times, one meets with these eccentric creatures, ridiculed by their sex and rejected by our own: they are of several species. In one, a chic masculinity is the effect of temperament and a great bodily vigor; one calls them *viragos*. These are less fearsome; they don't make good proselytizers, and all that suffices is a critique from other women to bring them to order. In others, the emancipatory tendency prevails, whether in the mind, or in the professions they make, or even finally in libertine excess. These are the worst: there is no fixed price with which the desire for emancipation can be managed in them. In certain epochs, sex consciousness gets mixed up; the cowardice of men becomes an auxiliary of the woman's audacity; and we see appear these theories of enfranchisement and promiscuity, of which the last word is PORNOCRACY. At this point society is finished.

Pornocracy combines very well with despotism, even with militarism: the Roman Empire has furnished an example with Elagabalus. Pornocracy unites equally with theocracy: This is what tempted the Gnostics from the 1st to the 11th centuries of our era, and to it the mystics equally tended, as late as the 17th century. In our day, one has seen pornocracy ally itself with bankocracy! Malthus and Enfantin are the double expression of modern decadence . . .

Don't complain, ladies, that I treat your ideas as things of little importance, as a man who hasn't sounded and measured the high import of your doctrines. I know in what spirit you live and have no difficulty avowing that it is this spirit, spirit of luxury and shame, spirit of confusion and promiscuity that, for the last thirty-five years, has been the plague of democracy and the principle cause of defeats for the republican party. Also I hold on to what the public says of you, *intus et in cute.*

Beginning with the cases that are beyond any doubt.

Parent Duchâtelet, in his book *Prostitution,* has remarked that public women were gluttonous, drunken, immoderate, quarrelsome, given to a chaotic and inscrutable gossip.[3] In these traits one recognizes the woman fallen into a state of nature or simple femininity: Where does this corruption come from? From excessive frequenting with men, which takes from them, along with their reserve, timidity, and diligence, the essential quality of their sex, that which makes the soul and life of the honest woman: modesty. Parent Duchâtelet could have added that the figure of these women alters in the same way as their mores: they deform and adopt the look, the voice, and the allure of men, and preserve nothing either physical or moral of their sex, except the gross material, the strictly necessary.

—What is there in common, you will say, between these prostitutes and us?

I would ask you first, ladies, what you mean by the word *prostitute*? Note that these women do nothing, after all, but exercise free love; that, if more than one began in being seduced, the mass of them elected to be prostitutes; that even, from the point of view of an amorous democracy, they act with a spirit of philanthropy and charity, as the Gnostics understood it; that for the rest of them, always following your maxims, erotic delectation has nothing immoral in it, being licit as well as natural; it forms the greatest benefit and the greatest part of humanity, and that consequently a pretty woman who, for the happiness of a man pricked by love, consents to give him the sacrifice of a day of her time, is perfectly in the right to receive compensation in exchange. She has all the more right, by exercise of the amorous function, insensibly to damage and degrade herself. There is not, there cannot be, free love, do you understand? The notion must be abandoned, in the name of conscience, in marriage. Either there is marriage, by which lovers unite forever, according to the law of devotion and in the highest sphere of love, or there is remuneration. Do emancipated women, who live in concubinage, have the pretention to give themselves for nothing? At the very least they receive pleasure, and the proof is that the moment the thing no longer pleases, she reserves for herself the right to withdraw. The lover who gives herself for nothing is a phoenix that doesn't exist except for the poets; this is why when she gives herself outside marriage, she is a libertine, she is a prostitute; she knows this so well that if, later, she finds someone to marry, she will present herself as a widow; she will lie; to impudence she will join both hypocrisy and perfidy.

Here we see how the commerce of men, as free love, affects a woman: it devastates her, denatures her, travesties her, and makes her appear like a man, hideous to behold. Now, I predict to you, all excessive frequentation with men, even if confined to simple conversation in salons, in academies, in bars, etc., is bad for the woman. It deflowers and insensibly corrupts. I say, moreover, it is impossible for a woman, not attending to men more than is expedient, to concern herself habitually with things not of her sex, and without this experience [i.e., in proper marriage—TRANS.] her natural grace suffers, and in some cases, her imagination consumes itself, her senses inflame, and the door of sin opens large before her.

A propos my last book on Justice, you have found it smart to say that it embarks on a new voyage in search of the *absolute*. You consider it a very unfortunate lapse for me, well known today for the war I have waged against the *absolute*, and who in the past has been well known for my attacks on property, to go thus in search of the absolute under another name. Also, a propos this absolute with which I am infatuated, you miss no opportunity in accusing me haughtily of misinforming people about justice. The accusation is serious: if I am convicted of absolutism, I should be suspect; I no longer merit being listened to in anything; I don't have the right, among others, to speak either of marriage or women. In truth, it is disquieting.

Examining below, not my conscience, which in absolute fact reproaches me for nothing, but yours, I have asked myself if you know yourselves what you mean when you speak of justice and the absolute. And this is what I have found . . .

If by ABSOLUTE one understands the *certain*, then certainly I believe in the absolute and I affirm it, since I believe in certain ideas, in ideas of an absolute certitude, such as the truths of mathematics, the law of the series, the succession of time, the relation of causality, the notion of equilibrium, etc. If by *ABSOLUTE* one understand the *universal*, I respond again that I am a partisan of the absolute, since I believe in universal ideas, since I admit universals and categories, to which I attribute a truth equally objective and subjective; and that of all these universal ideas or categories, the most universal to my eyes is *JUSTICE*.

But never, to my knowledge, has one considered these terms: the universal, the certain, the absolute, as synonyms, unless they are associated in this manner: when something has absolute certitude, the absolute becomes then an adjective that applies to all sorts of ideas and objects, in order to mark the highest power, ideality, or reality.

When I push back into the absolute, I understand, with all logicians it seems to me, an essence or entity that reunites in itself at once, and to an infinite degree, all power, all justice, etc. The absolute takes then a logical, ontological, aesthetic, juridical acceptation: nothing is clearer than this.

Justice, which I take as the foundation of my philosophy, is not absolute, even if it is for me a reality and an absolute certitude. The proof is that I can subtract from the notion of Justice all human legislation and all morality, but I cannot, with this same notion, give being to a fly; I will not discover the system of the world; I will not make a statue of a *gladiator,* I will not invent algebra. I will not even invent, with this sole notion of *law,* a political constitution, since, to apply the law, one has to understand in depth other relations not directly relevant to law; political, economic, geographic, historical relations, etc.; none of which prevents Justice from being absolutely certain of its nature, in all times and in all its decrees; absolute the way science and arithmetic are certain, limited to the formation of numbers that one can extend as far as logarithms.

You, ladies, on the contrary . . . understand neither justice, the absolute, the universal, nor certitude.

For you, nothing is certain, nothing is universal, nothing is just in itself. EVERYTHING IS RELATIVE, *mutable, variable,* like waves in the sea. To sustain the contrary, that is, to admit certain ideas, universal notions, immutable principles of justice, is to search for the ABSOLUTE, to degrade morality; wisdom consists in taking things according to circumstances and from the point of view that seems most profitable. Today republic, tomorrow monarchy; once marriage and family, later free love; sometimes socialist democracy, sometimes industrial and landlord feudalism; Christian of the Middle Ages, Protestant with Luther, deist with Rousseau, Malthusian speculator in the nineteenth century. Dare then to speak clearly, if you want to see yourselves clear;

admit what you have in your heart, and what judges you. What you qualify and discover as *absolute* in me, madame, is reason, truth, reality, justice, certitude, all morality, all natural and social law;—and your *relativism* is Pyrronism, the destruction of all reason, all science, and all morality, all liberty. For you society is arbitrary power, economic speculation, concubinage—I use the most honest phrase—in the family, prostitution of conscience, everywhere manipulation of credulity, cupidity, and all the bad instincts of man.

~

All truth implies harmony, symmetry, serial terms, that is to say, RELATION. The moment harmony is interrupted, the series mutilated, there is no longer relation; the *relative* does not exist.

Another cause of your error: certain beings, certain ensembles produce themselves by continuous increase; such are living beings, such also is justice.

You say, in your own logic: slavery is better than cannibalism, service is better than slavery, the proletariat better than serfdom, etc. Then, you conclude, slavery is relatively good, the proletariat relatively good, etc.; and, as one never arrives at the perfect, at the absolute, everything is relatively good and bad.

But all this is the myopic logic of people who reason only approximately, or who take conventional phrases as dialectical maxims. Truth, logical, philosophical, exact, severe, is altogether different. Justice, true to itself, in all its parts, develops *progressively* in humanity. To the extent progress is achieved, humanity raises itself above the condition of the animal, in order to enter a state of society and justice. The result is that slavery is not more true, either in itself or relatively, than cannibalism; it is still animalistic; serfdom, the proletariat, are still animalistic, fatalistic, progressively reduced by the action of liberty and justice . . .

Thus, your skepticism rests on absolutely nothing, only on confused ideas and arbitrary definitions: your philosophy, I repeat, is chaotic, promiscuous, I will tell you later that it is prostitution . . .

You speak of the *relative,* of *relative* truth, and you oppose this word to the *absolute.*

But there again you are not in the true, and you see only confusion. All truth is true from a double point of view: in itself, and considered individually; and as an integrated and constituent part of a system of things, of which full intelligence gives us, in effect, an aspect of the absolute.

Thus, each proposition by Euclid is true in itself, and abstraction is made of all geometry; and it is true like serial terms in geometry, of which the set is true also.—The theory of tides is true, independent of the Copernican system;—the circulation of blood, the system of nutritional functions are true facts in themselves, independent of any theory of reproduction; that which does not impede these functions is also true, in their relations with generation, the cerebral system, etc. Here we find the absolute and the relative; and you speak of imaginary things, in an uncertain light, when you oppose them to each other; they subsist together, and even when you take apart each idea, each phenomenon, each created being, and see that it still forms a whole, a universal, an *absolute* (even philosophy does not hesitate here to apply this term), you recognize that the *absolute* and the relative are once again identical.

Truth is double-sided; and its most luminous side is that of relation, since when one understands a proposition in itself, one doesn't understand the truth in all its scope; one knows something, but one doesn't know everything.

All this means for you, madame,[4] who professes to cultivate the ideal, that there is not really any ideal, there are only objects that more or less attract desire, concupiscence. The *ideal,* for all men who search within themselves, is a word by which one expresses the conformity of a being with its type. It speaks also of the faculty of mind by which, in view of realities that are always more or less defective, we find again the perfect model we suppose invincibly to exist in the thought of creative nature, in the reason of God. In this sense, the *ideal,* a thing not real, but perfectly intelligible, is an absolute, since it reunites truth, harmony, exactitude, proportion, force, beauty. We attain it not, this is certain; but we seek after it, as we seek after the law of justice; we degrade ourselves when we follow something else. The renunciation of the ideal is a sign of our decadence.

You, on the contrary, deny a priori this ideal, since you deny it as absolute, you deny, in your thought, that *absolute* is synonymous with truth, law, certitude. For you there is as a result, and paradoxically, only the ideal; and that which you call by this name is all that pleases you. This is the very essence of ugliness. The ideal is a word that you should accordingly delete from your dictionary, just as you should the *absolute,* the *relative,* the *certain,* the *universal,* because they signify nothing, absolutely nothing for you. You must replace them with another, called, in Latin, *libido,* in French: *fantasy.*

Today, the multitude of artists and people of letters know only one thing, fantasy, and, with fantasy, they estrange themselves equally from the *real* and the *ideal*. There is neither truth nor sublimity in their works; truths are fashionable merchandise, articles of pornocracy.

But we are not yet at the bottom of this. You mistake everything about the character of the ideal; after having denied the absolute, you make your GOD that which understands itself very well as a religion without principles, without law, without certitude, without universal ideas, without notion, without justice, without mores, in a century where all these things have been replaced by *fantasy,* that which implies inconsequence, contradiction.

I have explained, in the theory of progress I've tried to present, how progress had its principle in justice; how, outside of justice, any political, economic, literary, philosophical development became subversive and dissolute, how the ideal had been given as a means to bring us to justice, and how finally, if this same ideal, instead of serving as an auxiliary instrument of law, was taken as the rule and end of life, there would follow for society decadence and death. In a word, I subordinated the ideal to justice, the idea of which is, from the point of view of speculative reason, less universal; and the sentiment of which is, from the point of view of practical reason, less social than lawful.

You, on the contrary, subordinate law to the ideal, in the decadent manner of idolatrous polytheists: in this you accord perfectly with the modern bohemian, for whom the maxim is, as you know, *art for art's sake.*—For the principle of art for art's sake produces corollaries of all sorts, which enter naturally into your catechism: power for power, war for war, money for money, love for love, jouissance for jouissance . . .

The school of fantasy, by which you give to us, without knowing it, and by the sole fact of a perversion in your brain and a malady in your soul, an absurd metaphysic, is *jouissance,* it is vice, immorality, political degradation: it is PORNOCRACY.

For you who, on the contrary, see nothing in society but abstraction, who consequently recognize in it neither attributes, functions, relations, nothing of what constitutes existence and life, the social state is the result of relations that are, according to you, essentially mutable and variable. For you there is no constitution of society, no international law, no economic system: everything is governed by fantasy, by the whim of circumstances and according to the wisdom of that which chance, caprice of the multitude, corruption, or force has proposed for the management of the general interest . . .

For certain centralizers, society or the State is all; the individual, nothing; the first absorbs the second.—For you, society is nothing; the individual alone exists, male or female; society is a word that serves to designate the ensemble of relations of individuals among themselves (as if individuals could sustain these relations, and not create, ipso facto, an entirely concrete superior [i.e., still abstract—TRANS.] reality that transcends them!) The centralizers end up with communism, which is the same thing as despotism; you end up with anarchy or fantasy; but as fantasy and anarchy are impracticable by their nature, force exists to nominalists like you in the need for force; it is thus that, dividing the two extreme points of the horizon, tyranny is born.

I remember one day, in 1848, a meeting where I explained the principles of the People's Bank. Pierre Leroux[5] tried to refute my system, arguing that it contradicted, from one end to the other, the *law of the Triad.* Impatiently, I observed to the philosopher that the Triad, in the matter of finance, of discounting *[escompte],* was inapplicable, considering that everything goes there, as in accounting, under two terms: *debt* and *credit, active* and *passive, sale* and *purchase, consumption* and *production,* etc.: "Your political economy," wrote P. Leroux, "is false; your accounting false: I tell you, in the name of the Triad, that bookkeeping must be divided in TRIPLE parts, not in *two parts,* which is absurd!" P. Leroux then went on to accuse double bookkeeping of having engendered misery and the proletariat . . .

The old kings of France went so far as to pretend that money was nothing but a sign, they had the right to give to a 1-franc coin the value of 5 francs, 10 francs and 50 francs; they became counterfeiters.

I say, on the contrary, that money is a pure convention, a manner of abridging the multiplicity of exchanges; that at bottom, *products* are exchanged for *products*; that money is itself only a product, despite the privilege it enjoys; that, as commonly happened in primitive societies, one could again today easily go without it; that in any case, commerce is in its nature free and has no right to pay anyone.

Same thing for the Bank. Here Mr. Enfantin,[6] defending his [triple] synthesis, fights for his altar, for his hearth.

Since in *weighing* the intervention of a third term is necessary [for Enfantin], and the same is true in the act of exchange, so it will be the same in the operations of credit, which are nothing but a more complicated application of the use of money and exchange. The intervention of a third term will here then also be necessary; this intervention will come from the Bank of France, authorized by the State, from joint stock banks, equally authorized, from privileged stockbrokers, etc. For all these services, a right will be perceived to *discounts*, to *charges*, to *commissions*, or to *interest*; all these words express nuances of one and the same thing: the right of intervention.

I say, to the contrary, that the establishment of a social Bank has no need whatsoever of the intervention of a third power; that this third power is a pure fiction; that the State here represents only the *mutuality* of citizens, which mutuality originally supposes only *two* terms as in accounting, *debit* and *credit*, lender and borrower; that this is how a *credit union* organizes itself, of which there are many examples in Belgium; that consequently, credit-like commerce can and must one day work without any other fee than the *costs* of the operation.

Catholicism, the religion of divine right, which affirms the necessity of a priesthood, which makes the priest the intermediary between man's conscience and his liberty; the judge, an intermediary between parties;

the banker, an intermediary in commerce; the prince, an intermediary in all social and political relations; Catholicism, nonetheless, never went so far as to suppose, in marriage, the existence of any intermediary. The priest gave blessing to the spouses, but he left them the liberty to make their own choices; he did not meddle in the union. The same goes for the municipal officer in charge of civil marriage; he receives the *declaration* of the spouses and registers them, so that the world would know that this man and this woman are husband and wife.

Mr. Enfantin lacks the same scruple. Man and woman, he tells you, are the first two terms of the equation. But where is the third power that unites them? This power is once again society, he tells you, that of the prince or pontiff, authorized agent of its powers. Not only, then, does this intermediary witness the union, but he makes it: it is he who, in the Enfantinian theory, judges the aptitude of the spouses, their mutual *suitability*; it is he, in a word, who distributes to men their brides, to women their grooms, according to the science he has for their sympathies and their antipathies; it is he, it follows, who pronounces their separation, when their mutual love is extinguished; he who commits them to new bonds; the androgynous priest, in a word, makes and unmakes amorous unions, determining their duration. For everything is *relative*, the *ideal* changes, don't forget; love, finally, is FREE.

But if one supposes that here, as in the bank, as in politics, etc., the *go-between* has the right to tax, I wonder what can play the role of the same go-between in the conjugal relation? Up until now, we haven't had pornocracy; but what name would you give to the prince-pontiff charged with the purveyance of wives and husbands? What do you say of this synthesis? It has a name in the language of prostitution.

I'll stop: I've said enough to make it clear to whoever reads these pages that your metaphysics, that the metaphysics of Mr. Enfantin, is nothing but confusion, waste, chaos, realization of abstractions and negation of realities; that you don't understand the meaning of the words: *abstract, concrete, absolute, relative, certainty, truth, universal, law, thesis, antithesis* and *synthesis;* that all your philosophy reduces to a promiscuity of notions, and that the promiscuity of notions directs you to *pure fantasy,* in *law, science, art,* and *morals;* to the arbitrary in government, to speculation in business, to shocks in the realm of justice; to prostitution and hustling in love; in one word, to PORNOCRACY.

Notes

1. Proudhon's text is a response to feminist critics and also to writers who influenced them. The former he addresses without full attribution; in the edition from which I have worked, posthumously published in 1875, initials indicate their names. One was Jenny D'Hericourt (1809–1875), who wrote an influential response to Proudhon, incorporated into the book *A Woman's Philosophy of Woman* (1864). The other was Juliette Lambert, author of *Idées anti-proudhoniennes sur l'amour, la femme et le mariage* (1858). A background target for Proudhon is a utopian socialism associated primarily with the name of Saint-Simon and committed to positivist principles and social reforms (including the abolition of coverture laws and the legalization of prostitution), in coordination with a strong technocratic state.

2. Elsewhere Proudhon makes it clear that marriage is a means of sublimating jealous feelings that are nonetheless also indispensably part of the man's virile force.

3. Alexander Parent Duchâtelet (1790–1836) was a medical doctor who wrote a monumental social history of prostitution in Paris, published in 1836.

4. Here he addresses Juliette Lambert in particular.

5. A philosopher and political economist (1797–1871), associated with the Saint-Simonian sect.

6. Barthelemy Prosper Enfantin (1796–1864), social reformer and a founder of Saint-Simonianism, whose influence on his feminist critics Proudhon traces in a pamphlet by Juliette Lambert, presumably *Idées anti-proudhoniennes*.

ON PORNOCRACY

Stefan Mattessich

In tenth-century Rome, one aristocratic family, the Theophylacti, rose to power in the Holy See through a mother, Theodora, and her daughters, who manipulated the process of papal selection to their advantage through affairs, arranged marriages, scandal, incest, and murder. Sexual amorality also characterized the popes they backed; their sins ranged from simony to running brothels in the Lateran Palace to raping female pilgrims in Saint Peter's. Long referred to as the nadir, or "dark age," of church history, early nineteenth-century German theologians called this period the Pornocracy, or, alternatively, *Huenregiment,* Rule of the Harlots.

One event that prepared the way for the startling degeneracy of this era fell in AD 753–54, when Pope Stephen II struck a deal with the Frankish king Pippin, acquiring sovereign rights over Italian land in exchange for fealty to the Holy Roman Empire. Louis Dumont has singled this moment out as significant for the evolution of the modern state, which emerged as the church shifted from its otherworldly focus on private truth to public affairs. Likewise for Dumont, the moment was significant in the history of the modern individual, which he derived from a transposition of the priest's "out-worldly" asceticism to "in-worldly" engagement (1986, 49–50). On both registers, the effects were transitive: as the popes compromised the self-sufficiency of the church and acquired political power, they also assigned transcendent values to the new state and to the subjects who composed it. Authority and obedience, spirit and nature, soul and body were brought into a "hierarchical complementarity" that maintained the integrity of each through their displacement, on the model of the Incarnation.[1] In this light, we might think of the Pornocracy, which followed on the disintegration of the Carolingian Empire more than a century later, less as an anomaly, or a moment of pagan regression (a typical Catholic reading), than as a stage of secularizing history, in which modern institutions and subjectivity, with their "in-out" character, found their obscene other principle—the "old in-out," we might say, so memorably expressed in *A Clockwork Orange* by its depraved Beethoven-obsessed protagonist, Alex DeLarge.

To be sure, the word *pornocracy* tells us as much about the Protestant sensibilities of those German theologians as anything else—particularly as their sensibilities changed under the pressures of Enlightenment thought, value, and action coming from France. The Kantian internalization of absolute law as a duty receptive to political imperatives yet taken on by the introspective subject (closed off from the external world in his cultural sense of fusion or belonging, his *Gemeinschaft*) resonated with the paradoxical asociality of Rousseau's social contract. As the connotation of female power in the word *pornocracy* helps us to recall, the civilized life restructured by this social contract was often glossed in its ambiguous, artificial, vain, and meretricious dimensions as feminine. Rousseau acquired this misogynist bias in an ancien régime where monarchical power was so absolute (even for the nobility) that it emasculated everyone except the Bourbon kings; for this reason, it was typical to fix the exemplary trait of this power in the courtesan who exerted her influence behind the scenes, through networks and connections that lacked transparency and justice. Rousseau came to see a republican rule of law, predicated on the "natural" correspondence between inside and outside, essence and appearance, what you mean and what you say, in sharp contrast to a court and salon society where everything was reduced to a pure semblance.

The priority Rousseau gave to truth over illusion thus warranted an equally "natural" demotion of the feminine qua principle of unaccountable power. Equality under the law for men came to hinge on the restriction of women to roles of privatized dependence—or, since privatized dependence had for so long been the rule, on the latter's wider application, especially to women of the upper classes. Rousseau accounted for their lack of liberty in this arrangement by referring it to a sympathy or sentiment they could both manage and communicate. He further elicited from this unexpected "power" a model for the right political disposition of the (male) citizen, who, striving to align what he is on the inside with who he presents himself to be on the outside, speaking his mind in open deliberation with others and bound by nothing but a universal reason, required a sensibility not itself formed in the public realm. Privacy was a public good, provided it was shielded from public scrutiny or regulation—the private woman was also the (private) property of (femininity in) the man, and the social contract worked when the deal struck both inter-subjectively between them and intra-subjectively in the (male) citizen was upheld. So significant was this exchange of passive and active attributes across the private–public divide that Nancy Armstrong, in her historical account of the English novel, has suggested that "the modern individual was first and foremost a woman" (8).

This is less counterintuitive to say than it might appear, even in the context of a social contract theory for which, as Carole Pateman has argued, patriarchy furnishes a necessary structure for civil society, the public sphere, and the constitutional state. The underlying "sexual contract," with its presumption of a "male sex right" in the private sphere, nonetheless also conditions for Pateman the reciprocal rights and responsibilities of political society. Its "primal scene" of sexual coercion persists in displaced form through the parricidal transition from paternal subjection to fraternal equality that underlies the story of a masculine political birth. In what she calls "civil subordination," the modern individual becomes the locus of an equivocation, a (non) freedom, a (non)consent, and also a (non)paternalism that is sustained in the process of the individual's formation, even when this process entails women acquiring political and legal personality and embracing the central tenets of liberal democracy: self-ownership and property in the person.

This equivocation characterizes the shift from a filial (father–son) to a matrimonial (husband–wife) model of the social contract; justifications for democratic self-government, drawing on analogies between women and citizens, men and their elected representatives, thus operate no less conspicuously in defenses of the traditional family and conventional gender roles than in arguments for their liberalization. The same equivocation has also been evident when the state intervenes in the conjugal relation, either to shore up its heterosexist character in restrictive conditions for women or to relax the laws and rights governing the conjugal relation on both sides—for instance, where divorce, inheritance, custody, and property rights are concerned. In Pateman's view, it is when the marriage contract comes to define and control the private sphere—however flexible its terms might be—that the sexual violence or male sex right, in its foundational "scene," is both renewed and obscured.

Here, I would like to suggest, the word *pornocracy* acquires an intriguing historical efficiency, hinting at the displacement to which Pateman's "modern patriarchy" has progressively been subjected. As such, it signifies *not* a return of the pure semblance Rousseau linked to an uncontrolled feminine power but the strangely passionate investments in its serving as an exception that proves the rule of the social contract's sentimentalized "truth." By exception, here, I mean something like the "inherent transgression" that Slavoj Žižek sees as a fantasy construction dialectically sustaining the social laws of a community (2008, 34–35). Rousseau's foreclosure of feminine power from his conception of civil society would therefore function as its retroactively posited constitutive moment; *pornocracy* becomes a phantasmatic means of disavowing a legal order's arbitrary origin and the antagonism—above all between the sexes—that renders the order essentially unstable or "split."

One locus for such passionate investments in the nineteenth century was the figure of the prostitute, which came to signify both dissolution in public and private life and the redrawn boundaries between them, provoking laws and policies that helped to organize the new social, political, and economic spaces of liberal democratic capitalism. For T. J. Clark, writing about representations of the prostitute in the Paris art world, the way this figure "mixed up" sexuality and money for bourgeois society produced intense debates (and scandals) similar to theological arguments about transubstantiation (102). The prostitute stood for some as the ultimate debasement of the body in commercial society and for others as its highest (or at least right) valuation; but either way for Clark, the figure had the "unlikely plenitude" and "necessity" of a category that drew opposites of virtue and vice, liberty and license, body and soul, even truth and lies into mysterious coincidence. Love her or hate her, one was typically loving *and* hating the prostitute at the same time.

In this ambivalence we glimpse a pornocratic logic at work, signaling from even further back in the "in-out" history Dumont tells of the modern individual and state.[2] Of course, saying so raises, as an immediate caveat, the need to locate this logic in the act of reference itself, since what it refers to at the level of content is singularly this history at the level of expression. Pornocracy exists, if it does, as the feverish imaginary that has long accompanied its concept; it gives to thoughts, words, gestures, and indeed whole scenes of communication the spectral overtones of an arbitrary power that is both the other of law (what it displaces) and the otherness of the law (that displaces)—what Žižek would call its "Real violence" (1991, 204). It follows that using the concept requires a special genealogical caution. Before considering the critical value of the thesis for the present, then, let me first open the concept up on still more of its historical registers.

PROUDHON AND MARX

The principal point of reference for a modern conception of *pornocracy* is French anarchist Pierre-Joseph Proudhon's pamphlet *Pornocracy, or Women in Modern Times*.[3] Never completed and published posthumously in 1875, it set forth his theory of patriarchy as a crucial social protection for the artisans, shopkeepers, small farmers, and tradesmen in whose name he spoke (and from whose class he came). Addressed to his feminist critics and focused on the thinkers who influenced them, notably Barthelemy Prosper Enfantin, founder of the Saint-Simonian movement that had been active in the 1830s and '40s, the pamphlet was a polemic against a doctrine of "free love," which hinged on generic notions of an androgynous "humanity" vested above all in women, or rather in a representative "Woman" whose emancipation would, it was claimed, terminate the system of sexual exchange that had formed with the institution of private property.

Proudhon subscribed to his own versions of these generic notions. Instead of androgyny obtaining within each sex, however, he located it between the sexes and in the framework of an absolute sexual difference. Women, in his view, had a natural relation to the "ideal" and the beautiful; their role was to moderate an equally natural "force" in men by reflecting and amplifying its nonreciprocal qualities. The arbitrary character of the man's power over her was thus exemplified in her submission, which stood as both the limit and the delimiting condition of that power's sympathetic exercise in a "free" exchange of "services" for "favors."[4] But unless this common "humanity" found expression in the hierarchical complementarity of the monogamous couple, he asserted, both sexes lost their principle of restraint: arbitrary power in men turned possessive, the constraints on a natural jealousy were removed, and a feminine "ideal," bereft of the formal definition it found in men's mastery, became a pure phenomenality contaminating material life and love. The "humanity" espoused by Proudhon's feminist critics then revealed itself not only as a fiction, a "phoenix that doesn't exist except for the poets," but also as *the* fiction of modern society, grasped in the concrete abstraction of money. To realize equality between the sexes meant, therefore, only to preserve private property relations and concentrate sexual exchange on the social level, this time in the guise of an "emancipation" that concealed a more fundamental exploitation.

Behind the essentializing terms of this account, one easily discerns the historical process then underway: the proletarianization of Proudhon's class (the largest in France), "wage slavery," the disaggregation of families and communities in a new industrial mode of production that, making physical strength less of a qualification, precipitated women into labor markets. Against this backdrop, it made sense for men of Proudhon's social position to associate these changes with the fact of working side by side with women for a similar (low) wage. Indeed, everything Proudhon had to say on the "Woman Question" in his pamphlet spoke also about the ambivalence this sort of experience produced. The same went for the concept of *pornocracy* itself, which designated for him the condition that would follow from women's enfranchisement. Because this enfranchisement was *not* realized (far from it), there can be no question of any other than a symptomatic reading of the concept. Nonetheless, it does not follow that it had no descriptive power at all. Proudhon was, it turns out, shrewder in his understanding of modern history than that.

One senses as much in his reading of French society after the failed 1848 Revolution, the coup d'état of Louis Napoleon, and the establishment of the Second Empire, when political power came to be felt in still more novel ways—notably through financial speculation that gave the concrete abstraction behind "free love" the more definite social forms of easy credit, consumer spectacle, and a heightened status consciousness. A principal concern for Proudhon in his pamphlet was, indeed, with these latter stimulations of desire and the parallel demands they made to instrumentalize more intimate aspects and values of personhood, to sustain in the relations between men and women the "soft" violence of market (and sex) capitalization. The result was, he wrote, a "national prostitution" or, rather, what came down to the same thing, an "amorous democracy," in which law and right afforded registers for the specific intervention in the social substance that interested him: one making people producers of their own pleasures and agents of their own oppression. When Proudhon worried about the "need" for external limits that any removal of conjugal and libidinal constraints might engender—for the "enclosure," as he put it, of a market-based "community of lovers, children, and households" in the "unique family" offered by a paternalist "State"—he also perceived a power that sought not only control but legitimacy and consent.

This state form was, in part, a product of reforms implemented by the many Saint-Simonians who took up positions of authority in the industrial and banking sectors of the Second Empire. Proudhon spotted their technocratic bent in Enfantin's conviction that magistrates should arrange, and not simply ratify, marriages, "judg[ing] the aptitude of the spouses [and] their mutual *suitability* . . . according to a science . . . [of] their sympathies and their antipathies." The same blurring of private and public prerogatives played into another of Enfantin's theories, this one about the operations of credit in the economy, which required the "intervention of a third term" in the form of state-supported joint-stock banks, extending credit against equity shares in profit as opposed to simple debt financing at interest. Accordingly, Proudhon read the power of investment bankers to commoditize debt and profit through financial speculation in tandem with the sexual and sexualizing authority Enfantin granted magistrates. Both suggested a process of concentrating erotic wealth (or privatizing erotic assets) in the hands of elites at the expense of those who supported them in conditions of alienated service. Pornocracy, as Proudhon evocatively put it, was also a "bankocracy."

Distinctly eighteenth-century anxieties about aristocratic power animated this account—he also referred to the magistrates as "princes" and "pontiffs." But if, in this respect, he echoed Rousseau's sexual politics, it was with the signal difference that the locus of power had shifted into the technocratic state; it followed as an effect of modernizing reform rather than furnishing its absent cause. Tyranny was thus an inherent tendency of Rousseau's republicanism. In its social contract, and despite the superficial commitment to self-government asserted for it since the French Revolution, Proudhon detected a deeper mistrust of the capacity for people to manage their own affairs in the self-organizing forms of life he helped to innovate under a mutualist banner (through worker's associations, cooperatives, credit unions, and other institutions). The idea of a collective, indivisible, or "general will," unified and directed by a representative political class, only rationalized for Proudhon a fundamental absence of liberty; in Rousseau's ideal society, "the people" was simply the pretext for a transcendent and centralized state authority. Indeed, Proudhon, reading the abstraction of social contract theory into a general semantic and perceptual breakdown triggered by those interventions of magistrates and bankers in intimate life, saw *both* the social contract and the technocratic state in the light of the pure semblance Rousseau had attributed to court and salon.

Proudhon's feminist critics also worked within a republican horizon, feeling on the registers of sympathy and sentiment not only the androgyny they admired but also a chance to press political claims for basic rights. Such claims sounded like nonsense, or "fiction," to Proudhon, because they led to not only misrecognitions of the acquisitive energies released by consumer culture (as harbingers of egalitarian sexual and amorous relations) but also a "voluptuous ideality" that pushed social exchange into a "promiscuity of bodies" and "notions" so generalized as to vitiate the core metaphysical dualism structuring private and public relations on every level. This dualism presupposed, for Proudhon, Aristotelian categories and types that were intelligible but not "real"—what he called "absolute." Men and women, like chairs or hats, had a telic consistency that was inescapable if they were to register, to exist for others in a coherent field of experience. At the same time, they depended, as "complements" of each other, singularly on forms of monogamy and hierarchy that had their own teleologies. What obtained for everyone without these forms, Proudhon believed, was a kind of superadded impressionism, the world like Pissarro's branches and leaves dissolving in random brushstrokes and inscrutable intentions.

Proudhon was not alone among his contemporaries in sexualizing such breakdowns of a metaphysical superstructure, construing them as feminizations of male force and, mutatis mutandis, masculinizations of female beauty. Nor was he all that original in taking them as signs of a crude materialism that was, in turn, sexualized, assigned to a feminine nature that was, by contrast, "real" but not intelligible, sensuous but destructured, and anchored in the figure of the prostitute, generating the intense debates mentioned by T. J. Clark. Because Proudhon's stand, on one side of these debates, disclosed similar ambivalent investments did not mean such investments were less alien to any side, even those fixing in the figure of the prostitute the most radical versions of a modern sexual freedom—for instance, those stressing the inconsistent, mobile, and fragmentary desire of the "bohemian." The same held true for the androgynous "free love" espoused by the Saint-Simonians; and even if this picture perforce changed when the doctrine was taken up by Proudhon's feminist critics, his sense of its uncritical relation to bourgeois individualism remained pertinent enough. For this reason Marx, too, had no difficulty understanding French society during the Second Empire in the light of a "national prostitution"; moreover, he considered a utopian "social science" incapable of creating real material conditions or bringing about substantive change in the capitalist mode of production (1994b, 183–84). To the extent that the feminism of his time did, in fact, filter its agendas through such a reformist mesh, he also did not hesitate to align it under the heading of quasi-political action, language, and thought that he famously characterized in the reign of Louis Napoleon as "farce."

It did not follow that Marx ignored the stark contradictions in Proudhon's position on women's freedom; indeed, he perfectly encapsulated them in the category "Conservative Bourgeois Socialism," seeing Proudhon's commitment to patriarchy as part and parcel of a timid anti-communism, confined to the "wish for a bourgeoisie without a proletariat" and anachronistic forms of exchange and property relations. No less than his feminist critics, then, Proudhon failed to escape the semantic confusion that ran through the proximate public, private, and perceptual spaces of post-1848 French society, and which reflected for Marx, above all, a failure to grasp the material stakes in the dialectical transition from premodern to modern forms of economic organization. This failure appeared specifically in a misrecognition of the *losing* game finance capital played with industrial capital. For Marx, the instruments of the former fell under the rubric of a "usury" (or "interest-bearing") capital that he glossed as "imaginary" and "fictitious." Making money from money, finance capital was also unnatural in its generative capacities—"self-increasing" and "self-acting" (1909, 399). Its tendency was to accumulate debt at compound rates of interest and expand exponentially, sucking value from the real economy, leaving structurally unpayable debts, and redistributing wealth into the hands of ever smaller and more self-conscious elites. But this process was, as a whole, obsolete, or archaic, a spectral anachronism from an earlier feudal and mercantilist period, doomed in the struggle with an industrialism that had every interest in restricting banks to the function of facilitating investment (with productive credit) and appropriating (by taxation) the profit generated through land or asset ownership.

Marx had the same model as Proudhon for what happens when this process is encouraged: the Second Empire, which had enmeshed midcentury French society in what he called "world-redeeming credit phantasies" (1909, 711) and "cosmopolitan orgies" (1994a, 302) of financial fraud. But if Proudhon employed the concept of *pornocracy* to describe and explain the "void form"[5] financial speculation produced in society, Marx refrained from making the sexual connotations of his own metaphors explicit—the closest he came, aside from references to "orgies," would have been allusions to vampirism—sensing quite clearly that pornocracy, in its normative dimension, was only another spectral anachronism. To use it, then, entailed a performative contradiction: it implied in the designation (or at the level of expression) what it designated (at the level of content). Consequently, Proudhon, in his view, could not understand (a) the *neo*-modern character of his nostalgic reconstruction of the patriarchal family (inherited from the Rousseau he despised and as much endorsed by Louis Napoleon, for instance, as universal [male] suffrage), (b) the patently bourgeois rationality it preserved intact as a result, or (c) the "real point aimed at" by communist revolution: "to do away with the status of women as mere instruments of production" (1994b, 173).

PROUDHON AND FOUCAULT

This performative contradiction, however, remains interesting in ways Marx could not have anticipated from within his theory of history, which only uneasily accommodates the return (or ghost-like persistence) of finance capitalism in a postindustrial mode of production. This limitation goes straight to the heart of Marx's economic science, where a principal utilitarian maxim—whatever serves the individual also serves society "from each according to his abilities to each according to his needs"—combined with his account of the contradictions in capitalist production to support a prediction of the latter's revolutionary transformation. (Whatever produced a profit for the individual capitalist, that is, in Marx's view still served society, albeit not in the fashion complacently assumed by the capitalist.) This economic science prevented Marx from seeing clearly enough the configuration of political space as "mass" society, with its emphasis on what Hannah Arendt called a conformist "modern equality" reducing people to statistical aggregates, human action to a psychologized behaviorism, and human desire to the pursuit of satisfactions on the level of biological need (35). In particular, he could not have imagined how, from this, the liberal state form would mutate into a distinctly biopolitical governmentality. This mutation adds a singular function to state power, as Foucault reminds us: instead of limiting (or restraining) that market freedom, it also looks for *its own* limitation in it (2004, 102). This is not simply to emphasize state disengagement or a turn to deregulation; in addition, it suggests that market freedom *de*limits power, becoming the field of its exercise and the justification for a new prerogative over people's habits, feelings, intuitions, and beliefs. If this prerogative means power's identification with those it now subjects to a technocratic authority, it also works the other way around: people come to a sense of themselves, mutatis mutandis, in the identification with that technocratic authority, internalizing the latter's evaluative "gaze" and embracing the self-monitoring "responsibility" it commands.

Foucault speaks, in this regard, of an "art of government" that he derives from a radicalization, in response to twentieth-century totalitarian experiments, of the classical liberal tenet that economic freedom constitutes government's foundation, guarantee, and security. He identified the turning point in anarcho-capitalist reactions to Roosevelt's New Deal, but he caught its stakes still more precisely in the postwar German response to Nazism, which predicated the formation of the new Federal Republic on an economic rationality that would (once again) limit and find its own limitation in the "social irrationality of capitalism" (2004, 102). Instead of a welfare state providing cover for risks, the goal of policy makers became to provide individuals an "economic space in which they [could] take on and confront risks," but to do so through a more complete intervention in society as such, "in its fabric and its depth" (144–45). This liberation of individuals in a "social market economy" or an "enterprise society" found its principal antecedent in what the "ordoliberal" economist Wilhelm Röpke called an "eternal Saint-Simonism" (106) and identified, in Foucault's words, "with the birth of that vertigo which takes hold of the liberal art of government," leading it "to seek a principle of . . . organization in the application to society of a schema of rationality specific to nature" (115).

Foucault focused on a similar rubric of "vertiginous" control on the different plane of a "deployment of sexuality" that, beginning in the mid-nineteenth century with the differentiation of intimate life from reproduction (in the traditional family), involved the emulation of aristocratic sexual norms by bourgeois classes in their assertion of the body's "special character" as a form of capital. This "body," as Foucault put it, became the new "blood" and, as such, the vehicle of an "arrogant political affirmation" imposed on the lower classes "for the purpose of subjugation" (1978, 127). Such an instrumentalized bourgeois "body" bears within its nature the same "schema of rationality"—in *The Birth of Biopolitics* Foucault inscribes it in the "human capital" of an "entrepreneurial self"—and the same internalization of the evaluative gaze via a sexological expertise.

The latter takes its cues, this time, from an "erotic art," or non-Western *ars erotica*. In its alternate sphere of desire, to recall briefly the textures of this account in the first volume of *The History of Sexuality*, "truth is drawn from pleasure itself, understood as a practice and accumulated as experience; pleasure is not considered in relation to an absolute law of the permitted and the forbidden, nor by reference to a criterion of utility, but first and foremost in relation to itself; it is experienced as pleasure, evaluated in terms of its intensity, its specific quality, its duration, its reverberations in the body and the soul" (71). If the positive sensual qualities highlighted here point to an embodied "truth," its displacement in a modern society where considerations of (Kantian) law and utility become sacrosanct is also not a simple moment of transition: the former truth persists in the need one has for its alienated reflection, for what Foucault called "the pleasure of knowing that truth, of discovering and exposing it, the fascination of seeing it and telling it." This displacement into discourse conjures up a fetishized equivalent of pleasure in itself as a goal (or an aristocratic norm), at the same time as it delivers the reflexivized modern subject to its self-capitalizing imperatives.

His account echoes Proudhon's critique of a "free love" that sustained a commercialized (and perverse) sexual life by liberating people's desires. For Proudhon, Foucault's "arrogant political affirmation" ran its spectral reiteration of the ancien régime through the figure of the courtesan. Likewise, Proudhon associated the "real" but unintelligible materialism that resulted, and that led to a raw equivalence of bodies, values, beliefs, and properties—"service for service, product for product, idea for idea," and on the model of relations between "persons of the same sex"—with democratic equality, law, and right. Foucault had no need of a regressive neomodern patriarchalism (or, for that matter, homophobia) to make his case, but the theory of history on which he relied, and his derivation of the reflexivized modern subject, also did not proceed in the narrative form of a simple break from a premodern past, however gradual, uneven, or dialectic its construal.

This break was more discontinuous, involuted, and dream-like, as Foucault suggests in passages like this one, again from the introduction to *The History of Sexuality*: "How have we come to be a civilization so peculiar as to tell itself that, through an abuse of power that has not ended, it has long 'sinned' against sex? How does one account for the displacement which, while claiming to free us from the sinful nature of sex, taxes us with a great historical wrong which consists precisely in imagining that nature to be blameworthy?" (9). For Foucault, this "abuse of power," this "great historical wrong," placing the locus of sin in sex, serves as the pretext, or background, for the shift into a modern sexual freedom (where the "sin" is now "against sex"). At the same time, the burden (or "tax") of a newly compulsory self-consciousness—which entails beating ourselves up for believing sex "blameworthy," or for not being "modern" enough—engenders a scrutiny (or an evaluative gaze) reaching "the most tenuous and individual modes of behavior" and "everyday pleasure" through a process of incitement (11). In this process, the "displacement" of "sinful nature" into what we might call "natural sex" sustains, through the narrative scheme that would understand it as progress or liberation, the ground of the "original" sin. This ground remains as a prompting or propagating negativity in the reflexivized subject.

As tempting as it might be to see *pornocracy* as a name for the biopolitics of this subject—and Proudhon as proto-Foucauldian—a more modest claim would be that the concept situates the performative contradiction felt by Proudhon (and recognized by Marx) in the history Foucault reads into a modern consciousness. It indicates the self-objectifying and self-berating dynamic of that history in the subject, and above all at the point where discursive projections of the past sustain one or another positivized version of the present. Hence, Proudhon's fear of an aristocratic ethos persisting in a liberal bourgeois capitalism colored his view of the family as a domain of noninstrumental relations, when, in fact, the family was only ever the market, even if the market undermined it (or transformed it). But hence, also, a difficulty in too quickly dismissing either this fear or Proudhon's patriarchy in terms, for instance, of a puritan constraint or "great historical wrong," from and against which a modern sexual freedom and a "bankocratic" neoliberalism emerge. If a concept of *pornocracy* cannot be separated from the performative contradiction of its use for Proudhon, in other words, one can say that this performative contradiction *is* pornocracy. It constitutes a sign of the latter's reflexivization in the modern subject.

PORNOCRACY TODAY?

For sociologist Eva Illouz, the history of women's political enfranchisement and integration within labor markets from the late nineteenth century onward runs along three intertwined axes: the feminization of the corporate workplace, the psychologization of everyday life (starting with the introduction into society of Freudian ideas in the 1920s), and the institutionalization of feminism in the 1970s. Displacements of public and private boundaries on each axis led to a deeper synthesis of economic reason and intimate life, making "productivity an emotional affair" and reconciling "spontaneous emotionality" with "instrumental assertions of the self" (29). As men and women incorporated categories of thought and feeling from the experience of the other, a "communicative ethos," stressing self-awareness but also self-control, empathy but also self-reliance, came to coordinate sociability on both intra-and interpersonal levels. So strong have the tensions of these contrary imperatives been that an "emotional capitalism" ends up "destructuring the very gender identities it helped to establish in the first place," putting the emphasis firmly on an equality and fairness that makes for increasing "similarity" between the sexes (23). The rise of egalitarian norms in the workplace, as in intimate relations—especially inside marriage—engenders a "vast process of rationalization" (30) predicated on a quantification, or what Illouz calls a "textualization" of affects, which are alienated as objects of an evaluative gaze, cut away from their densely woven contexts (just as verbal signifiers lose their relation to a particular voice, time, and place in being written down), and given over to neutral procedures of self-management and self-actualization (35). The autonomous or "pure" emotion is (like a "pure" text) both a "definite object, external to the subject, to be observed and controlled," and also subjectively condensed and experienced tautologically without "any higher justification than the fact that [it is] felt." The only possible response to this "fact" is an acritical "recognition" that erodes symbolic efficiency even as it stimulates forms of discursive commensuration specific to experts or "knowledge producers," who mediate wants and needs for subjects in therapeutic fashion. Notwithstanding the symmetrical exchange of qualities between men and women in this account, for Illouz the principal characteristic of such subjects is a distinctly feminine double consciousness.

To put this claim a different way, the general condition for everyone in late modern societies comes to be modeled on an experience of self-objectification that has long been familiar to women, and not least under the burden of being a figure, or a figment, of "Woman" in debates around the proper arrangements of public and private life. Indeed, these debates are as intense today as they've ever been, given the still more radical reconfigurations of those boundaries in a neoliberal politico-economic order marked by state privatizations, eroding privacy rights (in a newly invasive national security state), flexibilized work, and networked sociability. "Never has the private self been so publicly performed" (4) than it is today, Illouz says, and in conditions of heightened uncertainty that further exacerbate the dissociative pressures of rationalization. As a result, that figure, or figment, is all the more volatile a node for explanation, frustration, and resentment.

We saw as much back in 2012, when Rush Limbaugh called Georgetown law student Sandra Fluke a "slut" and a "prostitute" because she argued contraception should be covered by health insurance. The analogy he draws between a rights-based claim and a commercialized sexual exchange works inside two distinct frames. In one, rights are associated with an illegitimate power, much as Proudhon saw tyranny as the inner logic of representative government and rule of law. The welfare state resembles, therefore, a court, breeding dependence (on elites) and dispensing privileges through its bureaucratic mechanisms; the court, meanwhile, resembles a salon, dominated by manipulative courtesans who not only stand in for emasculated courtiers (civil servants, public sector workers, or welfare "queens") but also exploit those mechanisms in the interests—particularly the sexual interests—of women as a class.

In a second frame, Limbaugh's obvious hostility to social democracy suggests the attitudes proper to a liberal capitalist state, and so also the technocratic interventionism that Proudhon denounced; Limbaugh's sexism has more in common here, we might say, with the modern patriarchy seen by Rousseau as an indispensable structure of civil society. This is why it follows that a neoliberal state grounding politics in the market remains, to its advocates, democratic, even though it exacerbates economic inequalities and hardens social hierarchies to a degree some contemporary commentators do not hesitate to call "neo-feudal." The only way to square these consequences with egalitarian or even simply legal norms is a) to assert as a value equality of opportunity but not outcome, and b) to sustain a paradoxically interventionist "sovereignty" in a permanent state of exception. Contradictions do not, of course, go away as a result; they require an imaginary resolution of the sort Limbaugh assays in a pornocratic fantasy that disavows arbitrary and unaccountable power *in* the demand that it be neither. The figure of the prostitute (or slut) is thus a screen in two senses: it both screens a projected power and screens it off from the scrutiny that would demonstrate its illegitimate character, indeed its affinity with tyranny. One of the more striking implications of this fantasy form is that, in it, Limbaugh himself, representing the agendas of corporate-financial power elites (in his role as radio host), also functions as this screen and so *is* the prostitute he denounces. One might even go so far as to argue that he stands in an exemplary relation to the feminized subject formed in the displacements of public and private boundaries that follow from the implementation of those agendas.

We can observe similar paradoxes when the figure of the prostitute is assigned a positive value, as Catherine Hakim argues it should be in her book *Erotic Capital,* advocating a fully legislated and liberalized prostitution as appropriate for a generalized market culture. Her argument hinges on the claim that both sexual conservatives (or "closet patriarchalists" invested in a "male sex right") and (second-wave) feminists collude in devalorizing qualities of look, style, grace, charm, fitness, and sexual competence in women. To assume relationships should be approached in a noninstrumental fashion—as ends in themselves, voluntary, freely given—is a ruse for Hakim; it amounts to advocating an updated form of veiling carried over from a premodern past where romantic love functioned for women as a containment strategy. In this historical narrative, liberation for women consists in claiming feminine qualities as "assets" and pursuing their "mercenary" enhancement and exchange (67–68). The prostitute (as, to be sure, a free agent rather than the instrument of a pimp) becomes the exemplar of the modern individual; "call girls" are equivalent to "party girls," and both signify not only women's long-denied expressive capabilities but those of the market that provides the clothes, makeup, manicures, gyms, and botox they need (141).

The political stakes of Hakim's argument come through in a further comparison between "men and women who earn money in the commercial sex industry" and "men who work in the financial services industry"—all of whom share an interest in profit-making over altruistic aims of social improvement. Here the normalizing thrust of her account works in two directions: the point is not only to empower prostitutes as bond traders by another name but also to assign the moral capital of empowered prostitutes to bond traders. The latter, then, become strangely feminized subjects of Hakim's liberation, signifiers of rights and freedoms that profit-making (in the "imaginary" and "fictitious" forms of asset-backed securities, derivatives, credit default swaps, and so on) transposes into discretionary powers that are clearly at odds with a democratic rule of law. In this manner, Hakim's project proves entirely congruent with the inequality and hierarchy that result from financializing interventions in social life.

Anthony Giddens, in his influential account of the rise in modern sexual culture of "intimacy" as a regulative ideal, does not share Hakim's presumption that a male sex right lies behind noninstrumental or egalitarian norms. Instead, he links instrumental reason itself to the traditional authority that is being superseded. In the transition from long-term marriage to short-term relationships, he sees what he calls "confluent love" drawing on the older resources of a non-Western *ars erotica* that was restricted to elite groups and "usually a female specialty . . . cultivated by concubines, prostitutes, or the members of minority religious communities" (63). Confluent love develops "in a society where almost everyone has the chance to become sexually accomplished, and it presumes the disappearance of the schism between 'respectable' women and those who in some way lie outside the pale of orthodox social life." He goes on to say, "Unlike romantic love, confluent love is not necessarily monogamous, in the sense of sexual exclusiveness. What holds the pure relationship together is the acceptance on the part of each partner, 'until further notice,' that each gains sufficient benefit from the relation to make its continuance worthwhile."

Giddens aims, in language like this, at an autonomous (noninstrumental) sexual choice that breaks with anachronistic conventions of romantic love and monogamy. If he worries that the rationality entailed in calculating "sufficient benefit" blurs ethical lines between manipulative and nonmanipulative behavior, he nonetheless concludes that confluent love is progressive, offering a "structural source" for the "possibility" and "promise of democracy" (188). As his use of the prostitute figure suggests, however, he also sees, in the "structure" it anchors, an overlapping of the prostitute's erotic knowledge with a sexological expertise (both constituting what "almost everyone" has); moreover, the mutual identification of subject and expert grounds for Giddens a logic of quantitative measure and control that characterizes the "justified authority" of a state that (or when it) guarantees symbolic efficiency in both private and public communication. That this state has neoliberal characteristics can be inferred from his well-known commitment to a Third Way communitarianism; but it also comes through in the distance he takes from Foucault, who, he claims, underdescribes the affective and cognitive aspects of sexuality that lend themselves to reflexive transformation (182).

Whatever the merits of this critique, it signals in Giddens an unwillingness to confront structural asymmetries and antagonisms, as many of his critics have pointed out. Lois McNay, for instance, identifies a tendency in Giddens to conceive of identity "solely as a mode of symbolic identification without considering its mediation in embodied practices" (2001, 42). This prevents him from fully addressing "involuntary, pre-reflexive, and entrenched elements of subjectivity" that resist change. Illouz, in her criticism of Giddens, similarly underscores the "resonance" of his analysis with a "psychological credo" that "celebrates equality in intimate relationships" and presumes its achievement as an "ultimate yardstick" of social transformation (30). Despite his different starting point, then, Giddens ends up where Hakim does, with a fantasy of sexual freedom that sustains Illouz's "emotional capitalism," via the link between a feminine double consciousness and the prostitute, in the kind of short-term contractual arrangements typically at issue in prostitution itself.[6] Indeed, the fantasy is the same whether the analogue for sexual freedom derived from these arrangements is instrumental or noninstrumental, and for two reasons: first, because, in both cases, the pertinent difference is with long-term contracts (marriage or otherwise, "social" contracts more broadly construed); and, second, because the subjectivity at stake is modeled not on the coldness of the prostitute in the purely economic transaction nor on the "sentiment" or jouissance of the idealized prostitute. It takes shape, rather, *in their combination*—in a "cold intimacy," as Illouz might put it (8).

Hakim and Giddens do more than use claims on democracy for ideological ends; they also reflect and reinforce a consensus in which their abstractions function as norms in the soul no less than in the state, civil society, or the public sphere. Given the depth of this consensus today, arguments for more grounded, more honest, or even more rational conceptions of democratic society have had to take those norms as starting points, working with what Judith Butler, for instance, calls a subject's constitutive implication or necessary "complicity" in social order (1997, 108). In her theorizing of resistance, she thus posits a desire *for* the law that founds this subject on its own prohibition—"an odd form of preservation," she writes, "eroticizing the law that would abolish eroticism" (103). On one level, this law is what Hakim sees devaluing women's expressive capabilities in the market; on another, or when the law is eroticized, it becomes the neoliberalized freedom that governs the incitement of desire in the exchange of erotic capital. But on both levels, the body discloses a negativity from which Butler extrapolates a repetitive (or reiterative) drive that, because it always fails, for the same reason leaves open the possibility of "inadvertently produced discursive complexity [that] undermines the teleological aims of normalization" (93). This "reiterability" for the subject is less an "unconscious outside of power," she claims, than "the unconscious of power itself" as it paradoxically grounds identity in an open-ended contingency (104).

Nothing guarantees this drive will become resistance. Indeed, even if it does, resistance is so close to submission, and so far from agency of a voluntarist stripe, as to raise the question of just what is gained in the formulation.[7] In practice, it may be that performative resignification as a verbal–symbolic mode boils down to an emotivism not far removed from Giddens's scruple about blurred ethical lines, or, rather, a commitment to "social transformation" that cannot easily reach beyond the establishment of "equality in intimate relationships" (as Illouz puts it). We sense this possible limitation in a self-resistant or self-different ethics when contingent relations to law, right, contract, or even reason and truth feel tactical, making it difficult to ascertain criteria by which one could know whether power is anything other than arbitrary and unaccountable. The absence of such criteria is one reason why egalitarian norms are so easily turned against themselves—as we see, for instance, when military occupation in the Middle East is justified in terms of "saving women" or war on terror associated with the defense of Western women's sexual freedom. We see a similar confusion in the Dutch tolerance test that Butler sharply criticized in 2008 for its equation of homosexuality with a modern citizenship that founds *its own otherness* on exclusions of non-Western others (2009, 105).[8] While she identifies, in this neocolonialist equation, what she calls a "restrictive idea of personal liberty" at work in a "liberal" or "progressive account of increasing freedoms," she also concedes that it puts her sexual politics "in a serious bind" (109), insofar as that founding otherness of the modern citizen also implies both its passionate attachment to the law (with its "odd form of preservation") and the possibility of resistance claimed for it.

One senses this "bind" for sexual politics on a number of fronts these days: where, for instance, military service by women, homosexuals, and transgendered people is construed as an equity issue; in a movie like *The Iron Lady,* which portrays Margaret Thatcher as a feminist model; or in a recent decision by Lisa Williams, president of San Francisco Pride, to block Chelsea (then Bradley) Manning from serving as grand marshal for its 2013 parade, on the grounds that she was a "traitor" to her country for her role in the Wikileaks release of the Iraq cables.[9] It also appeared in the controversy around sexual assault allegations made by two Swedish women against Julian Assange. Whatever his guilt or innocence, and however he might have personally related to a male sex right, the timing of these allegations suggested a strategy on the part of the American state to stop and stigmatize perceived threats (like Wikileaks). The strategy confused legal procedure with ad hominem attack, and it activated in the public sphere conflicting moral frames for understanding sexual violation in a manner that aroused ambivalent commitments on many sides to rights, due process, and civil liberty.[10] The result was a situation in which sexual justice was confused with political injustice, and both were rendered, if not indiscernible, then unactionable in any just fashion. What remains, in a status quo that normalizes, among other obscenities, indefinite detention, "extraordinary rendition," and targeted assassination, is an obvious ethical paralysis and a political need to cut the aporetic knot.

How one makes this cut is far from clear, given the depth to which these examples suggest what Nancy Fraser calls a "convergence" between or "uncanny doubling" of feminism and neoliberal order. Their shared locus, she argues, is a critique of a "traditional authority" that has for so long sanctioned women's subjection to men but also served as an "obstacle to capitalist expansion," a strategy for "confin[ing] economic rationality within a limited sphere" (114–15). Fraser's answer to the confusion this produces is to refocus social struggles for gender justice away from the cultural register of recognition to the politics of subordination and distribution, to reconnect with the anticapitalist critique of "structural and systemic processes in which many people are abstractly or impersonally mediated" (115). This gives clearly a way to sort the difficulties of debate and conflict legible in the aforementioned examples. But it still might not be able to cut that aporetic knot or escape the symbolic violence it indexes from within the framework of progressive history Fraser presumes; she underdescribes what Foucault foregrounds in his theory of governmentality, which takes aim at the "perverse" character of modern society and, by extension, the reasons why those difficulties are so intractable.[11]

Perhaps, here, an updated concept of *pornocracy* comes in handy—ironically, insofar as it pushes Fraser's "convergence" into an uncomfortable identity of interests, implying that gender justice *is* the same as, or coterminous with, the removal of obstacles to capitalist expansion. I do not mean to imply that capitalism leads to gender justice.[12] Nor do I mean to forget either the misogynist bias in the concept of *pornocracy* or its kinship with (ideological disavowals of) real violence. But if this bias and this kinship are included in the term, as what it signifies, perhaps it could designate the ontology of neoliberal biopower, its operation in social fields and at levels of desire, fantasy, disposition, and habitus, where actions are durable but also revisable. To the extent that giving neoliberal society the name of *pornocracy* helps to theorize this possibility of change, it may be worth considering the concept as a useful addition to our critical lexicon.

Stefan Mattessich teaches English at Santa Monica College. He is the author of a monograph on Thomas Pynchon, *Lines of Flight* (2002). His articles on contemporary literature and culture have appeared in *Angelaki, Theory & Event, differences, Postmodern Culture, ELH, English Studies of Canada,* and *New Literary History,* among other venues.

Notes

1. Dumont finds a still earlier instance of the priest's "out-worldly" sensibility transposed into the modern individual's "in-worldly" engagement at another key historical moment: the writing of a text by Pope Gelasius in AD 500 about the relations between the church and emperor. In Dumont's reading, Gelasius proposes a balance of power between the two that permitted the priest to remain "absolutely superior" to the king while at the same time "materially subject to him." The implied opposition between hierarchy and power in Gelasius's thinking placed the church within the empire and the emperor within the church, according to a formula of "hierarchical complementarity" (1986, 46–48).

2. It suggests something of the way Dumont elsewhere conceptualizes a modern "ideology" of the individual vis-a-vis a historical acculturation process cued to compromise formations or "combinations" of past and present value systems, in which "individualistic representations do not by any means get diluted or become less pungent . . . . Quite to the contrary, they become more adaptable and even stronger through . . . associations with their contraries" (1994, 14–15).

3. The first attempt in the English language to apply Proudhon's statements about pornocracy to modern society is by Karl Topfer. I came across his book in references made by Matt George in "Pornocracy of Fate: Mom's Tricks in *The Matrix*," where he makes an initial pass at reading the modern sexual field in a Foucauldian vein. For a fuller elaboration, see also George's "Rejecting the Specifically Sexual: Locating the Sexual Field in the Work of Pierre Bourdieu."

4. I quote from the translated selections of *Pornocracy, or Women in Modern Times* included in this volume.

5. "Void form" is still another term Marx used for finance capital; cited, without attribution, by Michael Hudson (423).

6. Carole Pateman sets the prostitution contract off from all others in the specific "distance" it entails for the woman who offers her body as a "service" in a sexually neutral, universalized, "egalitarian" transaction. Above all, when the prostitution contract becomes the exemplary contract—the "contractarian ideal"—the required abstraction is corporealized, internalized, even sexualized (191).

7. Not much, for many of Butler's critics; Seyla Benhabib, for example, sees in her inability to "answer the question 'how does anyone know that . . . resignification . . . has taken place?'" in any particular performance or speech act an insufficiently elaborated account of human intention and practical agency (340; cited in McNay 2008, 99). If such knowledge is beside the point for Butler, because there is no coherent self prior to action, only what emerges over time as an effect of repeated refashionings of discursive norms, rules, and laws, the claim she nonetheless makes on a subject's capacity for autonomous action by virtue of its necessary implication in a contingent symbolic order (or power) remains problematic. For McNay, Butler's poststructuralist stress on "language as an abstract system of signification rather than as a type of pragmatic interaction" yields a "'negative paradigm' of subject formation where the individual is [little more than] a passive effect of discourse" (167). Resistance then starts to feel distinctly more tenuous, if not phantasmatic.

8. The test, it will be recalled, used an image of two men kissing as a means of establishing whether (mostly non-Western) applicants for immigration visas had a requisite respect for "difference."

9. A lack of support for Manning from large LGBTQ organizations was sadly evident through her subsequent imprisonment. Andy Thayer, cofounder of the Gay Liberation Network, attributes this to their close alignment with the interests and donors of the centrist Democratic Party.

10. Consider, for instance, a 2013 Oxford University student protest aiming to prevent an on-campus video-link speech by Assange (about the restriction of

civil liberties in the digital domain) on the grounds that it abetted a "marginalization of rape allegations" (Hill). Butler adroitly frames the problem here (though in another context) as a "stop[ping of] speech with an unspeakable allegation" (cited in Aksan and Bailes). Her example is speech critical of Israel's policies toward the Palestinians, but the dynamic is the same: "If you speak, you are in an unspeakable place, have become a Nazi or its moral equivalent." She further sees in this strategy a "linguistic permutation of state terrorism, an assault that stops one in one's tracks, and secures the continuing operation of the regime and its monopoly on politically intelligible speech."

11. While Fraser orients herself in Foucault's work, critics sense a tendency to abstract formulation; Nicholas Kiersey, for instance, notes a lack of depth in her use of the governmentality concept (253). See also McNay (2008, 150–54) for a balanced account of objectivist bias in Fraser's thought, specifically with respect to her (overstated) criticism of cultural theories of recognition.

12. "Neoliberal capitalism's indispensable workers," Fraser writes, "are disproportionately women, and not only single young women, but also married women and women with children; not only racialized women, but women of all nationalities and ethnicities" (110). In David Harvey's estimation, neoliberalism has meant for women a "catastrophic" loss of rights, degrading low-wage labor, and a "trading in sexuality [that] varies from respectable work as hostesses and waitresses to the sex trade . . . one of the most lucrative of all contemporary industries in which a good deal of slavery is involved" (17).

Works Cited

Aksan, Cihan, and Jon Bailes. 2013. "An Interview with Judith Butler." Counterpunch, October 11. http://www.counterpunch.org/2013/10/11/an-interview-with-judith-butler/.

Arendt, Hannah. 1958. *The Human Condition*. Chicago: University of Chicago Press.

Armstrong, Nancy. 1987. *Desire and Domestic Fiction*. Oxford: Oxford University Press.

Benhabib, Seyla. 1999. "Sexual Difference and Collective Identities: The New Global Constellation." *Signs* 24:335–61.

Butler, Judith. 1997. *The Psychic Life of Power*. Stanford: Stanford University Press.

Butler, Judith. 2009. *Frames of War*. London: Verso.

Clark, T. J. 1984. *The Painting of Modern Life*. Princeton: Princeton University Press.

Dumont, Louis. 1986. *Essays on Individualism*. Chicago: Chicago University Press.

Dumont, Louis. 1994. *German Ideology: From France to Germany and Back*. Chicago: University of Chicago Press.

Foucault, Michel. 1978. *The History of Sexuality: Volume 1*. Trans. Robert Hurley. New York: Vintage.

Foucault, Michel. 2004. *The Birth of Biopolitics*. Trans. Graham Burchell. New York: Picador.

Fraser, Nancy. 2012. "Feminism, Capitalism, and the Cunning of History." HALarchives-ouvertes.https://halshs.archives-ouvertes.fr/halshs-00725055/document.

George, Matt. 2000. "Pornocracy's Fate: Mom's Tricks in *The Matrix*." *h2so4* (Fall): 34–39.

George, Matt. 2013. "Rejecting the Specifically Sexual: Locating the Sexual Field in the Work of Pierre Bourdieu." In *Sexual Fields: Toward a Sociology of Collective Sexual Life*. Ed. Adam Isaiah Green, 145–74. Chicago: University of Chicago Press.

Giddens, Anthony. 1992. *The Transformation of Intimacy: Sexuality, Love and Eroticism in Modern Societies*. Stanford: Stanford University Press.

Hakim, Catherine. 2011. *Erotic Capital: The Power of Attraction in the Boardroom and the Bedroom*. New York: Basic Books.

Harvey, David. 2005. *A Short History of Neoliberalism*. Oxford: Oxford University Press.

Hill, Amelia. 2013. "Julian Assange Finds No Allies." *Guardian*, January 23. http://www.guardian.co.uk/media/2013/jan/24/julian-assange-oxford-university-wikileaks.

Hudson, Michael. 2010. "From Marx to Goldman Sachs: The Fictions of Fictitious Capital." *Critique* 38, no. 3: 419–44.

Illouz, Eva. 2007. *Cold Intimacies: The Making of Emotional Capitalism*. London: Polity.

Kiersey, Nicholas. 2011. "Love Is a Battlefield: Post-political Control in an Era of Financial Crisis." *New Political Science* 33, no. 2: 249–57.

Marx, Karl. 1909. *Capital: Volume 3*. Chicago: Charles H. Kerr.

Marx, Karl. 1994a. "Civil War in France." In *Selected Writings*. Ed. Lawrence Simon, 301–14. Indianapolis: Hackett.

Marx, Karl.1994b. "The Communist Manifesto." In *Selected Writings*. Ed. Lawrence Simon, 157–86. Indianapolis: Hackett.

McNay, Lois. 2001. *Gender and Agency*. London: Polity.

McNay, Lois. 2008. *Against Recognition*. London: Polity.

Pateman, Carole. 1988. *The Sexual Contract*. Stanford: Stanford University Press.

Thayer, Andy. 2017. "The LGBTQ Movement Is an Intersectional Fail." Counterpunch, May 15. https://www.counterpunch.org/2017/05/15/the-lgbtq-movement-is-an-intersectional-fail/.

Topfer, Karl. 2001. *Theater, Pornocracy, and Aristocracy: The Orgy Calculus*. New York: PAJ.

Žižek, Slavoj. 1991. *For They Know Not What They Do*. London: Verso.

Žižek, Slavoj. 2008. *The Plague of Fantasies*. London: Verso.

PORNOCRATIC FANTASY AND THE CONTRACTARIAN CONCEPTION OF SEXUAL EXCHANGE

Amy Swiffen

Carole Pateman's book *The Sexual Contract* presents a criticism of classical social contract theory premised on the idea that the original notion of a consent-based rule of law made an exception for the subordination of women in the family. She extends this criticism to contemporary notions of contractual freedom through an analysis of contracts for "property in the person," which are contracts for services that are inseparable from the materiality of the body, such as sexual and surrogacy services. Pateman argues that the body is inseparable from the self, and as such, contracts for property in the person are also exchanging the autonomy of the body whose services are purchased. The possibility of such contracts subordinates the self of one of the parties in the act of exchange even when they are consensual. Pateman's phrase the "sexual contract" is an attempt to name the power relations that are translated in an economic exchange by the gender-neutral language of contracts. A sexual exchange contract is formally neutral but substantively gendered insofar as female bodies are the predominant object of exchange, given the relationship between the self and the body that Pateman assumes such contracts put women in positions of social subordination. The asymmetry of the contract recapitulates a power dynamic that remains obscured in discourses that assume a consensual exchange between two rights-bearing individuals. The "sexual contract" names what is missing, which is the background condition of female subordination.

In many ways, Pateman's argument anticipates the legal debate over sexual exchange in Canada, which has centered on decriminalization and/or legalization in recent years (Phoenix; van der Mulen;

Warnock and Wheen). This debate reached an important turning point in 2013 as several of the country's criminal laws relating to sexual exchange were ruled unconstitutional by the Supreme Court of Canada, on the grounds that they violate the constitutional rights of individuals engaged in exchanging sexual services. In particular, the laws were found to unreasonably violate the individual right to the "security of the person," which is protected by the *Canadian Charter of Rights and Freedoms*. A debate ensued as to whether Canada should adopt the "Nordic model" of regulating sexual exchange, which involves decriminalizing the selling of sex while instituting a criminal prohibition on buying, or whether Canada should decriminalize sexual exchange completely and treat it as an economic activity ("sex work").

To explore the relevance of Pateman's concept of the sexual contract to this legal debate, the paper also draws on the work of nineteenth-century libertarian thinker Pierre-Joseph Proudhon. It is hard to identify a thinker who would have been more opposed to the spirit of Pateman's *Sexual Contract* than Proudhon, who was a notorious antifeminist. Socialist and anarchist thinkers of the nineteenth century tended to be more open to the idea of women's emancipation, but Proudhon was a notable exception. He idealized an image of pre-French revolution peasant life in which wives were the property of husbands and men's position as heads of household determined their economic and political role in the community (Segalen). The reason for drawing on Proudhon is that his arguments against women's emancipation share with Pateman's concept of the sexual contract a critique of liberal conceptions of contractual freedom that sheds light the meaning of contracting bodily services. Remarkably, Proudhon agrees with Pateman that contractual freedom applied to "property in the person" does not eliminate women's sex-based subordination. In what follows, the paper analyzes the Supreme Court's ruling on prostitution laws in Canada in light of Pateman's concept of the sexual contract and Proudhon's concept of *pornocracy*. It argues that contractual framings of sexual exchange depend on a *pornocratic fantasy that supplements the reasoning by obscuring the fact that the autonomy of the body is part of the contractual consideration*.

THE CANADIAN CASE

The debate in Canada over the regulation of sexual exchange takes place at legal and political levels. Politically, it is concerned with whether the activity should be conceptualized as a form of labor/work or as a form of male violence (see Barry; Singer). Those who see sexual exchange as a form of male violence argue that selling sexual services is distinct with respect to other forms of labor because the exchange involves the autonomy of the body (Anderson; Overall; Jeffreys; Stark and Whisnant). The exchange, even if consensual, negates a person's bodily autonomy because the body is what is being exchanged for. These contracts are a manifestation of the subordination of women within the law. On the other hand, those who reject this view argue that sexual exchange should be understood as a form of labor and that the social stigma surrounding the activity is harmful to the women involved. The term "sex work" is used to convey the idea that what is being sold is a service, not an individual's self (Pattaniak; Lisborg). Proponents of this view emphasize how the buyer of sexual services does not have unilateral power in the course of the exchange and that sex workers can exercise autonomy in relation to the services they provide (Delacosta and Alexander). Contractarian proponents argue that the harm caused by sexual exchange derives not from the activity itself but from the social stigma associated with it (Ericsson; Kymlicka; Nussbaum 1999, 1998).

In Canada, this debate crystallized around a constitutional challenge to several of the country's criminal laws related to sexual exchange. While it has never been illegal to buy or sell sexual services in Canada, many of the activities surrounding the activity have been criminalized. The legislative objective of this regulation is not to prohibit sexual exchange but rather to regulate it as a public nuisance. For instance, until 2014 the *Criminal Code of Canada* prohibited keeping or being found in a "common bawdy-house" (s. 210),[1] living off the avails of prostitution (s. 212[1][j]), and communicating in public for the purposes of prostitution (s. 213[1][c]). These laws made it very difficult to exchange sexual services without being subject to criminal sanction (see *Bedford v. Canada,* para. 56). In 2010, three women from Ontario challenged the laws' constitutionality. They argued that they violated their right to security of the person under section 7 of the

Canadian Charter of Rights and Freedoms, which states that "everyone has the right to life, liberty and security of the person and the right not to be deprived thereof except in accordance with the principles of fundamental justice" (1982, c. 11, s. 7). The basic argument was that the criminal provisions created a situation where women must choose between compromising their physical safety or putting themselves at risk of criminal accusation.

Within Canadian constitutional law, the concept of "security of person" has developed to include bodily privacy and autonomy over one's body (Hogg). This was established in *R. v. Morgentaler* (1993), in which the Supreme Court of Canada (SCC) struck down criminal laws relating to abortion for infringing on a woman's right to the security of person by requiring her to carry a pregnancy or face criminal liability. The applicants in *Bedford v. Canada* (2010) argue that a similar logic should be extended to sexual exchanges, which, like abortion, implicate an individual's bodily autonomy (Galldin, Robertson, and Wiseman). A trial judge agreed and struck down the laws in question. The judge accepted the argument that sexual exchange implicates an individual's bodily autonomy and cited the Supreme Court of Canada in the *Prostitution Reference* to the effect that the impugned laws constitute "a more serious impairment of the individual's freedom than the avowed legislative objective [controlling public nuisance] would warrant" (*Bedford,* para. 471). Specifically, the judge found that the prohibition against living off the avails was overbroad because it could apply to individuals hired by those exchanging sex, such as bodyguards or bookkeepers. The public communication provision was found to disproportionately impinge on the security of the person by making it more difficult to screen clients and negotiate use of condoms or safe locations.[2] The bawdy-house prohibition was also disproportionate because it prevented individuals from working out of their home or fixed locations, thus pushing them on to the streets where it is more dangerous (Lowman, 51). Based on these findings, the trial judge held that the three provisions in the *Criminal Code* pertaining to prostitution were unconstitutional.

The governments of Canada and Ontario appealed the decision, and several groups were granted intervener status when the case was heard by the Ontario Court of Appeal in 2012. Pivot, Downtown Eastside Sex Workers United against Violence, and PACE Society argued that the laws increased the risk of harm to an already marginalized population (street-based sex workers) by preventing them from taking measures to mitigate risks (Bennett).[3] In contrast, the Women's Coalition for the Abolition of Prostitution (WCAP), an umbrella group representing multiple women's organizations, argued that only one of the provisions should not be struck down, that relating to public communication, which it agreed exacerbated vulnerability to male violence.[4] WCAP asked the court to uphold the other two provisions against living off the avails and bawdy houses on the basis of the argument that individuals should not be able to profit from the exploitation of sexual exchange. Its factum argued that in general exchanging sexual services is a form of sexual exploitation that can only be considered meaningfully consensual in exceptional cases. For the majority of women, the decision to exchange sex is a matter of survival and negotiating limited options. Consequently, the legal framework should regard sexual exchange as a form of exploitation that harms girls and women (Women's Coalition).

The Ontario Court of Appeal upheld the trial decision that the bawdy-house law was unconstitutional. It also agreed that the law against living off the avails was unconstitutional, but suggested it could be acceptable if it was limited to circumstances of exploitation. However, the court overturned the trial decision on the public communication provision, finding that while the law infringed on section 7 of the Charter, the legislative purpose of reducing public nuisance outweighed the infringement (*Canada v. Bedford* [2012]). The governments of Canada and Ontario again appealed the decision. The applicants also cross-appealed the constitutionality of the communication provision and the remedy for the living off the avails provision (*Canada v. Bedford* [2013]). In 2013, the SCC heard the case and ruled, in agreement with the trial judge, that all three provisions violated the right to security of the person in a way that is not justified in a free and democratic society. As Chief Justice McLaughlin wrote in the unanimous decision, the prohibitions do not merely impose conditions on how sexual services can be exchanged: "they prevent people engaged in a risky—but legal—activity from taking steps to protect themselves from the risk" (para. 60). The bawdy-house law was found to prevent working in a fixed location or meeting clients at different locations, which is safer than the street (para. 136). The law against living on the avails did not distinguish between "those who exploit prostitutes (such as controlling and abusive pimps) and those who could increase the safety and security of prostitutes (for example, legitimate drivers, managers, or bodyguards)" (para. 142). The communication law was found to "significantly increase" risk by preventing the screening of clients and making it more difficult to set terms for condom use (para. 71).[5] The SCC pointed out that the objectives of these provisions related to public nuisance and community health and safety, not the deterrence of prostitution more generally (paras. 132–47).

Two aspects of the SCC's decision are worth noting for the purposes of this paper. The first relates to the jurisdiction of section 7 of the Charter. The government of Canada tried to suggest that exchanging sexual services is an inherently risky *economic* activity, and that criminal liability is simply one of the risks that individuals assume when they choose to engage in such activity. The SCC agreed that section 7 does not protect any choice an individual might make.[6] It affords less protection to economic action than to matters that bear fundamentally on individual autonomy. In assessing the impugned laws using this standard, the SCC took a contextual approach and found that, while it is true that sexual exchange is an economic activity and some individuals do freely choose to engage in it, for many others it is not a meaningful choice. Due to "financial desperation, addictions, mental illness, or coercion from pimps, individuals involved in sex work often have little choice but to sell sexual services to survive" (para. 86). While all individuals engaged in exchanging sexual services retain some discretion, the majority "are not people who can be said to be truly 'choosing' a risky line of business" (para. 86). In effect, an overemphasis on contractual freedom obscures the contextual factors that determine the meaningfulness of the choice. Once these are considered, it is clear that individual autonomy is engaged by the activity of sexual exchange in a way that it is not in other kinds of economic choices. The SCC's reasoning involves an assessment at two levels: that of individual autonomy and that of the broader social context framing individual choices.

The second interesting aspect of the *Bedford* decision relates to the SCC's determination of the purpose of the impugned laws. The government of Canada argued that, even if the laws in question do violate the right to security of the person, it is justified by the objective to "deter prostitution" and "promote the values of dignity and equality" (para. 138). The SCC rejected this characterization, pointing to a legislative record in Canada that reveals how these particular provisions regulating the exchange of sexual services were designed to control the public nuisance aspect of an activity, specifically street-based exchange. For example, the purpose of the prohibition on public communication was not to eliminate sexual exchange but to take it "off the streets and out of public view" (para. 147). The laws responded "to the concerns of homeowners, businesses, and the residents of urban neighbourhoods," not to the interests of (mostly) women engaged in the activity (para. 146). Thus, for the SCC, at issue in determining the constitutionality of the impugned provisions was not the meaning of sexual exchange itself but the nature of the government's objective with the provisions. For this reason, it did not explore whether sexual exchange is properly conceived as a contractual exchange or as sexual exploitation. Rather, the focus remained on whether preventing public nuisance justifies the ancillary harm the laws cause to individuals involved in exchanging sex.

THE SEXUAL CONTRACT

The question of the meaning of sexual exchange contracts can, nevertheless, be analyzed beyond the conceptual limits observed by the SCC by drawing on selected strands of social and political theory related to contractarian reasoning. The idea of the "sexual contract" developed by Carol Pateman is based on a criticism of classical social contract theory and the notion of individual autonomy as constitutive of political power. Social contract theory developed during the eighteenth century at a time when the social organization of work and family in Europe was changing. Feudal economies based on family workshops and rural village networks were coming to be based on private property and the separation of work and ownership. Social contract theory emerged in the context of a need to conceptualize new political structures associated with these social developments. Pateman focuses particularly on a debate that took place between social contract theorists and patriarchalists. The latter believed political power was an evolution of the traditional authority of fathers in the family.

In contrast, social contract theorists sought to elaborate a social foundation for political power apart from the family. In *Leviathan,* Thomas Hobbes argued that political power was a social construct based ultimately on the consent of the governed. According to his theory, individuals implicitly consent to a social contract in which they relinquish a degree of natural sovereignty to a political sovereign, who enacts a rule of law that applies to all equally. Outside of such political structures, Hobbes hypothesized that humans would live in a "state of nature" characterized by a perpetual struggle for survival. By virtue of the capacity for reason, however, individuals recognize the benefit of a political association where the security of the person is guaranteed; consequently, they join together in a social contract that limits the sovereignty of each and grants it to the state in the form of a monopoly on violence.

Pateman's critique of social contract theory is that, alongside the advocacy of consent-based political power, Hobbes (like Locke and Rousseau) made an exception for the subordination of women in the classical marriage contract. She shows how all social contract theories denied that women could be party to the social contract directly. Instead, women were indirectly included through their husband, as parties to the marriage contract. For example, to varying degrees all social contract theorists accepted the legal principle of *coverture,* or the "one flesh" doctrine, which existed into the nineteenth century. Under coverture, a married woman's legal personhood was absorbed into her husband's. She could not divorce, sign contracts, hold property, or earn an independent wage. A husband's conjugal and chastisement rights were also considered to fall under coverture (Schwarzenbach).[7] Pateman argues that the separation between the private sphere and politics in theories of social contract is based on accepting these aspects of sex-based inequality in the marriage contract. Far from rejecting patriarchal power, therefore, social contract theorists divided it from paternal power by excluding the subordination of men by other men from the political sphere while assuming the subordination of women in private relations. This is why women fail to appear in civil society in the accounts of Hobbes, Locke, and Rousseau. The social contract is a "double pact" in which an implicit sexual contract among men subtends political equality and separates it from women's subordination in private relations (Pateman 1988, 182). In this sense, the shift from classical patriarchalism to contractarian logic involved not only a change in how political power is conceived but a connected change in how "male sex right" is understood (24).[8]

Pateman calls this the "sexual contract" and argues that it is evident in classical marriage contracts but also in contemporary contracts for sexual exchange and surrogacy services (1988, 80). The common feature of such contracts is the exchange of "property in the person" (55). In contractarian thinking, property in the person refers to an individual's right to his or her own body. What makes the concept interesting in the context of exchange contracts for property in the person is that it engages both the body as object (property) and bodily autonomy. Pateman argues that such contracts are inherently subordinating even when they are consensual because the body itself is also the object of the exchange. What is being contracted is not separate from the self of one of the parties to the contract. This immediately embodied aspect of both individual autonomy and what is being exchanged is obscured by Western conceptions of contractual freedom. The language of contracts frames the relation between the parties as an exchange between two equals, but in the case of contracts for property in the person, one of the parties is also the object of exchange.

Will Kymlicka offers a compelling example of more recent contractarian logic similar to what Pateman has in mind in her critique. Kymlicka suggests that a contract for property in the person is not problematic in the way Pateman describes because conceiving the body as a piece of property in this way has actually allowed individuals—including women—to gain legal rights over their bodies. It has provided a language through which claims for rights can be articulated and advanced. It is only an extension of this logic that would regard bodily autonomy itself as a form of property that can be exchanged if an individual wishes to do so. Kymlicka argues that subordination can occur in the context of such an exchange, not because the contract is inherently subordinating but because of the broader social context of women's inequality in which the contract is made. He states that if the world were "gender-free," contracts for property in the person could be simple expressions of individual autonomy (89). He also assumes that women's inequality will "be eliminated on the road to gender equality" (89). Assuming these two notions, sexuality would not be tied to power relations but would be seen neutrally as a basic human need. Contracts for property in the person (sexual exchanges, surrogacy services) would present rational alternatives to traditional family structures. Rather than marry, "individuals would naturally tend to short-term contracts for the sexual, domestic, and reproductive services they desire" (88). Kymlicka therefore conceives of sexual exchange as a legitimate contractual exchange and only contingently a form of subordination. However, to conceptualize contracts for property in the person as if women's subordination did not exist requires depending on the fantasy of a society that has already "protected the vulnerable and minimized the significance of gender" (88).[9]

One way to understand the difference in how Pateman and Kymlicka conceptualize contracts for property in the person is to consider the relation that each assumes between law and society. For Kymlicka, the exchange of property in the person is not a problem in itself; rather, the social context in which it occurs can make it problematic because of unequal power relations. For Pateman, in contrast, contracts for property in the person depend on the subordination of women in private relations. The "sexually indifferent" language of contractarian freedom obscures the subordination that Pateman sees as making it possible to treat bodies as objects of exchange in the first place (1988, 207). The parties' "embodied identity as a 'man' or a 'woman' . . . is deemed irrelevant" (2006, 78).[10] This is accomplished in Kymlicka's reasoning by positing the fantasy of a "gender-free" society as the basis for conceptualizing contracts for property in the person. The fantasy makes it possible to not take account women's inequality in the ensuing reasoning. It is in this respect, therefore, that Pateman describes the contractarian framework applied to sexual exchange as a "graphic example of men's domination of women" (1988, 207). The gender-free fantasy invoked by Kymlicka functions in the legal reasoning the same way as the sexual contract that Pateman identified in classical social contract theory. The fantasy obscures the way that contracts for property in the person are connected to women's substantive inequality in order to set a ground on which to build contractarian arguments.

At this point, it is relevant to think about the essentialism at work in Pateman's argument, which operates in two ways. One is in the presumption that the body is inseparable from the self, which means that one is never simply an abstract "individual" in an exchange but that the exchange contract is always already located in relations of power. The second is the presumption that the body is always already sexed. Rather than wade into a debate on the second presumption, however, this paper is only interested in the first, which relates to the claim that "property in the person" cannot be separated from the self that is party to a contract, because individual autonomy is inherently embodied. The point is not how sexual difference is ontologically conceived but rather how hermeneutics of gender equality in contractarian logic obscure female inequality. However, this is also a point where Pateman's account requires supplementation, as she does not explore the role of fantasy in contractarian logic identified above. To do this, the next section turns to the work of Pierre-Joseph Proudhon, specifically his critique of social contract theory and women's emancipation.

PROUDHON'S POLITICAL THEORY

Proudhon was writing at a time when a new ruling class of wealthy factory owners and bankers had gained power in France by purchasing land confiscated from the aristocracy after the revolution (Schapiro, 718). He was extremely critical of the way that the new bourgeoisie were building factories that threatened the economic independence of traditional peasant households, in which laboring and owning the means of production were inseparable. The household model of production could not compete with larger-scale factories, and many men who had been the heads of household and formerly self-sufficient, became wage laborers in the factories (Hall, 14). Unlike Marx, however, who attacked the way wage labor was inserted into production under capitalism, Proudhon saw the problem as one of fairness in the distribution of profits (Proudhon 1993). He believed that ownership and profit should always derive from the same source, direct labor, and sought to protect the interests of the "worker-owner" class (tradesmen, shopkeepers, artisans) who engaged in subsistence labor and exchanged surplus on the market (Schapiro, 719). Thus, while Marx wanted to destroy the legal concept of private property and overcome the division of work and ownership at a collective level, Proudhon wanted to limit property rights to the individual level (Hyams). For example, *What Is Property?* argues that income derived from loans, rent, or investments is unjust because it comes not from one's own labor but from the labor of others (those who pay the rent or work in the factory). Proudhon argues that private property conceived in this way is "theft" insofar as it generates profit for owners even though they do not labor directly. He blamed inequality under capitalism on this view of private property, as it puts those who are able buy the labor of others in a position to amass more wealth than others.

Proudhon favored legal reforms to protect artisan and household production against both large capitalists and the socialization of the means of production (i.e., the "dictatorship of the proletariat"). For instance, he advocated eliminating exclusive ownership rights over land in favor of property rights defined in terms of "possession," which implies rightful ownership over capital by virtue of making use of it (1993, 177). Ownership is not separable from the labor that makes a given property productive. Proudhon reasoned that property rights defined by possession would eliminate inequality by allowing individuals to own only that with which they directly labor; such a law would allow individual autonomy while impeding the concentration of wealth.[11] Proudhon used the term "mutualism" to refer to the form of society based on this type of property ownership arrangement (Ansart, 217–18).[12] He imagined that in a mutualist society individual worker-owners would enter into associations bound together by mutual cooperation, and that a "rule for all bargains" would emerge in the course of economic exchanges stipulating that parties must exchange things of equivalent value, not because there is a law that obliges it but simply because they mutually recognize each other as equal individuals (2004, 206). Proudhon's theory is based on the idea of a "social instinct" in human beings that produces spontaneous mutual recognition of equality (29). This instinct makes recognition a "natural attribute of free cooperative exchanges" (2011, 283). Hence, Proudhon rejected "transcendental" conceptions of justice as a source of legal authority (1969, 249). He felt that the theological approaches to law of Augustine and Thomas Aquinas positioned justice apart from humanity and created a hierarchy between justice and humanity.[13] His belief instead that justice was a product of natural instinct combined with human imagination meant that it was necessarily "immanent" to human consciousness (249).

Despite this humanist conception of justice, however, Proudhon was equally critical of social contract theorists' attempts to conceptualize political power as a social construct. He argued that this approach suffered from the inverse problem of theological conceptions of law. By suggesting that justice was dependent on a social contract, social contract philosophies subordinated justice to politics (1868, 97). For instance, Proudhon rejected Hobbes's idea that individuals in a state of nature live in war of all against all. He felt instead that in a state of nature individuals live in a state of mutual indifference. Individuals are estranged from one another, with "the rights of one [having] nothing to do with the rights of another" (1993, 48). As soon as individuals associate with each other, the social instinct for justice is activated and equality is spontaneously mutually recognized. There is no need for a special contract or political operation for the social instinct to produce justice. In this respect, Proudhon disagreed with Hobbes that political sovereignty comes at the expense of "natural" individual sovereignty. From Proudhon's point of view, any form of governance that subordinates individual sovereignty to a collective power represents the subordination of justice to politics, since justice is already within each individual in the form of a social instinct that is "independent of any legislative power" (2004, 221).

This view of natural justice led Proudhon to reject any form of state-based law. Because of this rejection, it has been argued that Proudhon offers a "non-sovereign" concept of law (Prichard). However, this assessment is true only if one equates sovereignty with state power, which Proudhon does not. He is clear that sovereignty is a natural property of the individual. He writes that in a mutualist society, "every citizen is king; for he has plenitude of power, he reigns and governs" (1848, 119).[14] With this statement Proudhon was not speaking of generic individuals. The "reigning" and "governing" referred to here is that of a husband / father in the feudal family, wherein men were the heads of the household and wives worked under their authority with their legal personhood subsumed. Recall, Proudhon essentially argued that political equality comes from the mutual recognition among men of their sovereign authority over the household. In this sense, his theory is not non-sovereign at all. It simply grounds sovereignty in private relations of subordination rather than public ones. Proudhon's critique of social contract theory is that it separated political recognition from the recognition of male supremacy in the household. Like Pateman, therefore, Proudhon felt that social contract theory divided political power from paternal power. In contrast to Pateman, however, Proudhon's problem was not that women's subordination might remain operative in the private sphere but that the exclusion of this subordination from civil society represented the subordination of natural justice (1875, 205).

In general, political and civil rights are counter to justice because they involve the state limiting the sovereignty of men in their private relations. To properly approximate justice, law should simply aim to recapitulate the norms that are "spontaneously upheld by a social group" (2011, 283). Thus, if a community excludes women from civil society, it is not a problem from the perspective of justice. In fact, to grant women legal equality in such a case would be an intrusion of the state into the autonomy of the community and the sovereignty of men. In this sense, Proudhon's concept of justice effectively elevated patriarchal norms based in local customs over political concepts of equality. Proudhon only opposed inequality between individuals who were naturally equal. Mutual recognition only occurs among "individuals of the same species," and "the difference of the sexes places the same sort of barrier between them as the difference of races places between animals" (1993, 185). Between males and females there is "no real society" and recognition of women's civic equality would be unnatural (Moses, 152).[15]

Proudhon's insistence on women's natural inferiority is elaborated in detail in a pamphlet titled *La Pornocratie, ou les femmes dans les temps modernes*. Here, Proudhon rejects historical materialist arguments that linked women's emancipation to general human emancipation and instead idealizes an image of pre-French revolution peasant family life in which wives were the property of husbands (Moses; Segalen). In this text, Proudhon also repeated his idea that women's legal emancipation represented state subordination of natural justice, however he specified how natural justice is also the proper regulator of relations in the family. If men's social instinct allowed them to recognize each other as equals and self-regulate accordingly, this same social instinct sanctioned women's subordination in the family. Consequently, women's emancipation from private subordination and entry into civil society as a legal person represented not just political repression but degeneration.

In *Pornocratie,* Proudhon referred to women's emancipation as "free love," not because it involved freedom but because it freed "second order virtues" of love, beauty, and pleasure, from the natural constraints of family life (1875, 3). Proudhon associated these virtues with women and suggested that they had their place within traditional marriage where they helped to socialize men and encourage the protection of children; but freed from the constraint of marriage, these female virtues enter the free market and become a corrupting influence on civil society (74). Proudhon warns that if women are emancipated, men will simply forego marriage in the face of access to love on the market, which would precipitate a general "political degeneration," as sensual pleasure would become the basis of social action in civil society (114). He used the term *pornocracy* to describe such a social order based on a "pure fantasy" of a free market for love and pleasure (139).

The term *pornocracy* is derived from the Greek word *pornokratiā,* meaning rule by prostitutes. Proudhon's use of the term was likely informed by the history of the Catholic Church, specifically a period known as the *Saeculum obscurum,* or the Dark Age (tenth century), which was dubbed "the Pornocracy" by eighteenth-century German Protestant theologians (Dwyer). During the *Saeculum obscurum,* a powerful family named Theophylacti dominated Roman nobility. They exerted a lot of control over economic and political affairs in Rome, and Theophylacti women had particular influence over the papacy (Brook). During this time, the Vatican was purportedly characterized by general sexual decadence and depravity (Stark). The Popes of the *Saeculum obscurum* would have been iconic pornocrats in Proudhon's eyes because he would see them as being controlled by second order virtues symptomatic of the influence of the aristocratic women. The pornocrat is only one side of the fantasy, however; the other entails the use of "property in the person" as a form of autonomy. It would seem that this aspect of the pornocratic fantasy is compatible with Pateman's concept of the sexual contract, in that it suggests that contracts for property in the person are based on a fantasy of a self that is separate from the object of exchange.

CONCLUSION

It is interesting to consider how the SCC's conceptualization of sexual exchange in *Bedford* relates to the concepts of the sexual contract and pornocratic fantasy developed in this paper. In one sense the SCC agrees with Pateman that sexual exchange contracts are not properly conceptualized as simply an exercise of economic freedom, but rather as a contract that inherently implicates bodily autonomy. If sexual exchange were merely a matter of work, then the consideration being exchanged would be separable from the body of the worker. Yet, in contracts for property in the person the consideration is part of the body itself. It is this distinguishing feature that allowed the Charter claim to go forward. The SCC recognized that if the impugned laws were having an impact "only in the context of economic interests," the right to the security of the person would not be engaged, as regulating risky markets is within the purview of Parliament (para. 45). If sexual exchange contracts were simply akin to economic exchange contracts the legal regulation (including the use of the criminal law) of economic activity would not present a constitutional issue. However, the SCC looked to the particular character of contracts for property in the person and determined that sexual exchange is not simply an economic action. This fits with Pateman's argument about the effects of an implicit "sexual contract" underlying consensual contracts for property in the person. This aspect of her analysis is compatible with the approach in the *Bedford* case. If we think about the meaning of "choice" as interpreted by the SCC, we see that sexual difference is invoked not as an essential category of being but rather as a contextual factor in evaluating the meaning of the role of the body in contracts for property in the context of sexual exchange.

In contrast, Kymlicka's contractarian logic is sustained in part on the fantasy of a "gender-free" society where sex-based inequality has been eliminated. The point of my critique has been to suggest that the fantasy of a gender-free society is "pornocratic" in so far as it separates individual autonomy from the fact that the body is an object of exchange. It further obscures sex-based inequality in which exchanges for property in the person occur by making possible forms of reasoning that do not take it into account. Drawing on Patemen's perspective, such pornocratic fantasies of women's freedom expressed through contracts for property in the person also sustain a fiction that the autonomy of the self can be separated from the body. The counterpoint is the assumption of a class of bodies available for exchange. In this sense, pornocratic fantasies obscure at the same time as they assume bodies available for exchange. They take the place of incorporating the fact that these bodies are effectively female. Pateman's point is that an individual's autonomy is inseparable from what is exchanged through contracts for property in the person, and hence these contracts are an inherently subordinating form of market exchange. The take away is that the gender-neutral idiom of contractarian logic combined with pornocratic fantasies of a society free from sex-based power relations seem to obscure the potential reproduction of female subordination through contracts for property in the person.

Amy Swiffen is a faculty member in the Department of Sociology and Anthropology at Concordia University. Her research is in the areas of sociolegal studies and sociological theory.

Notes

1. In the Criminal Code of Canada, a "common bawdy-house" means, "for the practice of acts of indecency, a place that is kept or occupied or resorted to by one or more persons" (s. 197).

2. It noted that a more narrowly defined provision that applied only when the communication caused some demonstrable public harm, such as street congestion or noise, could be acceptable.

3. See also Shrage; Bernstein; Ditmore.

4. The Women's Coalition was made up of the Canadian Association of Elizabeth Fry Societies, the Canadian Association of Sexual Assault Centres, the Native Women's Association of Canada, Vancouver Rape Relief Society, Action ontarienne contre la violence faite aux femmes, Concertation des luttes contre l'exploitation sexuelle, and Regroupement québécois des centres d'aide et de lutte contre les agressions à caractère sexuel.

5. After the Bedford ruling became effective, the Government of Canada introduced Bill C-36, which reflected the Nordic model of regulating sexual exchange: "Bill C-36 maintains that the best way to avoid prostitution's harms is to bring an end to its practice" (Government of Canada).

6. "Whether the s. 7 interest at issue is economic liberty or security of the person is not a distinction without a difference" (para. 45).

7. Even Locke, who argued that a father and mother had equal authority over children, accepted that women could own property, and was open to the idea of divorce, suggested that women were better off under the protection of men than as fully free citizens.

8. The concept of "male sex right" is drawn from feminist discourses that argue that sexual subordination by men is the foundation of women's inequality (See Rich).

9. It is interesting to note a fantasy present in other contractarian arguments about prostitution. Martha Nussbaum argues the criminalization of prostitution is based on stigma sustained by irrational prejudice (1999, 1998). To illustrate the irrationality, she makes analogies to professions that also involve taking money for the use of the body: a factory worker, a domestic servant, a nightclub singer, a professor of philosophy, a massage therapist, and a colonoscopy artist. She argues that, because these are analogous to sexual exchange in integral ways and are not considered legally problematic, sexual exchange should not be either. However, it is the final analogy that approximates most closely what Pateman is talking about with the idea of "property in the person." The colonoscopy artist is paid to receive anal probes for the purposes of testing medical equipment. This most parallels sexual exchange because the service cannot be separated from the materiality of the body. However, it is also the only profession on the list that is hypothetical. On this point, it is worth noting that this particular fantasy would generally be considered unethical in the context of medical research. Participants in studies testing medical equipment on humans can only participate if they are ill and have no other treatment options or the study offers the best treatment option (U.S. FDA 2014). In other words, similar to prostitution, the reality of the scenario Nussbaum presents is recognized as being potentially exploitative in ways that are not addressed simply through informed consent. Her invocation is a fantasy that obscures the exploitative aspect.

10. Pateman defines the prostitution contract as purchasing the "*sexual* use of a *woman's* body" (1988, 204).

11. Proudhon also advocated for price setting based on the concept of "synthetic value," which he defined as the value of a commodity measured by the amount of labor time that goes into producing it (2004, 92). Marx rejected this notion because he argued measuring labor value in terms of time is how labor is inserted into the capitalist mode of production already ("socially necessary labor time"). The problem is that this calculation is not based on the real labor involved but on the amount of "average" labor required. The idea of average labor is based on the labor of a worker with average training and average access to materials and equipment. In the *Poverty of Philosophy,* Marx posits that socially necessary labor time is calculated based on the idea of the most productive worker. In either case, the value of a commodity is not based on the real labor involved but on an abstraction of that labor measured in standardized units of time.

12. Proudhon envisioned mutualism as a federation of worker associations bound together by mutual cooperation involving small enterprises and small property owners controlling family-based production processes.

13. In different ways, both thinkers believed that justice emanated from a realm beyond human understanding and positioned God as the only one with full knowledge of justice.

14. "Tout citoyen est roi; car il a la plénitude de pouvoir, il règne et gouverne."

15. In *Justice dans la revolution et dans l'eglise,* Proudhon explains how women are inferior to men. They are physically weaker because their bodies are orientated toward pregnancy. Women's cognitive abilities lie somewhere between men and animals. Women also have a less-developed moral conscience because of this greater proximity to nature (See also Custers, 39; Ehrenberg, 138–39).

Works Cited

Anderson, Scott A. 2006. "Prostitution and Sexual Autonomy: Making Sense of Prohibition and Prostitution." In *Prostitution and Pornography: Philosophical Debate about the Sex Industry*. Ed. Jessica Spector, 358–93. Stanford: Stanford University Press.

Ansart, Pierre. 1967. *Sociologie de Proudhon*. Paris: Presses Universitaires de France.

Barry, Kathleen. 1995. *The Prostitution of Sexuality*. New York: New York University Press.

Bedford v. Canada. 2010. ONSC 4264.

Bennett, Darcie. 2013. "R. v. Bedford—The Decision in 705 Words." *Pivot* (blog), December 20. http://www.pivotlegal.org/canada_v_bedford_a_synopsis_of_the_supreme_court_of_canada_ruling.

Bernstein, Elizabeth. 2001. "The Meaning of Purchase: Desire, Demand and the Commerce of Sex." *Ethnography* 2, no. 3: 389–420.

Brook, Lindsay. 2003. "Popes and Pornocrats: Roman in the Early Middle Ages." Foundations 1, no. 1: 5-21.

Canada (Attorney General) v. Bedford, 2013 SCC 72, [2013] 3 S.C.R. 1101.

Canadian Charter of Rights and Freedoms. 1982. Part 1 of the *Constitution Act, 1982,* being Schedule B to the *Canada Act 1982* (UK), chapter 11.

Custers, Peter. 1997. *Capital Accumulation and Women's Labour in Asian Economies*. New Delhi: Vistaar.

Delacosta, Frederique, and Priscilla Alexander. 1988. *Sex Work: Writings by Women in the Sex Industry*. London: Virago.

Ditmore, Melissa Hope. 2011. *Prostitution and Sex Work*. Santa Barbara: Greenwood.

Dwyer, John C. 1998. *Church History: Twenty Centuries of Catholic Christianity*. Mahwah: Paulist Press.

Ehrenberg, John. 1996. *Proudhon and His Age*. Atlantic Highland: Humanities Press.

Ericsson, Lars O. 1980. "Charges against Prostitution: An Attempt at a Philosophical Assessment." *Ethics* 90, no. 3: 335–66.

Galldin, Karin, Leslie Robertson, and Charlene Wiseman. 2011. "Bedford v. Canada: A Paradigmatic Case Toward Ensuring the Human and Health Rights of Sex Workers." *HIV/AIDS Policy and Law Review* 15, 3: 5–14.

Government of Canada. 2017. Technical Paper: Bill C-36, *Protection of Communities and Exploited Persons Act*. Department of Justice, Ottawa: Canada. http://www.justice.gc.ca/eng/rp-pr/other-autre/protect/p1.html.

Hall, Constance M. 1971. *The Sociology of Pierre Joseph Proudhon (1809–1865)*. New York: Philosophical Library.

Hobbes, Thomas. 1997. *Leviathan*. New York: Norton.

Hogg, Peter W. 1997. *Constitutional Law of Canada*. 4th ed. Toronto: Carswell.

Hyams, Edward. 1979. *Pierre-Joseph Proudhon: His Revolutionary Life, Mind and Works*. London: John Murray.

Jeffreys, Sheila. 1997. *The Idea of Prostitution*. Melbourne: Spinifex Press.

Kymlicka, Will. 1991. "Rethinking the Family." *Philosophy and Public Affairs* 20, no. 1: 77–97.

Lisborg, Anders. 2002. "Bodies across borders: Prostitution-Related migration from Thailand to Denmark." In *Transnational Prostitution: Changing Global Patterns*. Ed. Susanne Thorbek and Bandana Pattanaik, 100–120. London: Zed Press.

Lowman, John. 2011. "Deadly Inertia: A History of Constitutional Challenges to Canada's Criminal Code Sections on Prostitution." *Beijing Law Review* 2, no. 2: 33–54.

Moses, Claire Goldberg. 1984. French Feminism in the Nineteenth Century. Albany: State University of New York Press.

Nussbaum, Martha. 1998. "Whether from Reason or Prejudice: Taking Money for Bodily Services." *Journal of Legal Studies* 27, no. 2: 693–724.

Nussbaum, Martha. 1999. *Sex and Social Justice*. Oxford: Oxford University Press.

Overall, Christine. 1992. "What's Wrong with Prostitution? Evaluating Sex Work." *Signs* 17:705–24.

Pateman, Carole. 1988. *The Sexual Contract*. Stanford: Stanford University Press.

Pateman, Carole. 2006. "What's Wrong with Prostitution?" In *Prostitution and Pornography: Philosophical Debate about the Sex Industry*. Ed. Jessica Spector, 50–79. Stanford: Stanford University Press.

Pattanaik, Bandana. 2002. "Where Do We Go from Here?" In *Transnational Prostitution: Changing Global Patterns*. Ed. Susanne Thorbek and Bandana Pattanaik, 217–30. London: Zed Press.

Phoenix, Jo. 2007. "Governing Prostitution: New Formations, Old Agendas." *Canadian Journal of Women and Law* 22, no. 2: 73–94.

Prichard, Alex. 2011. "What can the absence of anarchism tell us about the history and purpose of International Relations?" *Journal of International Studies* 37 (4): 1647–69.

Proudhon, Pierre Joseph. 1848. *La solution du problème sociale*. Paris: Pilhes.

Proudhon, Pierre Joseph. 1868. *De la justice dans la révolution et dans l'église*. Paris: A. La Croix, Verboeckhoven.

Proudhon, Pierre Joseph. 1875. *La pornocratie, ou les femmes dans les temps modernes*. Paris: A. La Croix, Verboeckhoven.

Proudhon, Pierre Joseph. 1969. "On Justice." *Selected Writings of Pierre-Joseph Proudhon*. Ed. Stewart Edwards, 248–53. New York: Macmillan.

Proudhon, Pierre Joseph. 1993. *What Is Property? An Enquiry into the Principle of Right and of Government*. Cambridge: Cambridge University Press.

Proudhon, Pierre Joseph. 2004. *System of Economical Contradictions, or the Philosophy of Misery*. New York: Kessinger.

Proudhon, Pierre Joseph. 2011. "Organisation of Credit and Circulation." *Property Is Theft! A Pierre-Joseph Proudhon Anthology*. Ed. Iain McKay, 283–94. Oakland: AK Press.

Rich, Adrienne. 1980. "Compulsory Heterosexuality and Lesbian Existence." *Signs: Journal of Women in Culture and Society* 5, no. 4: 631–60.

Schapiro, J. Salwyn. 1945. "Pierre Joseph Proudhon, Harbinger of Fascism." *American Historical Review* 50, no. 4: 714–37.

Schwarzenbach, Sibyl. 1990. "Contractarians and Feminists Debate Prostitution." *N.Y.U. Review of Law and Social Change* 18, no. 1: 103–29.

Segalen, Martine. 1983. *Love and Power in the Peasant Family: Rural France in the Nineteenth Century*. Chicago: Chicago University Press.

Shrage, Laurie. 1996. "Prostitution and the Case for Decriminalization." *Dissent* 43:41–45.

Singer, Linda. 1993. *Erotic Welfare: Sexual Theory and Politics in the Age of Epidemic*. New York: Routledge.

Stark, Christine, and Rebecca Whisnant, eds. 2004. *Not for Sale: Feminists Resisting Prostitution and Pornography*. Melbourne: Spinifex.

Stark, Rodney. 2014. *For the Glory of God*. Princeton: Princeton University Press.

U.S. Food and Drug Administration. 2014. "Inside Clinical Trials: Testing Medical Products in People." U.S. Food and Drug Administration Information for Consumers, November 6. https://www.fda.gov/Drugs/ResourcesForYou/Consumers/ucm143531.htm.

van der Meulen, Emily. 2012. "When Sex Is Work: Organizing for Labour Rights and Protections," Labour/Le Travail, 69: 147–67.

Warnock, Ceri, and Nicola Wheen. 2012. "Sex Work in New Zealand: The Re-importation of Moral Majoritarianism in Regulating a Decriminalised Industry." *Canadian Journal and Women and Law* 24, no. 2: 414–38.

Women's Coalition for the Abolition of Prostitution. 2013. "Factum of Intervenor—Supreme Court of Canada." http://casac.ca/sites/default/files/Factum%20-%20Womens%20Coalition.pdf.

FEMINIST PORNOCRACY?

FEMEN AND THE POLITICS OF RESISTANT NUDITY

Dina Al-Kassim

A scene at the April 2013 Hanover trade fair illustrates the peculiar symbiosis of pornocratic rule and struggle for celebrity enjoined by a global economy of sovereign subjectivity. Homogenizing market logics expressed as private sentiment and empowered agency feed the pornocratic economy by inflating and innovating the disciplinary imaginaries some mistake for liberty and sovereign intimacy.

> It was, recalls Shevchenko, a 24-year-old business studies graduate from . . . western Ukraine, "a very intimate moment." . . . "Suddenly there I was, looking into Putin's eyes, he into mine, just a metre between us before one of his men lunged to shield him from me and in those seconds I was just thinking to myself: "What a funny botox face—because of all the snips and tucks it's endured, it can't properly express what he's feeling." Alexandra Shevchenko (cited in Connolly)

Femen activist Alexandra Shevchenko here gazes at the mirror image of a potential future self, one reflecting every surgical stay of mortality and of our being in common. As a major player among the "shock troops" of sextremism known as Femen, Shevchenko and the pornocrat share a moment of recognition in the public eye as she launches herself topless upon the Russian president in full view of the assembled media throng and to the contagious surprise of Europe's most powerful woman and national leader, German chancellor Angela Merkel. Cementing the public disclosure of their relation, the eye lock can be read as an index of a postsoviet identity in crisis, where personality and celebrity are sought as the other side of real poverty and an ossified gender system, conduit of trafficking and sex tourism without end by Femen's account.

Cut off from its own expressive lexicon, the pornocrat's face beams back only images of bloated obscenity and grotesque invitation as Putin "seems to push his chest out, raise his eyebrows and purse his lips, producing a double chinned smirk, while Merkel puffs out her cheeks and frowns as bodyguards pounce on Shevchenko and her four fellow Femen members, tackling them to the floor" (cited in Connolly). If Femen nudity primly stops at toplessness, their public materializations unleash the farcical element only ever loosely held in check by public figureheads who contend with the rigorous body discipline of public appearance. The Femen intervention exposes this fact before the cameras: "I had observed from a distance a group of suited men. The closer I got to them, I recognised the really small one amongst them was Putin. He was so puny, not like the macho pictures you see of him riding a horse bareback, or fishing barechested," she said. "And that was when I realised: now is the moment and started to charge .... I jumped over the fence, pumping my elbows out at my sides and undressing as I ran towards him, screaming: 'Fuck the dictator'" (cited in Connolly).

Alternately tumescent and shrinking, fearsome yet fading, Putin appears less formidable when measured against the beauty system's exacting standards, and this fragilized masculinity, by turns ridiculous and obscenely leering, invigorates the Femen-ist who, seizing the opportunity to launch the insult, claims equality although only in the terms of erotic bondage. As one Femen-ist puts it, "We use women's sexuality as women's weapon" (Hutsol and Svyatski). Logics of saturnalian reversal or Bakhtinian carnivalesque fail to capture the restricted economy of Femen's pornocratic intimacy with heteropatriarchal power and the figures of sovereignty who front for it; for this we must reach into Achille Mbembe's notion of "commandment," a cycling entanglement of desire for glory wedded to a demand for absolute power, wherein the dominated "clothe themselves in cheap imitations of power to reproduce its epistemology . . . [while] power, in its own violent quest for grandeur, makes vulgarity and wrongdoing its main mode of existence" (133). Femen-ist nudity mirrors pornocratic vulgarity and machismo by borrowing its cheap lineaments to reproduce its logic of spectacular individuality, absolute agency, and freedom understood as the media capture of subjective singularity.

Yet a Femen-ist is no libertine. "We were invited to Germany. At first I was quite sceptical, thinking: 'What have we as feminists from Ukraine, which has no tradition of feminism, got to offer others, particularly in what we viewed in Ukraine as forward-thinking western Europe?'" she says. "But we soon realised they were extremely keen to work with us because we're completely rethinking feminism" (cited in Connolly). Citing a 30 percent pay gap between German men and women in the context of the legalization of prostitution, the Femen-ist business graduate cannily shifts the map of value to suggest that Ukrainian lack may expose neglected realities in the West, where the gains for women's sexual freedom mask entrenched inequalities.

Femen's recourse to a resurgent pornocracy may contain a kernel of refusal directed at what Angela McRobbie has called the "new sexual contract," one that prompts the new young woman to abandon critique of hegemonic masculinity in exchange for "incitements to become wage-earning subjects" adapted to "post-feminist masquerade" (fashion and the beauty system as modes of power). "The sexual contract now embedded in political discourse and in popular culture permits the renewed institutionalization of gender inequity and the restabilization of gender hierarchy by means of a generational-specific address which interpellates young women as subjects of capacity . . . endlessly working on a perfectible self" (726). Referencing Joan Riviere's 1929 observation that "women who wish for masculinity may put on a mask of womanliness to avert anxiety and the retribution feared from men," McRobbie argues "post-feminist masquerade is a strategy or device for the re-securing of patriarchal law and masculine hegemony." Reading masquerade back into commandment's aesthetics of vulgarity, sextremism poses the question of how "the economy of pleasure has become inseparable from vice" (723).

Isomorphic with the pornocracy it protests, Femen shares the pornocrat's stringent body discipline and investment in mass media spectacle as a substitute for public culture. Rule by media, which assumes the total failure of democratic forms while exploiting them, is an essential fact of pornocratic regimes that suppress and suffocate public speech using all the tools of censorship, fear, and coercion. Femen's tactical response necessarily moves in tandem with efforts to restrict public engagement and criticism to farcical protest and a weak refusal that effects no social change. A convulsive tango danced between topless female youth and patriarchs, rightwing and government thugs, figureheads and perverse potentates—Berlusconi, Putin,

Trump—this is the opiate of the medias, and so much so that television outlets actually hire Femen to stage performances, thereby staging the news. Though resolutely "postfeminist" in bent, Femen's rhetoric of performance and self-promotion is firmly anchored in a patriarchal logic of public and private decorum characteristic of a prior age. Thus the destruction of patriarchy, their stated goal, is not, in fact, the point. Rather, they promote pornocracy through other means that many critics identify as Islamophobic, misogynist, and homophobic, and this seeming contradiction demands that we think the phenomenon of Femen not through the analytic of sex/gender but as one among the indices of the postsoviet, postcolonial deployment of sexuality, and thus as a contemporary industry of the pornocratic subject.

PORNOCRACY RULES

Proudhon's defense of marriage, *Pornocracy, or Women in Modern Times,* provides exemplary language to illuminate the isomorphism between the many-headed hydra of pornocracy—Strauss-Kahn, Putin, Institut Civitas, Marine Le Pen, Trump—and the Femen breast. Penned only two years after the Crimean War, this antifeminist pamphlet offers a version of heteropatriarchal union, one that subordinates mere pleasure, chided as inconstant hedonism practiced by feminists, to the interests of the greater good and social justice achieved only through marriage. Proudhon's rant against the dangers to the body politic posed by the luxury and decadence of capitalist women was already a traditional view by 1858. Prefigured in the luxury debates of the eighteenth century and long associated with the civic threat of *effeminatus,* linkage of the ills of capital with sex and enfeebled gender was a commonplace of the strain of political writing exemplified by his pamphlet (see Berg and Eger Basingstoke). Extolling the "voluptuous commerce" of marriage, Proudhon asserts,

> It is thus that marriage becomes for spouses a cult of conscience, and for society the very organ of justice. A sacred marriage . . . immunizes them, vis-à-vis others, against all crime and felony; while concubinage, a union of man and woman, secret and solemn, but formed solely in view of pleasure . . . is the habitual resort of parasites, of thieves, of forgers and assassins.

Secret and solemn unions that eschew publicity, neglect marriage bans, and dissolve at pleasure's end are here allied with criminality, dependence, fakes, and murderers because private intimacy without public sanction earns no immunization of its actions; whereas, in marriage, even crime can be secreted by virtue of marriage's prior *publicity*. In exposing the bonds of marriage, the man of exchange and the woman of favor are indemnified against the stain of "mutual prostitution." Depicting man as master of the household and woman's "goading beauty" as complementary to his force, Proudhon upholds the domestic circulation of value and energy as the primitive form of all political society. The paterfamilias, strengthened and augmented by domesticity, contributes his mastery to the whole of his social network, thereby entering into the social industry of wealth and "dignity and virile liberty." The wife, engulfed in the "embryonic organ of justice," sustains the private intimacy of domesticity while the public man becomes the very "minister of feminine fidelity," communicating in public and to the state the value that she embodies and sustains. Without this natural sharing out of labor, value, and matter, Proudhon asserts, there can be no basis for civil society. If heteropatriarchal marriage supplies the primitive organ of justice, the husband represents this organ by veiling it in public.

Proudhon reveals a structure of inner and outer, secrecy and disclosure, that governs the border of public and private and that conditions feminine liberty by avowing it to self-exposure and self-promotion. The unmarried woman and, in particular, the sexually active unmarried woman open the state to threat not because she herself is a felon but because her unguarded and unmediated beauty and eros cannot temper itself as justice. And as an ancillary effect of the secrecy of concubinage, her public persona can only be expressed and lived out as a form of exposure that is not properly public because not properly mediated or veiled by man. In her, the organ of justice is laid bare and erased by the same body, for only the state of marriage can confer on her the right to a public mask, the persona bestowed by marriage. The unmarried woman who appears in public without a minister of feminine fidelity is a foreigner, a persona non grata or, in Proudhon's charge, a "feminist." She is, in other words, not public at all but outside the bounds of the social commerce that founds and delimits what can enter the public sphere. She appears as a form of exposure threatening both the secrecy and the publicity of the norm, and she materializes in public the possibility that family life is, indeed, the mutual prostitution he abhors.

Resisting pornocracy, Proudhon's portrait of a lady sketches the contours of a problem for the normative account of marriage. If women's criticism of the marriage form and refusal to enter into it are neither private nor public disclosures, then departures from the norm can be perceived only as a violent exposure of private life and a failure to conform to public decency. This general economy of propriety relegates feminine criticism and difference to heterogeneous excess. Thus, Proudhon's feminist can only be violently transgressive for having never gained the immunity from crime and prostitution guaranteed by the public form of privacy that is the marriage bed.

Marriage, what he calls the embryonic organ of justice, and the Femen breast are bound together by the logic of the family that Proudhon spells out. Pornocracy, with its economy of exposure and despotic rule, positions autonomous subjectivity as criminal technology of the self defined against the state logic of family life.

In its claim to individual agency, sovereign subjectivity, and the state of exemption, Femen offers a contemporary reassertion of Proudhon's pornocratic doublet wherein to say "Ukraine is not a brothel," a slogan of their antisex tourism campaign, exposes the speaker as excess, which in turn becomes the defense or tactic of revolt.[1] In a context saturated with pornocratic challenges to Proudhon's social good, even criticism of pornocracy partakes of the failures he identifies in defense of marriage. When queried, Femen always represents their tactics as transgressive women's empowerment, radicalism and revolt; this is the case in all their propaganda and media coverage. The Femen breast is asserted as "speech" and "weapon" defiantly facing the pornocrats, who would enslave women by controlling their bodies. Femen, like Proudhon, takes aim at pornocracy to denounce the abuse of women's bodies in prostitution and other crimes; and equally, neither Femen nor Proudhon can imagine a program of sex worker's rights or a politics of women's equality under the law. In other words, Femen makes no claims for social justice because they remain within the restricted economy of the pornocratic imaginary and thus can and do only publicize the private body.

Femen has also absorbed the image of the artist's sovereign exemption from the commonplace. Rather than pursue a critique of the strange elitism that binds mass media to the institutions of high culture, Femen exploits this vestige of sovereignty. As a postfeminist formation, Femen appropriates a selection of tropes from feminist art practice and especially from activist body art and its strategies of self-exposure, yet this appropriation is evidence of a loosening of normative homogeneity within the image of the equality of women.[2] Whereas bra-burning and other tactics of collective protest inscribed the image of a group or class in the national imaginary of an activism made-in-the-USA circa 1968, Femen's topless antics have only in rare cases been staged to make or materialize a collective claim. Bra-burning, for instance, can signify a protest against the authority of church or state to regulate women's health and publicness through vice or dress codes; it can be performed singly or in groups; it need not entail personal nakedness. In 1968 the Miss America Pageant was protested by a group of women who threw bras as well as other tools of the beauty standard into trash cans; this is the protest credited with stigmatizing the Women's Liberation Movement. In fact, no bras were burned there, but the assault on the overvaluation of beauty as found in the pageants, where state and nation compete, shows that the attack on the beauty standard as sign of pornocratic power was well underway. In this paradigmatic protest of a modern pornocratic tool—the Miss America pageant dates only from 1921—what is remembered is not the message but the suggestion of exposure as political tactic.

Pornocracy is perfectly suited, then, to explain, describe, and interrogate the Femen phenomenon, which constructs itself in opposition to a faded apparition, all that remains of a middle-class fantasy of women's domesticity as the site of production of masculine power and potency—what Proudhon renames the masculine "fidelity to femininity." This faded fantasy of gendered order and public peace contains a threat wherein women circulate beyond domesticity to contaminate the abstract sphere of public relations with their unstable, inconstant passions. Here the public good is exposed to contagion and the image of its own vulnerability in a queer form of sovereign detumescence. This is the vice that Proudhon names *pornocracy,* or government by harlots. To stage its singular antics, Femen requires the pornocratic phantasm with its coupling of vice to corruption of power founded in an improper mixing of public and private. This interdependence has the effect of authorizing the dichotomy of publicity versus the body qua private property as a generator of profanation or subversion.

Femen's attachment to pornocratic figures and extreme denunciations of commercial sex thus do not constitute a heterogeneity against the pornocratic logic of its targets. They do not subject their own desires for glory to self-inspection but are satisfied to project interior needs outward in a dynamic gesture that Georges Bataille defined as the very psychological structure of fascism. Closer to the violent subversion of a sado-masochistic ritual, fierce Femen nudity leaves intact the social institutions governing female beauty and women's domesticity by the very act of violating them theatrically in public. And so, the postfeminist topless protest takes its place alongside other forms of repressive desublimation that we have learned to read through the texts of Marcuse and, more recently, Slavoj Žižek.[3] It would seem we have nothing more to learn from Femen than this conventional confirmation of dialectical method.

That would be true but for two objections. The first we might call historical: the pornocracy that Femen mirrors no longer finds its anchoring point in a normative heteropatriarchal structure realized by bourgeois domesticity, for the domestic is the very thing imperiled by the new global economy. As an aspiring member of the EU,[4] the Ukraine was, by the mid-2000s, notorious as a major source of sex traffic; its political economy could therefore be viewed as actually "pornocratic" in this connection. However, by the time Femen assembled in 2006–9, NGO and government-education campaigns had made a significant impact on sex trafficking, which moved to neighboring countries rather than disappearing, while Ukrainian sex workers shifted their trade to tourism.[5] This is to say that the economy was dependent not on a clean break between public and private as alleged by Proudhon and upheld by the Femen tactic of "my body, my rules," but on an international circuit of domestic sex work for international tourists. In other words, the Femen-ist opposition to sex work and hostility toward sex workers echoes Proudhon's (post–Crimean War) family values at the very moment that sex work became a main driver of tourism. Rather than expressing a cultural heterogeneity of protest, Femen remains in-sync with pornocracy as its rebellious partner.

In this moment of crisis consciousness, Femen found a wealthy patron in Jed Sunden, an American mini-media mogul, who could provide salaries, lodging, and media access.[6] Hutsol and Svyatski became manager, creative director, and public relations team. Their bookings grew. More girl band than activist movement, Femen reached for stardom; this fact becomes the condition for the second objection to the explanation by way of repressive desublimation.

The aspiration for celebrity encodes a political and cultural stasis of postsoviet economy in the Ukraine. Their shock tactics aim only to oppose and provoke without the accompanying persuasion that the "intolerable image" is believed to awaken in the viewer and target alike.[7] Self-sovereignty in the mode of celebrity renders them surplus "pretty women" in search of a self on the model of the spectacular subjectivity of Proudhon's bourgeois wife, who is now wandering the streets of the newly rudderless pornocracy, itself the consequence of neoliberalism become "culture." On the one hand, the economy diminishes middle-class domestic spaces—both real and imaginary—while the disappearance of the domestic sphere of intimacy takes with it the gender ideals espoused by Proudhon. On the other hand, the fantasy of gender, sex, family, and sentiment formerly guaranteed by the threat of pornocratic rule does not evaporate with its material base but lingers on in symptomatic forms, adrift from its former anchor in the materiality of a classed apparition, namely home and hearth secured.

Shaming while claiming to be shameless, Femen's sovereignty is declarative; they assert their agency and desire to strike fear in the hearts of men; their political gesture is limited to the "obscene" retort intended as the foundation of another gain, spectacular or hypervisible celebrity. In seeking personal glory or celebrity, Femen abandons the class of women, along with any claim to a collective and universal freedom, opting instead for another dependency on mass media. Their imagined agency is, thus, hollowed out in the embrace of recognition by mass media, which, in turn, displaces their political intentions and substitutes for those the aims of their patrons. Can celebrity enact political agency when captured in the pornocratic entanglement of paid protest?

Exposed in this network of what Lauren Berlant calls "cynical practical realism" (48) as protest for hire, Femen appear as both inauthentic and insincere yet earnestly making a living; this form of commercial political passion is ironized by their manifesto's denunciation of sex work, a party line at odds with sex-positive feminisms across a range of political identities that seek to destigmatize sex work, to render it safe, legal, and healthy. "We demand the recognition of prostitution as sex slavery, and the immediate abolition of the sex industry."[8] Not content with naming all sex work slavery, the Femen Manifesto invokes a colonial metaphor under the heading "Requirements," where they demand the "complete extermination of prostitution as an egregious form of exploitation of women by criminalizing the clients, investors and organizers of slave trade. To recognize that sex industry is the most large-scale and long-term genocide against women." Femen announces its anti–sex work policy in imitation of what is now called the Swedish Model but against the grain of more than a century of feminist work to decriminalize sex workers. A characteristic move of a resurgent abolitionist strain in contemporary feminism, the claim that sex work is not work but a tragic destiny to which women are driven either by poverty or entrapment, invokes the autonomy of women only as an abstraction attached to bodies that must be saved. As Rosalind Petchesky puts it, "Nowhere is the paternalistic zealotry of rescue feminism more evident than in the abolitionist . . . attempt to criminalize all forms of commercial sex work. Abolitionists erase entirely any distinction between consensual and coercive sex work" (263). Sovereign autonomy over a female body that may be displayed in public toplessness but can never become a subject of work nor an agent of capital, this "ownership" of the self's body is imagined as equivalent to the liberation of chattel slaves.

Topless protest and the cult of celebrity supplement the refusal of sex tourism and trafficking while rendering voluntary sex work impossible, for the pornocratic market celebrated by the Femen-ist admits no collective or multitude. The spectacular individual is here the sadly inarticulate Inna Shevshenko, whose insufficiencies in the area of political speaking can be measured by the collapse of her discourse in the "dialogue" with a perplexed but respectful Amy Goodman and a weary Tariq Ramadan. Celebrity's ever-augmenting demand, which appears to escalate but only repeats, subjects these young women to the impossibility of alternatives. Their complicity with celebrity and sensation, matched by the media's tropism toward sextremism of any form, is the quotidian banality of a pornocratic economy, a marriage of sensation and representation that was operative even in Proudhon's time, though the art of the "sex scandal" would not flourish in print culture until the 1880's.[9]

The sovereign's obscenity knows no bounds, but what understanding might we glean from his mirror image in postfeminist performance and resistance? Departing from Proudhon's antifeminist treatise on the dangers of expanded suffrage and representative democracy when extended to women, one might remobilize "pornocracy" to describe the nexus of hypersexual publicity and wanton defiance of democratic forms enabled by the privatization of public goods today. In this light, the claims of postfeminism to sovereign choice and public exposure, as exemplified by Femen, emerge as stations in the restricted economy of commandment examined by Mbembe as an "aesthetics of vulgarity" in the postcolony, where obscenity greases the wheels of local logics and value circuits. If postfeminist antics mirror the pornocrat's obscene disavowal of collective values, this is because both insist on a species of neoliberal subjectivity achievable only through mediatic publicity misrecognized as sovereign power.

NUDITY, GOD'S SIGNATURE

"Clothed men who observe nude bodies: this scene irresistibly evokes the sadomasochistic ritual of power" (55). So Giorgio Agamben reflects as he describes a museum performance staged by Vanessa Beecroft, known for her use of naked women, sometimes models, sometimes not, positioned in impassive groups throughout the white box of a gallery space. The philosopher calls up Pasolini's trench-coated fascists in *Salò* and pictures of uniformed American soldiers jeering at naked Arab men in Abu Graib to say that contemporary sadism also stages this "image." State violence resonates through the museum or the street, wherever the vulnerability of the body is foregrounded in this way, whether in the reality of torture or the fictional reflection on it.

Agamben's essay "Nudity" (collected in the volume *Nudities*), pursues the double inscription of violation and exposure by stating, "Nudity, in our culture, is inseparable from a theological signature" (57). Approaching nudity as an aesthetic medium in Beecroft's installations by excavating the "signature" of innocence and corruption, the state of grace and the fall, he complicates the purity of nudity by proposing that it is always a doubling or divided condition in which no pure nudity exists, only relations of nudity and experiences of denudation; thus, nudity is that which appears or fails to arrive. It is never merely bare.

Agamben distinguishes the known specter of torture and violence from the gallery performance, which inverts the gaze as the "perfidious" boredom of the "youngest girls" is now aimed at the "defenseless spectators." Invoking the trope of the Last Judgment, where the resurrected face clothed angels with their naked and vulnerable new bodies, "Nudity" finds that even under conditions of late capital without believers, God's signature is legible in the staging and reception of the performance. This reversal, in which it is the clothed spectators who feel their vulnerability while the seminude, putative objects channel a gaze of judgment, calls nudity into question—not by a superior nudity or a new nudity but by the very failure of innocent nudity to appear. Positioning the nonappearance or manifest absence of nudity in the midst of all this nakedness, Agamben distances the Sadean violence that is contained within the lettered field of reference and unleashed in the contemporary context of torture. What is at stake in the choice of this simple, decathected, alienated, partial, and abstracted nudity when examples of terror come so readily to mind, when even the slinky bodies of mannequins ranged in a phalanx are enough to unsettle a viewer as entangled with suggestions of violence as his own reflections show?

Only the tension between beauty as regime of power and the experience of nakedness can break the spell cast by a tradition that retains, even in negative or inverted forms, the theological signature of nudity. This is relevant for the claims of transgression, resistance, and resignification that are cited by Femen spokeswomen as motives or explanations for their topless tactics. Were the Femens not beautiful women or, rather, were their naked bodies presented in their quotidian form rather than glorified by empowerment's claim to agency and sovereign will, their exposure might "defuse the theological apparatus" by which they profit. The paradox of Femen's nudity is to retain, while seeming to upend or reject, the very apparatus of pornocratic corruption that their slogans decry. The framing of the Femen body by professional photographers and documentarians, with carefully painted breasts and salon-dyed hair garlanded with flowers, itself attests to the refusal to embrace nudity as "a simple, inapparent human body." Not the body in common, not every woman's body, but the spectacular body unwilling to relinquish the mystifications of beauty, which permits the circulation of value and power in our inherited pornocracy, this glorious body repeats and reproduces the apparatus of an antifeminist pornocratic regime.

BETWEEN THE FINGERPRINT AND THE MASK

Yet Femen is also the mixed product of opportunism, cynicism, and rebellion in the street that eludes the analysis in "Nudity," with its focus on the archeology of the theological thread and very mannered examples of pornography. The cold gaze of the mannequins in Beecroft's performance is choreographed and performed on command. The agency of Femen protesters is less uniformly distributed; their stars and leaders seek out a sovereign subjectivity enacted in and produced by the state of exemption they hope to gain. They "speak" for all women. Their anger is ferocious; they practice fierce expressions, writhing, screaming, and other manifestations of fury to be performed on cue. They still believe, as the mannequins do not. The nudity is not the whole point.

Alternately donning a mask of theatrical rage or the beauty queen's frozen smile, the Femen-ist aims to provoke a spectacle of police violence, or at least containment. Though staged for the camera, these scenes are nonetheless difficult to watch as impossibly thin, half-naked young women are dragged off camera by uniformed guards, while their torsos and faces are ground into sidewalks by the combined force of their own unstoppable flailing and institutional authority. As seemingly indestructible as a Sadean heroine, the Femen-ist actively seeks to create images of this kind and trains to kick, bite, scream, and squirm to prevent being peacefully escorted off the stage of protest, thus guaranteeing a theatrical image of physical conflict with the law. Rehearsing the role of woman's fury, the Femen-ist cultivates the discipline of a particular affective and discursive apparatus, as detailed in the 2014 documentary *I Am Femen* and in multiple testimonials and journalist accounts. A militant cult of the personality, Femen announces its demand for agency and sovereign power in direct terms. "I'm proud of the fact that today naked women are not just posing on the cover of *Playboy*, but can be at an action, angry, and can irritate people" (cited in Cochran).

Performed for the camera, the Femen persona is embedded in the living matter of the mask and its identity that Agamben argues is constitutive for contemporary subjectivity under biometric power. In a speculative genealogy of this alienation, he references the etymology of "persona" and returns to Roman practices as anchor for his discussion of affective alienation in identity. Offering an allegory patched together out of histories of science and dramatic arts, he quotes the slave become freedman and philosopher Epictetus to address the weakening dialectic of mask and persona in the contemporary moment. As moderns, we are all actors, Agamben says in "Identity without a Person" (also in *Nudities*), but "the actor (like the sage, who takes the actor as a paradigm) must not identify completely with his part, thus confusing himself with his stage persona: 'The time is coming,' Epictetus admonishes, 'when actors will believe that their masks and costumes reflect their very selves'" (47). By these lights, Femen appears to mistake the mask of public nudity for the person, herself, but why is this?

"Persona," we learn, means "mask," and refers to the habit of identifying or recognizing someone through the elaboration of family lineage, household, and citizen status. A Roman was a persona by birth, social role, and identity. Personality was conferred by this situation of social recognition. Thus a slave had neither standing nor familial reputation, no ancestry, no mask, and no name that would confer a "persona" with juridical capacity. These deficits made the slave illegible as personage, while the slave's freedom, once acquired, could not erase the absence of lineage. Failure to possess a mask meant one never acceded to the "political dignity of the free man" endowed with persona. One could be a person only by dint of the recognition accorded one's ancestors and one's name; thus, the mask was a possession that could be handed down yet never acquired.

From this model of social recognition, Agamben moves to the player of roles, the actor, whose task is to inhabit fully an assigned persona, which is neither chosen nor uniquely fitting. Again, the mask is not won but conferred through a social recognition that precedes the one who dons it. In this allegorical staging of a not-yet fully alienated being, the person balanced his use of the mask by deciding when to wear and when to refuse it. Such self-knowledge allowed for ethical self-regulation of social and personal demands. The allegory of the mask and the persona establishes a sediment of reference and experience that exerts a phantasmatic pull on our present-day claims of identity, autonomy, and personal sovereignty, which we see activated as claiming actuality, if not as actuality itself, in the pronouncements of Femen. The ethical balance of mask and actor collapses under pressure of the alienation of mass media and its mass culture. This collapse conditions subjectivity both before the camera seizes the image and after media has appropriated one's representation.

The anti-representational character of technology prompts Agamben to ask what relation we can have with identities regulated by and through technological means, and at the extreme end of this development, with the biometric details of contemporary identity. Agamben, following Benjamin, is concerned with alienation produced by a kind of reproduction that undermines the relation of representation between actor and mask, identity and persona. Technologies of identity circulate reproductions of identity in the traces of bodily presence (biometrics) that exponentially distance the person from the effects of identity. This gap or erasure of contact expands possibilities for appropriation, inversion, and reversals without also conserving the potential for creative misuse, reuse, or resistance; this is to say that, against the grain of a commonplace that holds aesthetic reappropriation and resistance are the sovereign right and power of the arts, biometric identity dissolves the possibility of creative resistance or of repurposing our image. This further alienation of representation, alive in the retinal scan but nascent in the finger print, contains within it the evacuation of the person and leaves only identities circulating without reference. Before we dismiss this view as lapsing from a poststructuralist attachment to the infinite possibility of reappropriation or the inescapable division of every sense, the insight that something is sundered between the person and the mask by the technologies of recognition deserves further consideration in the context of nudity's recent deployments. And let us not forget the slave, never recognized for the adroit manipulation of a mask and thus not accorded the value of persona.[10]

Describing the origins of Bertillonage and fingerprinting, Agamben notes that these technological representations of the human trace were introduced to identify criminal recidivism in a world where recognition had become impossible. "Human beings removed the mask that for centuries had been the basis of their recognizability in order to consign their identity to something that belongs to them in an intimate and exclusive way but with which they can in no way identify" (50).

Technologies invented to track the recidivist in the metropole, where scale prevented regulation through recognition, these early forms of biometrics predate photography (which secures a likeness to be circulated impersonally), and were, in a sense, more personal than the image because they required the intimate presence of the person. For instance, Bertillonage involved extensive measurement of the skull and body, mapping identity well beyond hair, complexion, and eye color, to produce a description easily distributed even among the public. Fingerprinting, in particular, was conceived as a way to record identities of the colonized, who all look alike to colonial administrators, and prostitutes, who must be identified in ways that eliminate the dependence on intimate recognition. Thus, the production and circulation of forensic description, fingerprints, and finally, mug shots, owe as much to the desire to preserve distance and distinction between police and deviant profile as they do to a drive to contain and label. The imprint of the person was gathered to secure the long-distance circulation of the identity; this arrangement of social relations and representation culminates for Agamben in a loss akin to the fall from grace that is the origin for him of the nakedness of the world and that still bears the legible trace of its theological signature. The distance between identity or identification and recognition is itself secured and policed by the intercession of technologies that measure and record the trace of the other. The identity card does not recognize us, foreign or native, performance artist or prostitute; it gathers the traces of the body as registered by machine perception to produce "something with which I have absolutely nothing to do, something with which and by which I cannot in any way identify myself or take distance from: naked life, a purely biological datum" (50). No longer the eyewitness but the retinal scan, no longer the touch of the other but the photo recognition of the fingerprint. This is the mediation of identity that causes Agamben to register a gap rather than a tightening of the networks of connection; the intensification of the body as point of interpenetration of power's knowledge, to paraphrase Foucault, leads not to more or greater possibilities for subjectivation but to an implacable distance between the effects of the body in its identification and the fading purchase of the person on his own bodily traces and identity.

Agamben writes, "As part of the unstoppable drifting of political power toward governmentality—in which a liberal paradigm curiously converges with a statist paradigm—Western democracies are preparing to establish an archive containing the DNA of every citizen, as much to ensure security and repression of crime as to manage public health" (51). This gap between, on the one hand, forensic identification of and with the body and, on the other, the progressive disappearance of the person, troubles any flat insistence that the body speaks above and beyond its capture in identity. Claims to "my body" are caught in this very gap and are not relieved of this burden of history by declarations of sovereign autonomy. Situating the contemporary moment in this historical genealogy, a mere thumbnail sketch, Agamben concludes, "If, in the final analysis, my identity is now determined by biological facts—that in no way depend on my will, and over which I have no control—then the construction of something like a personal ethics becomes problematic. What relationship can I establish with my fingerprints or with my genetic code?" (52). By his own account, identity-without-the-person befell women, the poor, criminals, the colonized, foreigners, and Jews well before its universalization as the condition of all identity, thus well before it affected the unaffectable.[11] Agamben's analysis of identity without the person, while seemingly an example of universalism in crisis, of what we might call a white identity politics feeling its limits, affirms the affinities between governmentality in its various forms and statist or totalitarian rule. This encroaching sameness operates according to differing local logics and rationalizations while reaching the same conclusions globally in contemporary biometrics.

> Like every apparatus, biometric identification captures a more or less unconfessed desire for happiness. . . . To this one can add the fleeting and almost insolent pleasure of being recognized by a machine, without the burden of the emotional implications that are inseparable from recognition by another human being. The more they have lost all identity and all real belonging, the more gratifying it has become for them to be recognized by the Great Machine in its infinite and minute variants: from the turnstile of a subway entrance to an ATM machine. . . . I am here if the Machine recognizes me or, at least, sees me. . . . I am not forgotten if the Great Memory has recorded my numerical or digital data. (52–53)

Does this not hold for the celebrity-seeking Femen-ists who say explicitly that they do not exist without media coverage, who are dependent on mediatized spectacle, paid performance, and private donation, who cannot embody the fiction of an autonomous speaking body that their slogans promise?

More to the point, Agamben identifies an affective escape into technological identity where machine recognition recuperates the person but with a difference. "Virtual" recognition not only compensates the loss; even better, the hollowed-out form of exposure improves on the original by replicating "me" and my opportunities for gratification. "I" become spectacularly available to myself in the impression of a world that registers, reports, records, and is ever alert to my movements through space.

How, then, might the inheritors of pornocracy establish a personal ethics from this identity without the person, when all are reduced to the biological datum that must be thought with the naked body, whether vulnerable and open or militantly exposed, rather than against it? For the Femen-ists, this question misses the mark entirely. The naked body will unmask those who deceive; these are "political breasts": "This nudity is a different nudity!" says Shevshenko.

THE LAST FEMEN

Femen channel a modernist image of the artist's autonomous subjectivity even as little of their language, gestures, images, pranks, and protests resembles a recognizable feminism. Anna Hutol denounces as elitist the learned feminism of social justice movements and university scholars while saying that Femen is a feminism for all women *(I Am Femen).* This repudiation of feminist knowledge mirrors the loss of ethical reflection in the "identity without the person" sketched by Agamben, for whom election of the mask, like its refusal, was a moral choice and an ethical exercise recognized by the social group. Before the biometric dispensation, the person was not only the criminal, the colonized, or the prostitute; before identity, there was the person. While Femen advances the most archaic "weapons"—bare breasts—to signify "liberty," their signature gesture may in fact be the counterpart to governmentality's biometrics. Like the forensic trace, this gesture is equally able to forgo the past, the accumulation of text and history, the archive of prior resistances and ways out that never stuck. Is this not a Femen-ism analogous to the identity without the person, a featureless mask of bodily signs? And within this new economy of the oldest profession is there not a lesson to be gleaned from the philosopher? To paraphrase Agamben, what relation can I have with these images of my breasts, which are claimed to speak for me and in my stead?

Their iconography took off in 2016, perhaps as a result of their popularity after relocating to France. At their online store you can browse "apparel and accessories" with maladroit English slogans such as "We all different but the same," "My body my rules," or "Every woman is a riot." A new item in Femen swag, the "Boobsprint," comes in the original yellow and blue of the Ukrainian flag adapted to the Femen logo, as well as the republican tricolor for "type France." You can have yours signed by one of the four Femen superstars: Inna Shevchenko, Iana Zhdanova, Sasha Shevchencko, and Oksana Shachko.

Other slogans signal the twin features of Femen's claiming of sovereignty through an aesthetico-nationalist positioning. "My body is my manifesto" keys the aesthetic slant of their brand while the i-Phone cover signals the national symbolic with its tricolor brandishing "Nudité Lutte Liberté," also available on a coffee mug. The body as manifesto is supplemented by a lengthy text rich in clichés. Solanas, Césaire, Breton, and Marinetti as garbled by an online translation site: difficult to call this practice citational, it carries the history of revolutionary resistance like so many indistinct smears on a new sneaker, impossible to efface yet equally impossible to embrace as inheritance. Faint trace as tactic is the market feint of appropriation in and through which a history of struggle becomes a stylization of "choice."

Feminist psychoanalysis, one of the variants of disdained learning that postfeminism leaves behind, tells us that the body is more than a vehicle of speech, essential though it is for the performance of speech acts. From the feminist archive we hear the echoes of a meditation on our entanglement in and with the body, where the body is "sexuality, understood not as 'intentional' disposition, but as unconscious fantasy structuring bodily desire" (Butler, 117). The psychoanalytic understanding of the body poses certain problems for the Femen-ist if the body is asserted as the intentional body or the intended use of the body—"My body, my rules"—without remainder (shame, desire, fantasy); if the body is reduced to utterance, to a juridical notion of protected speech, or to a weapon, then what kind of body is this? It is a metaphysical body without an unconscious, not a body at all, but a substrate for ideological and biometric inscription. The peculiar denial of eros in the body that is made to speak here is an index of a more general solipsism and denial of others. And the message is so uniformly directed to a male patriarchal figure that this comes to mean that the ideal audience for a Femen protest is the pornocratic authority, the unredeemable sovereign of sovereigns, for which the Pope and Putin are mere stand-ins or interchangeable mannequins. Matching image for image, the Femen-ist positions women only as fans of the spectacular sovereignty of Inna et. al. Inc.

Dina Al-Kassim is a critical theorist who works on political subjectivation, sexuality, and aesthetics in transnational modernist and contemporary literature, arts and cultures, including the Middle East and South Africa. She is the author of *On Pain of Speech: Fantasies of the First Order and the Literary Rant* (2010), which examines *parrhesia*, subjectivity, and the politics of address in the practice of literary ranting.

Notes

1. *Ukraine is not a Brothel* debuted at the 70th Venice International Film Festival in 2013, where Femen members appeared on the red carpet topless and wearing slogans "I am free," "Naked war," and the truly mind-bending "Women are still here." Nominated in six categories at the AACTA, the film won for Best Feature Length Documentary and Best Direction in a Documentary in 2014.

2. Self-exposure and performance as feminist resistance are detailed by Amelia Jones (1998).

3. For Žižek, "repressive desublimation" crystallizes the Frankfurt School uptake of psychoanalysis. Arguing that for Adorno and others, postliberal societies are characterized by a form of social repression that works through license rather than prohibition, Žižek's gloss presents us with a power that commands us to "Enjoy yourself!" Thus base or "archaic urges" coexist with social domination (16).

4. The Ukraine-EU Association Agreement, signed in 2014, points the way forward with Ukrainian political leaders predicting EU status; as recently as July 2017, Vice Prime Minister Ivanna Klympush-Tsintsadze said that EU membership "will become a truth."

5. The 2012 *UN Global Report on Trafficking in Persons* estimates that sex trafficking reaps €2.5–3 billion annually and involves roughly 140,000 victims in Europe

alone. This estimate is based on a rate of €50/client and a "perhaps 50 million sexual services annually," though the numbers are speculative due to the difficulty of detection and the fact that many figures are based on self-reporting by clients. "The trafficking originating from the Russian Federation and Ukraine, although still prominent, appears to have decreased in the last ten years in all West and Central European countries. This decline coincided with an increase in detected victims from the Balkans, particularly Romania and Bulgaria, but this trafficking flow also appears to have decreased after 2005" (50). The report is silent on the question of whether this decrease correlates with an increase in sex tourism to Ukraine, as claimed by Femen.

6. The story of Sunden's financial backing for Femen, reported in several news outlets, was picked up by a number of right-wing Christian websites as well as by *Pravda*'s English site; many of these sites refer to *Il Foglio*'s report of March 15, 2013, which explained that Femen members received monthly salaries of €1000 while the leader, Inna Shevchenko, drew €2500, in contrast with the then-average Ukrainian monthly income of €500. In December 2011, when Sunden stopped funding them, *Il Foglio* removed the original report and replaced it with a letter explaining that Sunden, whose impetus to finance the group came from his interest in promoting their antisex tourism campaign, had a change of heart when Femen lost sight of their specific original target and "expanded" to general criticisms of religion, the 2012 EU Football Championship, and politics.

7. For Jacques Rancière, the "intolerable image" refers to a shock effect meant to awaken sensibility and unmask sovereign power (83).

8. From the June 5 Femen statement of their protest at the Montreal 2015 Grand Prix of Canada.

9. The mobilization of the sex scandal to sell newspapers is a technique of an older mediatic form retained in the arsenal of new media. For a concise account of the rise of the sex scandal as popular entertainment in the British penny press, see Michael Foldy. For comprehensive coverage of sex work and the vagaries of abolitionism historically, see Magaly Rodriguez Garcia. The pin-up girl selling Coke or boosting military morale looms large as a grandmotherly antecedent for Femen, though the group's own portfolio repetitively cites from a nationalist arsenal of Marianne and pornocratic patriots. For a history of the pin-up as patriot and the commodification of the bare breast, see Joanne Meyerowitz.

10. That is, not accorded the resources of nonrecognition and the assertion of a "new humanity" that is not dependent on the human figure as developed by Agamben.

11. "Affectability" is a term given new currency by Silva's analytic of race.

Works Cited

Agamben. Giorgio. 2011. *Nudities*. Trans. David Kishik and Stefan Pedatella. Stanford: Stanford University Press.

Bataille, Georges. 1985. *Visions of Excess*. Trans. Allan Stoekl. Minneapolis: University of Minnesota Press.

Benjamin, Walter. 2010. "The Work of Art in the Age of Its Technological Reproducibility" [First Version]. *Grey Room* 39 (Spring): 11–37. (Orig. pub. 1936.)

Berg, Maxine, and Elizabeth Eger Basingstoke. 2002. *Luxury in the Eighteenth Century: Debates, Desires and Delectable Goods*. London: Palgrave.

Berlant, Lauren. 1997. *Queen of America Goes to Washington City*. Durham: Duke University Press.

Butler, Judith. 2003. Afterword to Shoshana Felman's *The Scandal of the Speaking Body: Don Juan with J. L. Austin, or Seduction*. Stanford: Stanford University Press.

Cochran, Kira. 2013. "Rise of the Naked Female Warriors." *Guardian*, March 20. http://www.theguardian.com/world/2013/mar/20/naked-female-warrior-femen-topless-protesters.

Connolly, Kate. 2013. "Femen Activist Tells How Protest against Putin and Merkel Was Planned." *Guardian*, April 12. https://www.theguardian.com/world/2013/apr/12/femen-activist-protest-putin-merkel.

"Femen BoobsPrints." N.d. https://www.pinterest.com/femen0126/femen-boobsprints/.

Foldy, Michael S. 1997. *The Trials of Oscar Wilde: Deviance, Morality and Late Victorian Society*. New Haven: Yale University Press.

Garcia, Magaly Rodriguez. 2016. "Ideas and Practices of Prostitution around the World." In *The Oxford Handbook of the History of Crime and Criminal Justice*. Ed. Paul Kneppner and Anja Johansen, 132–54. Oxford: Oxford University Press.

Hardy, Alain, dir. 2014. *I Am Femen*. Caravel Production.

Hutsol, Anna, and Victor Svyatski. 2015. "We Have Authority." Pineapples and Caviar, November. https://pineapplesandcaviar.wordpress.com/2011/08/15/anna-hutsol-and-vitaly-svyatsky-femen-kiev/.

Jones, Amelia. 1998. *Body Art: Performing the Subject*. Minneapolis: University of Minnesota Press.

Mbembe, Achille. 2001. *On the Postcolony*. Berkeley: University of California Press.

McRobbie, Angela. 2007. "Top Girls? Young Women and the Post-feminist Sexual Contract." *Cultural Studies* 21, nos. 4–5 (July/September): 718–37.

Meyerowitz, Joanne. 1996. "Woman, Cheesecake, and Borderline Material: Responses to Girlie Pictures in the Mid-Twentieth-Century." *Journal of Women's History* 8, no. 3 (Fall): 9–35.

Petchesky, Rosalind. 2015. "Owning and Disowning the Body." *The Oxford Handbook of Transnational Feminist Movements*. Ed. Rawwida Baksh and Wendy Harcourt, 252–70. Oxford: Oxford University Press.

Rancière, Jacques. 2009. *The Emancipated Spectator*. Trans. Gregory Elliott. London: Verso.

Silva, Denise Ferreira da. 2007. *Toward a Global Idea of Race*. Minneapolis: University of Minnesota Press.

"Ukraine EU Membership 'Will Become a Truth.'" 2017. *BBC*. http://www.bbc.com/news/av/world-europe-40522646/ukraine-eu-membership-will-become-a-truth.

United Nations Office on Drugs and Crime. 2012. *UN Global Report on Trafficking in Persons*. https://www.unodc.org/documents/data-and-analysis/glotip/Trafficking_in_Persons_2012_web.pdf.

Žižek, Slavoj. 1994. *Metastases of Enjoyment: On Women and Causality*. London: Verso.

THE PORNOCRATIC BODY IN THE AGE OF NETWORKED PARANOIA

Eyal Amiran

And I don't need to see any more
To know that I can read your mind

—Alan Parsons Project, "Eye in the Sky" (1982)

My subject is the relation between the pornocratic body and the scopic regime produced by the networked age. Pornocracy, to borrow from Pierre-Joseph Proudhon's *Pornocracy, or Women in Modern Times,* here designates the way the sexual exhibition of the body is understood to secure political power. In the networked age, the totality of visibility promised by a new scopic regime, together with the shift in digital media from representation to projection, makes the public body, and with it pornocracy, subject to a new imaginary. Under the networked regime, a global imaginary threatens to make any body, including the pornocrat's, as irrelevant as it is visible.[1] Contemporary pornocrats counter this trend, which diminishes the power of pornocracy, leading them, or the governing apparatus, to extreme forms of self-revelation. While the Marquis de Sade gets credit for imagining total enlightenment, or full frontal visibility (Judovitz, 171–98), the new regime ushered in by global surveillance exchanges his rational positivism for big-data mining, for an archive of objects that then serve as parts in a psychological machine. Neither this age nor Sade's has quite managed to treat bodies as interchangeable things, as Sade's philosophy recommends, but now the universal perspective produced by spectacle comes closer to making the exhibition of the body, and with it the securing of pornocratic power, irrelevant.

The idea of a total scopic regime, a world in which nothing is hidden, has been heralded by aerial photography, x-rays, night vision, and other technologies that flatten out the distinctions between inside and out, day and night, public and private. In *War and Cinema,* Paul Virilio argues that visualization in general has evolved along with military technologies. "Just as weapons and armour developed in unison . . . so visibility and invisibility now began to evolve together," producing radar, sonar, and spy satellites (72). These technologies are not so much about the image as they are about perception and perceivability, detection, and exposure. The imagined teleology of intelligibility is the capacity of the apparatus to spy anything everywhere. In what is now a familiar formulation, a technical sergeant describes the global reach and effect of the military's Distributed Global System:

> It spans the globe and it eats data, and it eats lots and lots and lots of data. This is global. This is getting information anywhere at any time, shooting people from anywhere, at any time. . . . It's like borders don't matter anymore. And there's a huge system that spans the globe that can just suck up endless amounts of your life, your personal data. . . . And we're not the only ones that have this—this is going to become commonplace, if it's not already. ("National Bird" 11:50–13:06)

Akira Lippit writes that the shifting of perspective from locality to systemic vision becomes universal with the advent of the atom bomb, an x-ray that penetrates the body and makes divisions of here and there, inside and outside irrelevant (81–91).[2] These precursor technologies produce global visualization and lead to what Rey Chow calls, after Heidegger, "The age of the world target." In the networked age, they become an imaginary government over and in relation to the world.

Several of these themes can be found, by way of introduction, in "The Magic Bush," a 2014 *South Park* TV episode about the ambiguous power of exhibition under the networked scopic regime. In this episode, Eric Cartman learns that Butters's father has a new drone. The drone is said to be the father's ("Your dad has a fucking drone?!")—and its object, as we soon learn, is the mother. "We can spy on everyone!" says Cartman. As Cartman explains later, we live in a world where privacy no longer exists. "We can see that girl from *Hunger Games*' butthole," he explains (11:30). The drone makes visible even those places where the sun don't shine: it's not about the pornographic gaze so much as about total visibility, which the pornographic image exemplifies. To dramatize this point, just when Butters shows Cartman the drone, Butters's father returns home; Cartman picks up the drone and leaves, pulling the garage door down behind him, while Butters and the viewers remain inside in the dark, visibility having disappeared with the drone.

Flying the drone, the children record Craig's mom Laura Tucker as she disrobes, and Craig's dad sees the drone and comes to Butters's home to complain. But the drone has been returned to its place in the garage, and Butters's dad is none the wiser. "These things don't fly themselves!" says Craig's dad, raising the question of the agency of the drone (later Butters's dad wants to return it to the store, saying "it flies by itself"). It was, we know, flown by the children, but it represents a larger power: Cartman finds he must post the video of Craig's mom on the internet so the children can explain how they came to have it. Likewise, while none of the adults would confess to seeing this video, it's a joke that everyone already has (the video has had over 300 million views). Everyone is fascinated that Laura's pubic hair is untrimmed—natural, as she explains, and nothing to be ashamed of. "What happened to Laura could happen to anyone," says Randy Marsh at a town meeting. The town sets up neighborhood-watch drones to watch for rogue drones. Randy's neighborhood-watch drone spies on the sexual lives of the residents—depicted as a video in the controller display (12:25)—and gets shot down by a police drone. The residents blame the drones for having "minds of their own" (14:55), which makes them "more than spooky." Cartman has a solution: "If there's one thing we've learned, it's that drones can't resist Craig's mom" (19:14). The children dangle a sex doll of a woman from Butters's father's drone, and all the drones—police and civilian—follow it out of town. In celebration, South Park salutes Laura for having done "something miraculous" to overcome her exposure (20:30): future generations, according to a minstrel at the event, will tell "how Craig's mom flew through the town and led all the drones away."

In this episode's reading of the new scopic regime introduced by drones, the exhibition of the body, the subject of surveillance, has political consequences. Networked aerial surveillance produces a spectacle of the body and induces a paranoid state in South Park. This paranoia leads people to think both that they are always exposed and that the machine has a mind of its own. They project their motives on the machine and in turn become governed by their consensual hallucination, their new imaginary. The episode acknowledges the degree to which the image of the body puts the (unremarkable) actual body on the defensive. It is not Laura who becomes the leader, but a doll that represents her (leading the drones out of town), and she has to disavow the embarrassment her exposure is assumed to have brought her. The body is not pornographic; rather, it is made so by those who watch it online. In pornocracy, the body exists as spectacle, and the specular machine does not find a particular body irresistible so much as interchangeable and, as the doll in the episode hints, inanimate. This notion is invoked by the magical, mythical, and pseudo-religious future life imagined for Laura's body in the episode.

To occupy the place of power and to guarantee political power, the spectacular body faces contradictory requirements. It must be revealed or unveiled, made spectacle, made an object, in order to be special. Walter Benjamin argues in "The Work of Art" that when media technology brings the politician's body into personal relation with the voting public, it empties that relation of personality (128 n.23).[3] Laura's supposed sexual abjection is required for the body to have pornocratic power, political power obtained by the body's sexual exhibition. (A picture of Laura in her usual public capacity would not have that effect.) As Karl Marx says in the *Brumaire*, executive power "finds its strength in its very weakness and its respectability in the contempt that it calls forth" (43). The scopic regime governed by satellite imagery, drone technology, and networked surveillance, under which in principle (if not quite in fact) everything can be seen at any time, exposes the body but also denies it importance, substituting for it the paranoid apparatus.

To return from South Park back, as it were, to the real war (but of course *South Park* is a shot in that war), the image produced by surveillance technologies sees what cannot be normally seen, leaving nothing unnoticed or unnoticeable. A recent instance is sexual surveillance shot with the aid of military technologies like drones and infrared photography. The sexual focus underscores their ability to see what is hidden—images of sexual bodies being, as in the *South Park* episode, the paradigmatic example. Joining the omniscient perspective that sees the world from above, this vision seems to complete the cinematic projection of Jean-Louis Baudry's apparatus theory.[4] In one widely circulated infrared video, a night scene is alleged to show a sex act between a man and a donkey in a rural setting. Several video-sharing sites introduce this clip as a drone video of an ISIS fighter.[5] The somewhat obscure data displayed on the image, however, shows that it was shot in the Kabul time zone in 2011; as a stationary image it comes not from a drone but probably from JLENS, a "dirigible device tethered to the ground and constantly searching for threats to coalition forces, especially at night" ("Drone Video"). The footage is grainy, grey on grey ("grey on grey . . . as shadows that have lost their bodies," Marx says in the *Brumaire* [44])—a fog, more fantasy or projection than reproduction.[6] Because these technologies expose private space as part of the surveillance imaginary, they encourage us to read images such as this one as exposure, even when, as here, the image is nearly opaque.

Another exemplary object is "Drone Boning" by Ghost+Cow Films, a sweeping landscape video shot from a drone that just happens to pass over couples having sex. These couples would not be seen from ground level—they are on rooftops or on hillsides away from other vantage points.[7] The drone's POV, in contrast, knows and shows all, so it's no coincidence that it passes over these scenes without modulating its speed or focus, any more than that the sexual body is the object of its indifferent panopticism. Likewise my argument does not hinge on literal visibility, but concerns the imaginary of perception. So other recent ideas of space penetrated by modern technologies also help construct or reconstruct the imaginary of the emergent scopic regime: the phone-activated sonar Batman uses to map interior space in *The Dark Knight,* for example, the sound maps of cities posted online,[8] and the sand submarine in Thomas Pynchon's *Against the Day,* which visualizes underground worlds.

A second feature of the scopic regime of digital surveillance that makes it a potent imaginary is the reversal in the nature of photography (or representation more broadly) that the digital medium entails. Since the demise of analog and the arrival of Photoshop, Auto-Tune, and digital object manipulation software, photography and other traditionally representational technologies can no longer be counted on to witness a reality they document. That idea, always (contra Sontag) suspect in photography, no longer defines the imaginary of the medium. Instead, photography, like digital audio recording, reproduces the domination of the apparatus over its world. I'm not interested in revisiting debates about simulation; instead I am pointing out that in the digital age, at least in principle, the world of objects to be photographed or recorded is granted us by the machine. We do not witness the object; we witness our ability to imagine it. A program called Optic Nerve has collected images from 1.8 million Yahoo UK users every time they turned on their web cams (Ackerman and Ball).[9] Hence web-based data visualization and analysis software like Voyant Tools become components of photography. The networked apparatus does not "see" or "hear" anything, any more than cell towers listen to phone conversations, but it is imagined to do so. It is an ideal machine, inspiring or reproducing a projection of the world. Networked media has a particular quality of paranoid world-making. In surveillance video and photography, public culture, as exemplified by the work examined here, sees the threat of an imaginary apparatus that appears to manipulate people from a distance. The influencing machine as a psychological concept dates at least to the eighteenth century, and was identified by Victor Tausk in 1919 (Armstrong, 101–5; see also Tanner). It is not only CCTV and satellite mapping and government spying and data mining and email surveillance that activate this scopic construction in the new media age, but the paranoid logic that this apparatus produces.

This is not the place to argue for the importance of paranoia in political culture, but a paranoid imaginary is required for pornocracy. In paranoia, the world or the object of thought, like the influencing machine itself, is a projection of one's own needs or qualities, themselves always already social, and is understood to be about the fantasist. It repeats us, even when it is against us (see Figure 1). The pornocratic body is not natural but magical; it appears powerful because it personifies public attention, which then recognizes itself in that body. As Marx says about Napoleon, the body appears ready to enforce the popular will, but instead is identified with that power: rather than identifying himself with order, Bonaparte "identifies the cause of order with his person" (57).[10] The influencing machine has been important to discussions of paranoid schizophrenia, important also to readings of many so-called outsider figures like Daniel Paul Schreber, Francis E. Dec, and Yayoi Kusama, who conceptualize a world against but also as analog to the narcissistic body. Like the pornocratic

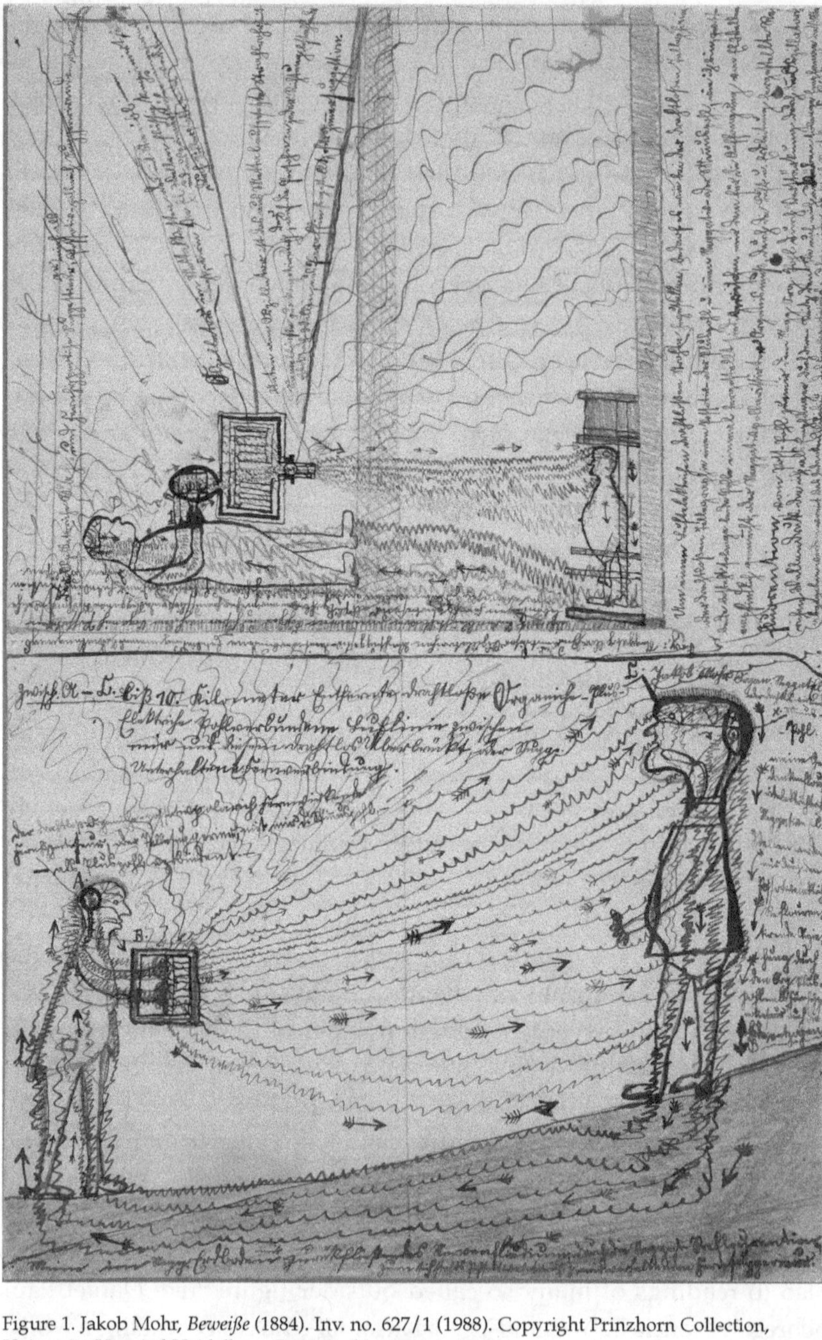

Figure 1. Jakob Mohr, *Beweiße* (1884). Inv. no. 627/1 (1988). Copyright Prinzhorn Collection, University Hospital Heidelberg. Reprinted by permission.

body whose expression of political structure appears to be personal, they are structured by a paranoid cultural logic and testify to its power over popular imaginaries. This paranoid construction is useful for analysis of public politics, for example as discussed by Richard Hofstadter in "The Paranoid Style in American Politics" (1963), a survey of conspiracy theories in the United States from those of the Illuminati to the Cold War's Red Scare. These theories do not posit a machine per se, substituting for it a conspiratorial apparatus that controls public space from afar. For Hofstadter, paranoia is the general condition of American society, so despite his liberal perspective (Sedgwick, 142–43), he is in line with such arguments as Victor Burgin's in *In/Different Spaces* (a reading of racialized national space as paranoid [129]), and Robert Meister's in *After Evil* (an analysis of psychological models of cultural reparation), that see paranoia as a state of identification common to any political endeavor.[11]

The pornocratic body seems to stand, like the figures and personified organizations in my examples, outside the machine that produces it and which it helps to project.[12] Narcissistic political figures like the stage-grabbing Donald Trump, whose wife has so often been put on display, and Vladimir Putin (KGB agent and star of a call-in TV show who is often photographed bare-chested), rely on the infantile and paranoid logic of the pornocrat, which puts their bodies at the center of the scopic regime.

Like any paranoid logic, however, the position pornocrats occupy is threatened by the indifference of the world and needs constant maintenance. Control of the scopic regime has been dealt a blow, for example, by the disappearance in March 2014 of Malaysia Airlines flight 370. How could it be, people immediately asked, that governments can't find an airplane? The plane's ability to elude visibility occasioned competing conspiracy theories. "Could missing MH370 have stalked SIA flight to the north? Possible, say netizens," writes the *Malaysian Insider*.[13] Maybe the plane was hijacked by terrorists, and the government is plotting to conceal it, said relatives. The FBI and Interpol are looking for it ("French"). Years later, the news covers airplane bits and pieces that continue to be found in the Pacific ("MH370 Search: Two More Pieces") (see Figure 2). The object cannot be allowed to be lost, though eventually the search must be officially called off.[14]

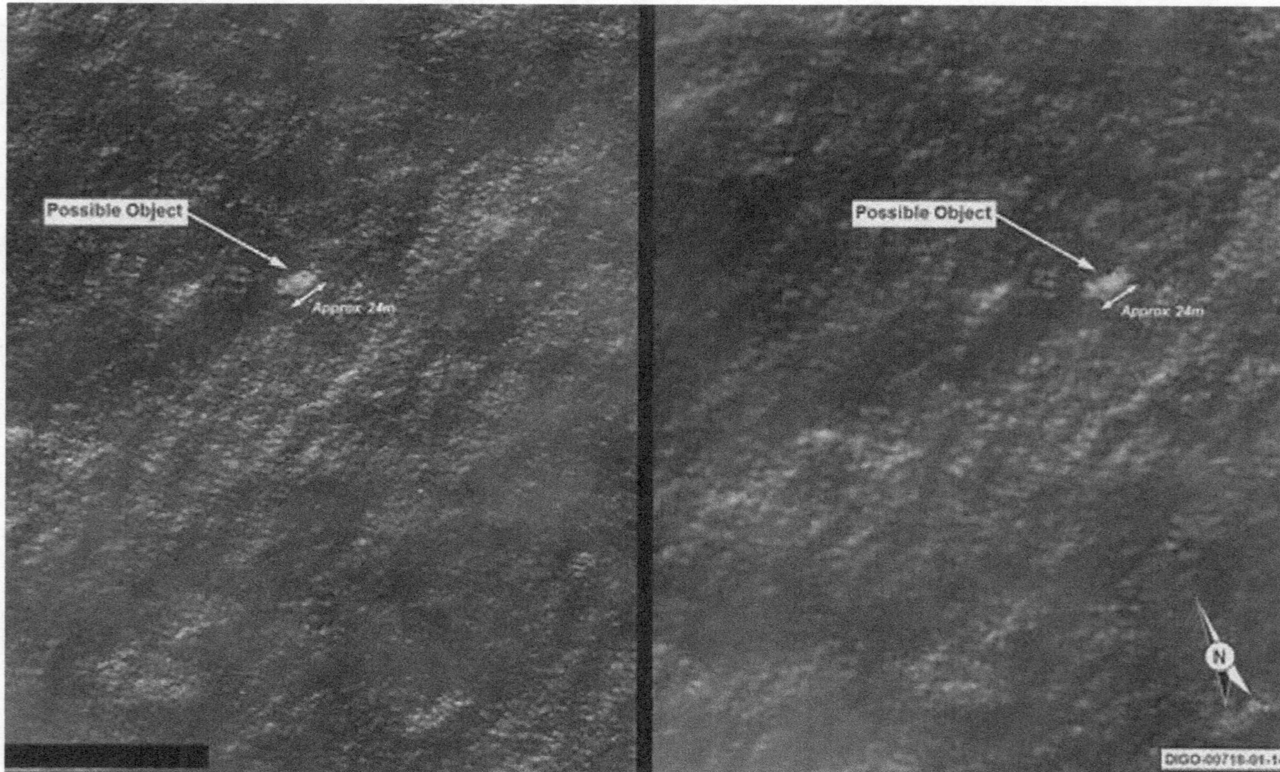

Figure 2. "Malaysia Airlines flight MH370: Satellite Images Show Possible Debris." *The Guardian,* March 5, 2014.

The correlative threat is that the exceptional (or out-standing) pornocratic figure would be ignored by the world to which it posits an outside. The spectacle that makes the body visible deprives it of presence, making its special status as body ambiguous or, as Marx says, grey. The body can echo the system that produced it, but only inside the system. To see this threat I turn to "Collateral Murder," the classified military video Wikileaks made public in 2007. This video, which shows an attack by U.S. troops in Baghdad, exposes the ambiguous place of the body in the paranoid machine's field of vision. In the footage I read here, suspected enemy fighters, including two men later found to be journalists whose cameras are identified as weapons, are killed by soldiers in an Apache helicopter. The helicopter's gun camera takes the video. (The "murder" in the title refers to the killing of an unarmed man shown later in the video.) The audio records the conversation between a commander, who views the images sent by the helicopter to headquarters in the United States and authorizes each strike, and soldiers in the helicopter. This apparatus projects its own world, seeing the opposition in its own terms. Its object, which it is the function of the camera to make visible, is understood as a dialectical element in a system that constitutes both Apache and Iraqi, gun camera and the camera identified as a gun.[15] The people we see in the video are targets because they fit this system, not because they fight the helicopter (they do not). The soldiers identify the people they shoot as already dead bodies—as, in Judith Butler's phrase, "shadowy contentless figure[s] for something not yet made real" (Meijer and Prins, 281; see also Butler, 27).

"Collateral Murder" thus reflects the paranoid logic of the digital apparatus. It should not be read as though the relation of its particular features to its centrality in public discourse is accidental, but as reflecting a structure of actual relations that, when circulated as this video, reinforces the idea of this structure much as images of consumer products reinforce their consumption. We hear the gunner and commander:

> minute 3:33 "All right, we just engaged all eight individuals."
> 3:53—"All right, you're clear."—"I'm just trying to find targets again."
> 4:03 "Got a bunch of bodies layin' there."
> 4:20 "You shoot I'll talk."
> 4:29 "Currently engaging approximately eight individuals KIA, RPGs and AK-47s."

4:37 "Move to that location once Crazyhorse is done and get pictures. Over."
5:10—"Nice shootin'."—"Thank you."

These exchanges homologize two sides of paranoid action: engagement and disengagement, seeing bodies and being bodies, dialog and action as opposite terms where visibility is death. In this scopic regime, "once you can see the target, you expect to destroy it," explains W. J. Perry, former U.S. Under-Secretary of State for Defense (Virilio, 4).[16] Vision targets the body, which then helps constitute the surveillance apparatus.

This is bad news for anyone who would exhibit the body's singularity. In the paranoid imaginary that we can understand based on these important, if selected, surveillance media, the location of a body is produced by the apparatus (see Figure 3). The soldiers continue:

18:51—"I think they just drove over a body."
18:52—"Really?"
18:58—"Maybe it was just a visual illusion, but it looked like it."

It is not clear whether the figures on the ground are physical. They merge with the ground.[17] The body that is the target of the system is not outside the structure that produced it. The networked influencing machine devalues the body, not because we've seen it all but because the machine sees bodies much as it does any other thing: they become hard to recognize as people, like the Iraqi body. Maybe it was there. Maybe it was not. This problem besets not only the abject target of power, but any body within the specular system that would unveil bodies.[18]

Pornocracy needs to counter the potential invisibility or indeterminacy of the public figure. The pornocrat cannot afford to stop revealing. Hence Putin's bare-chested escapades ("Putin on the Ritz," as one internet meme has it). Spreading his fingers for the camera, Trump explains that in a certain department that corresponds, according to popular myth, with the size of the hand, he is very satisfactory: "I guarantee you there is no problem. I guarantee" (Greenfield). His three wives are proof; when the competing 2016 primary campaign of Texas senator Ted Cruz publicized a photograph of Trump's third wife nude,

Figure 3. Wikileaks, "Collateral Murder."

Trump was scandalized, but in response retweeted "an unflattering picture of Mr. Cruz's wife next to a glamour shot of own his wife, Melania, a former model" ("Cheesed Off"), accepting the logic of exposure. To give another example, Indiana house majority leader Jud McMillin had to resign when in 2015 he sent sexual images of himself with a girlfriend to his contacts list (Kaufman). The impulse to leak this video helps confirm the point, although, like Anthony Wiener (the sexting New York congressman), his political career did not survive the treatment, at least in the short term.

To discuss the pornocratic counterattack, I choose the leaked surveillance tapes of private telephone conversations between Prince Charles Philip Arthur George, the English public figure, and Camilla Parker Bowles, his then special friend (later his wife), on December 18, 1989 (known as "Camillagate"), and those between Princess Diana Spencer, Charles's wife, and her friend the TV actor James Gilbey, on December 31, 1989 (known as "Squidgygate"). The development of television in the UK has been "tied intimately to the democratization of access to spatially and socially restricted imperial ceremonies, especially rites of accession and imperial weddings" (Bernard, 343).[19] The Camillagate and Squidgygate tapes were not public to begin with, but it is hard to imagine them being made without the expectation of exposure they have had. These are by nature public objects, always already "overheard," to borrow the term from John Stuart Mill's "Thoughts on Poetry and its Varieties," and the royal speakers are "waving a little flag" in their head, as we will see. In these recordings, Charles and Diana want to tell all, and the leak only confirms their wish. As Alan Bennett writes, "Where the Queen is concerned everyone is a spectator": "the odd overheard remark" is not unguarded or natural (78). It is not known who recorded the tapes (a "Scanner enthusiast," reportedly)[20] or how they came to be released. James was calling from his car phone, so he is said to have been a soft target, but the technical difficulties of the espionage and what some claim had been efforts to edit the recordings have occasioned paranoid theories that the tapes were produced or leaked by MI-5, the domestic intelligence agency.

These media leaks reinforce the sovereign position, the bodily exceptionality, of their objects, but exhibit the ambiguity of and ambivalence about the body that exposure entails. The royal bodies should not be read apart from the mediated structure that reveals them (the king cannot today have "two bodies," allowing the king to turn king mode off). Charles and Diana fight the ambiguity of the body by rehearsing scandalous exposure that, as it happened, got real:

> CHARLES: "He thought he might've gone too far."
> CAMILLA: "Ah well."
> CHARLES: "Anyway, you know that's the sort of thing one has to beware of. And sort of feel one's way along with—if you know what I mean."
> CAMILLA: "Mmmm. You're awfully *good* feeling your way along."
> CHARLES: "Oh Stop! I want to feel my way along you, all over you, and up and down you, and in and out . . ."
> CAMILLA: "Oh, Charles!"
> CHARLES: "*Particularly* in and out!"
> CAMILLA: "Oh, that's *just* what I need at the moment."
> CHARLES: "Is it?"

It seems an odd conversation in which to call someone "Charles," as though the official quality of the exchange never goes away. Nor does the repetition of avowals remove the need for repetition or the doubt that it creates in the process of overcoming it:

CHARLES: "Oh, God. I'll just live inside your trousers, or something. It would be much easier!"
CAMILLA: *[laughing]*"What are you going to turn into, a pair of *knickers*?"
[Both laugh.]
CAMILLA: "Oh, You're going to come back as a pair of knickers!"
CHARLES: "Or, God forbid, a *Tampax*! Just my luck!" *[laughs]*
CAMILLA: "You are a complete idiot!" *[laughs]*"Oh, what a *wonderful* idea!"
CHARLES: "My luck to be chucked down the lavatory and go on and on, forever swirling round on the top, never going down."
CAMILLA: *[laughing]*"Oh, Darling!"
CHARLES: "Until the next one comes through."
CAMILLA: "Oh, perhaps you could come back as a box."
CHARLES: "What sort of box?"
CAMILLA: "A box of Tampax, so you could just keep going."
CHARLES: "That's true."

Charles imagines an eternal return through the sewer system. Camilla encourages his abjection, and even proposes he could return, in a kind of karmic justice, as a cardboard box. When Charles says, "Until the next one comes through," he is acknowledging the formal substitutionality of the English monarchic bloodline that this exchange allegorizes. His substitutionality as cardboard box is all too consistent with his body's indifferent place in the world of objects.

The conversation ends with Beckettian protraction when Camilla encourages Charles to "press the button":

CHARLES: "Going."
CAMILLA: "Gone."
CHARLES: "Night."
CAMILLA: "Bye. Press the button."
CHARLES: "Going to press the tit."
CAMILLA: "All right darling, I wish you were pressing mine."
CHARLES: "God, I wish I was. Harder and harder."
CAMILLA: "Oh darling."
CHARLES: "Night."
CAMILLA: "Night."

The homology between "button" and "tit" superimposes the apparatus and the body. The body, like the dead bodies in "Collateral Murder," is terminated by remote control, subject to the apparatus. It wants to be seen, to be touched, to expose itself, but fears invisibility, abandonment, detachment.

"Squidgygate," so-called after James Gilbey's pet name for Diana Spencer, is similarly co-constituted, or "mutual," as Diana says. It offers exposure of the body, but acknowledges the prospect of defeat. "I don't know *what* I'd do," says James. "Do you know, Darling, I couldn't sort of face the thought of not speaking to you every moment. It fills me with real horror, you know." "It's purely mutual," says Diana. "Is it?" asks James. "I really hate the idea of it, you know. It makes me really sort of scared." James says several times he is scared of something, while Diana says she is brave. But her bravery, a public function of her office, is also a kind of surrender. She is the outsider to the State system of her husband and his family that, of course, she is so visibly part of. She identifies with the abjected outside of that system even while, elsewhere in the conversation, she occupies the privileged center, and commends James for locking his car, in case anyone threatening should be about. She recounts a visit to a charity in which she had an exchange with a bishop:

DIANA: "No, with the Bishop: 'I understand people's pain, people's suffering, more than you will ever know.' And he said: 'That's obvious by what you are doing for the AIDS.' I said: 'It's not only AIDS, it's anyone who suffers; I can smell them a mile away.'"
GILBEY: "What did he say?"
DIANA: "Nothing. He just went quiet. He changed the subject to toys; and I thought, 'AH! Defeated you!'"
GILBEY: "Did you? Marvelous, Darling. Did you chalk up a little victory?"
DIANA: "Yes, I did."
GILBEY: "Did you, Darling? Waving a little flag in your head."
DIANA: "Yes."
GILBEY: "How marvelous. You ought to do that more often. That flag ought to get bigger."
DIANA: "Yes, my surrender flag." *[laughs]*
GILBEY: "You haven't got one, have you?"
DIANA: "Yes."
GILBEY: "What, a big one?"
DIANA: "Well, medium."
GILBEY: "Is it? Well, don't wave it too much."
DIANA: "No."

Diana is official when she is petty, and triumphs over the center—the bishop—when she identifies with what Stefano Harney and Fred Moten call the "surround." But she is identified with the flag by displaying her ability to "smell" pain and suffering (or: she thinks the poor "smell"). The bishop cannot smell the poor because he is too secure at the center; she can, because she is not secure, because she identifies with the smelly poor. Having put forward an abject idea of her body, she must next disavow it. She always covers her footsteps, she says.

These surveillance recordings reveal contradictions built-in to the public body. They help guarantee the exceptionality of that body, but they also make the exposed figures common. Charles in particular seems more honest and real than he does in official portraits. That is bad for pornocracy. As real people, Charles and Diana threaten to become unworthy of spectacle, even as their visibility is harder and harder to secure. With constant trying, for example, Donald Trump achieved the status of caricature, as when he said that his daughter Ivanka is so fine that if she were not his daughter, he would have dated her:[21] "Yeah, she's really something, and what a beauty, that one. If I weren't happily married and, ya know, her *father*" (Solotaroff).[22] His recognizable style is a branding achievement. He joins the other efforts I have examined here to prop up pornocracy. Trump has endeavored valiantly to reoccupy the place of the contested body whose spectacular revelation would guarantee political power. Shooting someone in the middle of Fifth Avenue in New York, he said, would not cost him votes. (Is shooting merely his incidental metaphor?) The Debordian spectacle has fallen. "We love you, spectacle, get up!" seems to be the cry, though the threat is actually coming from another direction, as I have been suggesting—from the scopic imaginary that no longer cares how tall Trump's tower is. Pornocracy must fight, like the Georgian politicians recently blackmailed online by an undisclosed entity. The entity posted sex videos of Georgian politicians and threatened to post more. "Sex and having a sex life are nothing to be ashamed of," said President Giorgi Margvelashvili in a public statement that recalls Laura's speech in *South Park*. "I address those dark forces, who intend to blackmail our population and our society: we will find each of you and you will not be able to frighten and terrorise people" (Forestier-Walker). But (recalling the paranoid speculation about Squidgygate) the source of the blackmail is probably the government itself: according to news reports, in 2012 the Georgian Ministry of Interior announced that it had found an archive in the ministry containing "24,000 [sexually explicit] videos, hundreds of hours of material" (Forestier-Walker). The government exposes itself in order to shore up pornocracy, and then must deny it or prosecute itself.

Given the subsumption of the body into the global apparatus, it is all but expected that defiance of the scopic regime would involve the reassertion of the body. Google's massive Street View project, which aspires to map or project every corner of lived experience, has generated for this reason its share of resentment. An image in Jon Rafman's popular selection from Google View shows a child hiding in an alley as the camera passes by. There is no such thing as hiding. In other photos from this archive, youth in a generic run-down city street moon the passing car-camera (see Figure 4) and, elsewhere, give it the finger, as though to reassert the body, not only of the person who acts, but as something that would resist interpolation in a system that records everything equivalently. But these bodies are already dead to the influencing machine the way Schreber was to his father. As the symbolic aftermath of its own demise in figures like Berlusconi, Putin, and Trump, the pornocratic body fronts the interests, economic and political, that turn the wheels of the scopic regime. In the networked age,

Figure 4. Jon Rafman, "Google Street View archive."

the exhibition of the exceptional body is almost empty as a gesture, the last Munch-like scream of pornocracy.

Eyal Amiran is professor of comparative literature and film and media studies at the University of California, Irvine, and editor of the journal *Postmodern Culture*. He has published on electronic culture in *Discourse, Minnesota Review, symplokē*, and elsewhere. His recent book is *Modernism and the Materiality of Texts* (2016).

Notes

1. Christian Metz proposed the term "scopic regime" in 1982; see Gregory, 190. "Imaginary" refers to Cornelius Castoriadis's concept, revisited by Benedict Anderson and others. Unlike the public space understood by Jürgen Habermas to reflect reasoned conversation, the imaginary is a common fantasy that can be understood symptomatically from cultural practice.

2. Compare also Lisa Parks's notion of the "diachronic omniscience" afforded by satellite archaeology (91). She emphasizes the satellite image's "inability to tell all" (95) and urges a critical distance from the satellite's implicit claim for omniscience: "It is *in the image* that citizen-viewers must struggle for the autonomy of the look to maintain its separation from the orbital gaze of the military intelligence and the military gaze of filmed entertainment" (103). This is a worthwhile position to hope for from within the big-data imaginary.

3. In "Hitler's Diminished Masculinity," he argues that Hitler establishes his relation with the public by projecting the sartorial image of a bourgeois man of leisure.

4. For Baudry, because projection in the cinema hall directs the audience from a god-like position outside the audience's field of vision, it produces an authoritarian experience that determines how viewers experience the world of the film. Projected film is always in part about the perspective of projection.

5. This video has been republished on several websites. Apparently it was posted first by LiveLeak.com on October 4, 2014 ("Coalition Drone").

6. Greyness that blends the body into the background distinguishes the foreigner in Kristeva's account: "gray, imperceptible" (6). Drone photography is for now distinguished by a phantasmal graininess that has been said to make it in principle pornographic: "UAV videos are more like the peeping tom's camera shoved in a hole in a bathroom wall that seduce the viewer to looking closer at scenes of killing" (Thompson).

7. "Drone Boning" has been covered in an article for the *Daily Mail*, "Are Drones the Future of Porn?"

8. For the sound of cities, see http://www.soundcities.com/; see also the London underground sound project at http://www.soundsurvey.org.uk/index.php/

survey/waterways/ and at http://www.telegraph.co.uk/news/uknews/road-and-rail-transport/10257633/What-do-London-Underground-stops-taste-like.html.

9. Correlatively, in the "internet of things," the world of networked appliances and toys, the television watches you: TVs with voice activation "'listen' to every conversation held in front of them and may share any details they hear with Samsung or third parties" ("Not in Front"). Supporting President Trump's allegation that President Obama ordered wiretapping surveillance of Trump Tower before the presidential elections of 2016, Trump's counselor Kellyanne Conway explained that microwave ovens can be used to spy on people (Memoli).

10. "The elected National Assembly stands in a metaphysical relation, but the elected President in a personal relation, to the nation. . . . In the President this national spirit finds its incarnation" (Marx, 33). And elsewhere: "Only when . . . he himself now takes his imperial role seriously and under the Napoleonic mask imagines he is the real Napoleon, does he become the victim of his own conception of the world, the serious buffoon who no longer takes world history for a comedy but his comedy for world history" (76).

11. I thank Philip Anselmo for pointing me to Burgin's discussion of paranoid space.

12. As Harney and Moten write, "Politics soldiers on, claiming to defend what it has not enclosed, enclosing what it cannot defend but only endanger" (18).

13. TMI was blocked by Malaysia's internet regulatory body on February 5, 2016, on grounds of national security and closed on March 15, 2016. I cite an alternate posting of the article.

14. As though to shore up their credit as influencing machine, Google Maps released their 2014 "Pokémon Challenge," requiring players to map Pokémons around the world. The game acknowledges the disappearance of nature, or something that has duration outside the symbolic world of Google Maps. A story about the 2016 release reports that a player using the app stumbled on a dead body (Cockburn), which was startling because, rhetorically, the Challenge has no outside. Compare Andrejevic's notion of "digital enclosure" (2–3).

15. The dialectic structure is not symmetrical, as Jameson explains (19–21). For a discussion of asymmetry in digital FPS games as a pretended Hegelian symmetry, see Chamayou.

16. "If I can see it, I can kill it," according to Rick Sondag, executive vice president of Liteye Systems, which sells a counterdrone "death ray," at the Commercial Unmanned Aerial Vehicle (UAV) Expo in Las Vegas (Thielman). On military vision as targeting, see also Garrett Stewart.

17. A camera operator at a "remote duty station" explains in the documentary video *National Bird* that, after a drone strike, the camera operator must "follow through" (15:54): after the strike, "you can see, like, the body parts. You can identify, like, 'that could be the lower half of his body, that could be a leg'" (16:00–16:08). In a December 29, 2013, article in the *Guardian*, the operator, Heather Linebaugh, refutes the idea that remote drone operation can isolate enemy combatants from noncombatants. I thank Alex Rivera for the reference.

18. Compare David Marriott's discussion of the black body as a "black hole" in *Rhizomes.* As Marriott writes, "The wretched are neither a foundation nor anti-foundation, but are the figure of a dislocation at the heart of modern sovereignty. Only thus do they come into being. What manifests itself as the law's inner decay in the colony is the fact that rule of law is, in the final analysis, incomprehensible without the wretchedness that ruins it, without which law's ultimate justification or legitimation would not exist sovereignly" (23).

19. While I do not follow the convention of seeing television as democratizing, it is important to note, with Bernard, the relation between mediated spectacle and the legitimacy of "political pageantry" (344). In *Televisuality: Style, Crisis, and Authority in American Television*, John Thornton Caldwell considers exhibitionism characteristic of televisuality, as Parks notes (33).

20. So it says in the Camillagate transcript.

21. "When asked how he would react if Ivanka, a former teen model, posed for *Playboy,* Trump replied, 'It would be really disappointing—not really—but it would depend on what's inside the magazine.' He added: 'I don't think Ivanka would do that, although she does have a very nice figure. I've said if Ivanka weren't my daughter, perhaps I'd be dating her'" ("Trump jokes").

22. In the 1959 film *The White Warrior,* based on Tolstoy's *Chadži-Murat,* the king has the same idea. "It's really a terrible pity that you happen to be my goddaughter," he tells Maria. "You inspire me with feelings of quite a different kind." It's a king's kind of idea.

Works Cited

Ackerman, Spencer, and James Ball. 2014. "Optic Nerve: Millions of Yahoo Webcam Images Intercepted by GCHQ." *Guardian,* February 28. https://www.theguardian.com/world/2014/feb/27/gchq-nsa-webcam-images-internet-yahoo.

Andrejevic, Mark. 2007. *iSpy: Surveillance and Power in the Interactive Era.* Lawrence: University Press of Kansas.

Armstrong, Tim. 1998. *Modernism, Technology and the Body: A Cultural Study.* Cambridge: Cambridge University Press.

Associated Press. "Trump Jokes about Dating his Daughter." 2006. *USA Today,* March 7. http://usatoday30.usatoday.com/life/people/2006-03-07-trump_x.htm.

BBC News. 2015. "Not in Front of the Telly: Warning over 'listening' TV." February 9. http://www.bbc.com/news/technology-31296188.

Benjamin, Walter. 2002. "The Work of Art in the Age of Its Reproducibility." In *Selected Writings, Vol. 3, 1935–1938.* Ed. Howard Eiland and Michael W. Jennings, 101–40. Trans. Edmund Jephcott et al. Cambridge, Mass.: Harvard University Press.

Benjamin, Walter. 2003. "On the Concept of History." In *Selected Writings, Vol. 4, 1938–1940*. Ed. Howard Eiland and Michael W. Jennings, 389–400. Trans. Edmund Jephcott et al. Cambridge, Mass.: Harvard University Press.

Benjamin, Walter. 2005. "Hitler's Diminished Masculinity." In *Selected Writings, Vol. 2, Part 2, 1931–1934*. Ed. Michael W. Jennings et al, 792–93. Trans. Rodney Livingston et al. Cambridge, Mass.: Harvard University Press.

Bennett, Alan. *The Uncommon Reader*. 2007. London: Faber and Faber.

Bernard, Rosemarie. 2001. "Mirror Image: Layered Narratives in Photographic and Televised Mediations of Ise's Shikinen Sengū." In *Religion and Media*. Ed. Hent de Vries and Samuel Weber, 339–75. Stanford: Stanford University Press.

Burgin, Victor. 1996. *In/Different Spaces: Place and Memory in Visual Culture*. Berkeley: University of California Press.

Butler, Judith. 1998. *The Psychic Life of Power: Theories in Subjection*. Stanford: Stanford University Press.

"The Camillagate Transcript." 2016. Geocities. http://www.geocities.ws/rickanddarvagossip/camillagate.html.

Chamayou, Gregoire. 2011. "The Manhunt Doctrine." *Radical Philosophy* 169 (September/October). http://www.radicalphilosophy.com/commentary/the-manhunt-doctrine.

"Cheesed-off Wisconsinites Dump Donald Trump." 2016. *Economist*, April 6. http://www.economist.com/blogs/democracyinamerica/2016/04/wisconsin-primaries.

"Coalition Drone Filmed Daesh/Isis Raping a Donkey." 2014. LiveLeak. http://www.liveleak.com/view?i=9a0_1412420896.

Cockburn, Harry. 2016. "Pokemon GO Virtual Reality Game Leads Teenage Girl to Dead Body." *Independent*, July 12. http://www.independent.co.uk/news/world/americas/pokemon-go-uk-release-date-teenager-finds-dead-body-playing-game-a7128441.html.

"Drone Boning." N.d. Vimeo. https://vimeo.com/109274211

"'Drone' Video of 'ISIL Member' Having Sex with Donkey Not of ISIL Member, Not Drone Video." 2014. AATTP, October 14. http://aattp.org/drone-video-of-isil-member-having-sex-with-donkey-not-of-isil-member-not-drone-video-video/.

Farrell, Paul. 2014. "French and Chinese Satellites Show Trash in Ocean as Potential Sightings of the Missing Flight MH370." *Guardian*, March 23. http://www.theguardian.com/world/2014/mar/23/mh370-poor-visibility-indian-ocean-search-effort.

Forestier-Walker, Robin. 2016. "Georgia's Very Public Sex Tapes and the Secret Police." *Al Jazeera*, March 19. http://www.aljazeera.com/blogs/europe/2016/03/georgia-public-sex-tapes-secret-police-160319063729861.html.

Foster, Olivia. 2014. "Are Drones the Future of Porn?" *Daily Mail*, November 7. http://www.dailymail.co.uk/femail/article-2821900/Are-drones-future-porn-Sex-skies-latest-trend-female-friendly-erotica.html.

Greenfield, Patrick. 2016. "Artist Threatened with Lawsuit if She Sells Nude Donald Trump Painting." *Guardian,* April 17. http://www.theguardian.com/us-news/2016/apr/17/nude-donald-trump-painting-illma-gore-lawsuits?CMP=share_btn_fb.

Gregory, Derek. 2011. "From a View to a Kill: Drones and Late Modern War." *Theory, Culture and Society* 28, nos. 7–8: 188–215.

Guardian. 2016. "MH370 Search: Two More Pieces of Debris from Plane Found in Madagascar." June 10. https://www.theguardian.com/world/2016/jun/10/mh370-search-two-more-pieces-of-plane-debris-found-in-madagascar.

Harney, Stefano, and Fred Moten. 2013. *The Undercommons: Fugitive Planning and Black Study.* New York: Minor Compositions.

Hunt, Elle. 2017. "Malaysia Airlines Flight MH370: Underwater Search Called Off." *Guardian,* January 17. https://www.theguardian.com/world/2017/jan/17/malaysia-airlines-flight-mh370-search-called-off.

"The Infamous Squidgygate Transcript." N.d. Geocities. http://www.geocities.ws/rickanddarvagossip/diana_gilbey.html.

Jameson, Fredric. 2009. *Valences of the Dialectic.* New York: Verso.

Judovitz, Dalia. 1995. "'Sex,' or, the Misfortunes of Literature." In *Sade and the Narrative of Transgression.* Ed. David B. Allison, Mark S. Roberts, and Allen S. Weiss, 171–98. Cambridge: Cambridge University Press.

Kaufman, Scott Eric. 2015. "Indiana GOP's House Leader Resigns after Texting Sexually Explicit Video of Himself Cheating on Wife to Everyone on His 'Contacts' List." *Salon,* September 30. http://www.salon.com/2015/09/30/indiana_gops_house_leader_resigns_after_texting_sexually_explicit_video_of_himself_cheating_on_wife_to_everyone_on_his_contacts_list/.

Kristeva, Julia. 1991. *Strangers to Ourselves.* Trans. Leon S. Roudiez. New York: Columbia University Press.

Linebaugh, Heather. 2013. "I Worked on the US Drone Program." *Guardian,* December 29. https://www.theguardian.com/commentisfree/2013/dec/29/drones-us-military.

Lippit, Akira Mizuta. 2005. *Atomic Light (Shadow Optics).* Minneapolis: University of Minnesota Press.

"The Magic Bush." 2014. An episode of *South Park,* Season 18, Episode 5. Directed by Trey Parker.

Malaysian Insider. 2014. "Could missing MH370 Have Stalked SIA Flight to the North? Possible, Say Netizens." March 17. https://sg.news.yahoo.com/could-missing-mh370-stalked-sia-flight-north-possible-225900110.html.

Marriott, David. 2016. "Judging Fanon." *Rhizomes* no. 29. http://www.rhizomes.net/issue29/marriott.html.

Marx, Karl. 1975. *The 18th Brumaire of Louis Bonaparte.* New York: International.

Meijer, Irene Costera, and Baukje Prins. 1998. "How Bodies Come to Matter: An Interview with Judith Butler." *Signs* 23, no. 2: 275–86.

Memoli, Michael A. 2017. "Kellyanne Conway on Surveillance: We Have 'Microwaves That Turn into Cameras.'" *Los Angeles Times,* March 13. http://www

.latimes.com / politics / washington / la-na-essential-washington-updates -more-than-just-spying-microwaves-why-1489416182-htmlstory.html.

"National Bird." 2016. An episode of *Independent Lens*. Directed and produced by Sonia Kennebeck. http: / / www.pbs.org / video / 3000298620 / .

Parks, Lisa. 2005. *Cultures in Orbit: Satellites and the Televisual*. Durham: Duke University Press.

Rafman, Jon. N.d. Google Street View archive. 9-Eyes. http: / / 9-eyes.com / .

Sedgwick, Eve Kosofsky. 2003. *Touching Feeling: Affect, Pedagogy, Performativity*. Durham: Duke University Press.

Solotaroff, Paul. 2015. "Trump Seriously: On the Trail with the GOP's Tough Guy." *Rolling Stone*, September 9. http: / / www.rollingstone.com / politics / news / trump-seriously-20150909.

Stewart, Garrett. 2012. "Surveillance Cinema." *Film Quarterly* 66, no. 2 (Winter): 5–15.

Tanner, Christopher. 2004. "The Influencing Machine." *Cabinet* no. 14 (Summer). http: / / cabinetmagazine.org / issues / 14 / turner.php.

Tausk, Victor. 1933. "On the Origin of the Influencing Machine in Schizophrenia." *Psychoanalytic Quarterly* 2:519–56.

Thielman, Sam. 2015. "Anti-Drone 'Death Ray' Can Blast Vehicles Out of the Sky from a Mile Away." *Guardian*, October 7. https: / / www.theguardian.com / technology / 2015 / oct / 07 / drone-death-ray-device-liteye-auds.

Thompson, Rachel. 2013. "The Seductive Killing Screen." *In the Moment* (blog), *Critical Inquiry*. https: / / critinq.wordpress.com / 2013 / 06 / 17 / the-seductive -killing-screenrachel-thompson-in-2008-the-defense / .

Virilio, Paul. 1989. *War and Cinema: The Logistics of Perception*. Trans. Patrick Camiller. London: Verso.

Wikileaks. "Collateral Murder." Full version. https: / / collateralmurder.wikileaks .org / .

PORNOCRACY'S QUEER CIRCULATIONS

Natasha Hurley

I want to know why we started learning somewhere down the line that a president is always a clown. Always a john and never a hooker. Always a boss and never a worker. Always a liar, always a thief, and never caught.

—*Zoe Leonard*, "I Want a Dyke for President"

Let's face it: the world has never been run by sex workers. When Pierre-Joseph Proudhon wrote his proleptic diatribe against pornocracy, defining it as rule by prostitutes and recalling the tenth-century papacy, he was looking backward to a historical period that did not exist as such to name his anxiety about a feminist political future that has yet to come. As *Pornocracy, or Women in Modern Times* makes clear, Proudhon's fear of feminine sexual power is, moreover, underwritten by a deep distrust of same-sex relations. The term *pornocracy* thus operates as a catachresis that disavows the form of political rule it claims to identify: improperly naming (and so dismissing) the phenomenon—rule by harlots—that it purports to designate. In this essay, I read Proudhon's cautionary tale about a coming pornocracy as a theory aimed at managing sexual circulation: the circulation, primarily, of women and queers with respect to state and economic power. That the world has never been run by sex workers doesn't mean the world has never been run by people who care deeply *about* those who engage in transactions that exchange sex for money. The phantasmatic edge of pornocracy's paranoia does not mitigate the term's enduring conceptual and material effects. The ironic shape of life under conditions of pornocracy is rather best articulated by countercultural denizens, who never use the word *pornocracy* at all. Zoe Leonard's 1992 broadside "I Want a Dyke for President,"[1] first circulated at the height of the AIDS crisis, encapsulates the paradox nicely: a president is "Always a john and never a hooker. Always a boss and never a worker."

In light of pornocracy's retrograde political potential, at least in the hands of Proudhon, it is worth asking what the concept excavates and animates for a contemporary politics of gender and sexuality as matters of sexual circulation. In taking up the history and potential of *pornocracy* as a term for understanding the vexations of gender and sexuality under capitalism, I propose in this essay not merely to diminish pornocracy but to take seriously the ways it exposes gender and sexuality as problems of circulation within and beyond Proudhon's incendiary pamphlet. To do so, I attend to pornocracy in its historical unfolding, first of all as a fantasy of circulation that bears down specifically on sexual dissidence by women and queers. This genealogical approach to the term involves tracking its circulation as well. Despite the fact that the term *pornocracy* names something that has never existed, it nonetheless serves to crystallize for us a structure of sexual management that exposes the hypocrisy of our economic and political order.

In pursuit of these aims, the pages that follow assemble detritus from the history of pornocracy's evolution and circulation as concept in an effort to track the contradictions that estrange the term from what it claims to name, to consider some modern deployments of the term *pornocracy,* and to assess the strategic deployment of pornocratic logic in the hands of feminists and queers who counter its constraints on sexual circulation by insisting on more sexual circulation. By thinking through pornocracy-as-fantasy-of-sexual-circulation that itself circulates before, after, and through Proudhon's thought, I ultimately argue that any rehabilitation of *pornocracy* as a concept for understanding contemporary gender and sexuality demands an exploration of the queer forms it takes and conceals within itself: queer in its sexual politics, but queer as well in what it simultaneously names and unnames, knows and unknows about itself. Pornocracy's queerness, in short, resides not merely in the concept's capacity for naming a subversive mode of gendered and sexual sociability but also in its simultaneous aspiration for dampening that very possibility. What Proudhon fears most about pornocracy—its redistribution of sex and gender roles—is arguably what makes the concept a site of political possibility consonant with the world-making capacity of sexual life outside of heteronormative contracts. And yet his elaboration of pornocracy precisely as a thing to be feared—and addressing that threatening elaboration directly to feminists—has the effect of shrouding pornocracy's disruptive potential within a discursive framework that upholds traditional sexual mores and gendered forms of economic privilege. It may be for this reason that pornocracy understands itself to be diagnosing scandalous behavior while fixing firmly in place norms of gender and sexuality that reproduce fundamental asymmetries of both economic and gendered forms of power. To read pornocracy as a theory of circulation is not merely to redeem a queerer pornocracy by redeeming the very circulation that Proudhon diminishes. Rather, it is to read pornocracy's circulation as a diagnostic rather than predictive tool for describing the contradictions of gender and sexuality under capitalist conditions.

PROUDHON'S PORNOCRACY

In the nineteenth century, when women's rights emerged as a site of contestation for many ideas that we read now through the lenses of feminist and queer theory, Proudhon embraced radical social change in economic terms, all the while fearing the effects of that change when it came to gender and family organization. Pornocracy would displace the family, which he took to be the bedrock of all things sexual, gendered, economic, and republican. "The law of the sexes," he writes, "depends on that of the family, and it extends also to the order of society." For women to take up space in public would amount to prostitution, at least in Proudhon's estimation: out with the family and power to the whores. This sort of thinking arguably continues to haunt critiques of capitalism that lack attention to the materialities of gender and sexuality. Proudhon's writing on pornocracy might thus be seen as both an untapped archive for queer thought and method (where his term indicates gender dissidence and queer life even as he diminishes them) and a site from which to theorize the roguish political structure that gives form to that diminishment. Pornocracy as a concept does not arguably queer anything, but it exposes, precisely by concealing within itself, the privileges and contradictions structuring the gender and sexuality of political power. In this way, I will suggest that the sexual form Proudhon's *Pornocracy* pamphlet so paranoiacally names (rule by harlots) stands at odds with the sexual form that enables that very act of naming (rule by sexually hypocritical political bosses).

By tracing the development and deployment of *pornocracy* as a concept, we begin to see its double-edged status as a rhetorical weapon: its use as an epithet against feminist ideals, its symbolization of male political excesses, its economic disavowals (and underpinnings), and its gestures to the horizons of queer possibility (however dystopian) as a potential site for reanimating the concept for modern life. After offering an account of the term's historical circulation, and its significance for Proudhon, this essay concludes with a reparative consideration of pornocracy's feminist and queer political aesthetics that includes an account of its conservative reparations.

PORNOCRACY'S QUEER ENCRYPTIONS

Were we to engage in the thought experiment of inverting the nightmare of political life that Proudhon describes in *Pornocracy, or Women in Modern Times,* we might end up with something like the dream of today's queer theorists and sex radicals. The pamphlet outlines a philosophy of social life driven by a fear that the nuclear family would be undermined, that monogamy would be threatened, that prostitution would be legal, and sex and gender roles disturbed—all concerns that have frequently found relatively earnest embrace in many queer world-making projects today. Proudhon explicitly fears the reorganization of gendered and sexual social life. Under pornocracy, he insists, "things would become between man and woman what we see between persons of the same sex: service for service, product for product, idea for idea. Without doubt there would be love, since we conserve, in this express aim, the sexual distinction." This fear of a queered heterosexuality (where "things" become "what we see between persons of the same sex") features men and women living, as he says, "in a zone of liberty and concubinage; not arousing jealousy." Marriage would be displaced as "the very organ of justice," society would "not hold to 'an indissociable monogamy,'" "modesty" could be "sold" as "prostitution," "sex consciousness [would get] mixed up," and free love would reign, even if it would be, as Proudhon insists, "an abomination."

As tempting as it might be to read Proudhon's theory reparatively, not as nightmare but as queer or feminist dream, doing so would make the mistake of too easily equating Proudhon's fearful prognostication with modern queer political aspiration. Such a project would also replicate the mistake (which Proudhon himself made) of extracting it from both his own broader economic vision and the historical conditions of pornocracy's circulation before and after Proudhon. Without dismissing the potential for a utopian embrace of pornocracy, we might better understand Proudhon's concept as a prolepsis of our present. The linguistic form and social life of this vision have yet to be understood fully for the contradictions they consolidated and mobilized and that continue to haunt modern thought about accepted forms of sexuality and politics in public. Proudhon's treatment of pornocracy, in other words, is striking less for the queerness it suspects at the level of political content and more for what it encrypts within itself about the sexual form of politics under capitalist conditions.

To the extent that Proudhon's pornocracy is an argument against non-monogamy, sex in public, prostitution, and even same-sex relations, it makes distinctive features of queer social life central (in its very refusal of them). As a paranoid theory, pornocracy also makes itself fully available for deployment in the interests of conservative and sexist forms of political rule. But what is strangest about Proudhon's work is less its queer sexual content than the very structure of its relationship to sexual politics. Pornocracy does not merely name an argument about political rule; it enacts one. When Proudhon insists that pornocracy would result from women gaining political power, he refuses to see that in doing so, he upholds one philosophy of sexual circulation (putatively benign male power that treats women as sexual currency) at the expense of another (malign female power, which presumably amplifies feminized sexual currency to the point of perversion). A structure of reading the sexualization of political rule is thus encoded within *pornocracy* as that concept circulates in the world. This formal feature of pornocracy depends, fundamentally, on the right of speech and diagnosis for the one who defends the status quo and the noncirculation of gender and sexual labor beyond their traditional spheres.

PORNOCRACY'S CHECKERED PAST

Proudhon did not invent the term *pornocracy* to characterize the perversions of both political power and the family when women take power publicly. He did secularize its figuration of scandalous religious culture to theorize a broader political phenomenon, but in so doing he only confirmed the force of its religious precedent (ironic, given Proudhon's professed aversion to religion)[2] while also disguising the historical contradictions of its unfolding. *Pornocracy,* we know, was coined to name the period in Roman Catholic history known as the Saeculum obscurum (the Dark Ages).[3] While the *OED*'s definition of the term as the "Dominating influence of harlots or prostitutes, specifically on the government of Rome during the first half of the tenth century," implicitly recognizes the gap between "rule" and "influence," later circulations have tended to displace that gap and shore up its catachrestic form. Hence, the term makes visible a political and economic history of gender and sexuality to which misrecognition is a central, even constitutive, feature. Some names for this misrecognition include disavowal, hypocrisy, and gender-as-usual. If we grasp, at the heart of pornocracy, the difference between what it names and the norms of speech, gender, and political economy that it enacts through that naming, we can better trace the effect both of the term's movement through the world (as content) and of the ways its deployment exceeds that content (as form).

What *pornocracy* names is not just a system of political rule but also a site of historical shame and political disavowal. Further, that "porn" persists in modern usage beyond its etymological referent, "prostitute," enables a reframing of pornocracy beyond the terms of its historical usages. By the time Proudhon seizes on the term, the *porn* of *pornocracy* had also come to name explicit sexual representations (pornography as a genre) and the forms of sex work that produce them. Proudhon is the inheritor of an intellectual tradition in which democracy and pornography are entangled—so much so, that the fusion of the two words continues to seem inevitable, even to scholars today. Despite Proudhon's relative inattention to economics in his pamphlet, his ideas about how "things" are between persons of the same sex find curious resonance in his theory of mutualism, which emphasizes co-operatives and small-scale systems of circulation (see Proudhon 2011a;

2011b). At the heart of Proudhon's theory of mutualism is, as he puts it, a fundamental principle of "exchange in kind."[4] Such a principle would seem to find an echo in the "service for service, product for product, idea for idea" that he associates with (and dismisses in) relationships between persons of the same sex.

PORNOCRACY AS POLITICAL PORTMANTEAU: PORNOGRAPHY AND DEMOCRACY

One reason that the word *pornocracy* flows so easily from the lips of commentators ready to critique anything ranging from funding for Planned Parenthood to the circulation of pornography is that the term neatly combines in one linguistic portmanteau two phenomena that have long been controversially associated with each other: pornography and democracy. Lynn Hunt's work in *The Invention of Pornography* charts the entangled history of both, a history that tracks back to eighteenth-century France in particular:

> Democracy was established against monarchy through pornographic attacks on the feminization of both the aristocracy and monarchy. It was accelerated in and after 1789 by especially vicious attacks against the leading female figure of the ancien régime, the queen herself. At the same time, the fraternal bonds of democracy were established in pornography, at least and perhaps more broadly, through the circulation of images of women's bodies, especially through print media and the effect of visualization through pornographic writing. . . . Women were thus essential to the development of democracy and, in the end, excluded from it. (329)

Through images, tracts, pamphlets, and novels ranging from *L'École des Filles* to the writings of the Marquis de Sade and beyond—many of which staged the scene of pedagogy as the scene of sexual schooling—women and the exchange of knowledge among them came to consolidate those "fraternal bonds" of democracy. What scholars such as Joan de Jean and Lynn Hunt contribute to historical understandings of the relationship between pornography and democracy is the centrality of gender to bringing them together. Hunt's insight on the matter is twofold, and each side the fold offers is an important part of the prehistory of Proudhon's conception of pornocracy. On the one hand,

Hunt claims that "early modern pornographers were not intentionally feminists *avant la lettre,* but their portrayal of women, at least until the 1790s, often valorized female sexual activity and determination" (44). On the other hand, the circulation of these women as the sexual agents of pornography had a rather different effect: consolidating communities of male producers and consumers. As Hunt puts it, "Pornography as a structure of literary and visual representation most often offered women's bodies as a focus of male bonding. Men wrote about sex for other male readers" (44). She is careful to stress that pornography ultimately disrupted sexual difference as much as it reinforced it. Pornography was tied not just to women but to libertine culture, early modern queer subcultures, and to matters of class, all of which complicates even further any reduction of the cultural work that pornography does in the period preceding Proudhon to a concern specifically with women. It is precisely because of its unpredictability and its far reach that pornography would seem to have revolutionary potential. Hunt argues that "as new biological and moral standards for sexual difference evolved, pornography seemed to become much more dangerous. It had to be stamped out" (45). In its context as an overdetermined site of cultural and political meaning, pornography, in Hunt's succinct formulation, "names an argument, not a thing" (31).

This argument, however, created the conditions under which Proudhon could advance his view of pornocracy as a political structure. As Hunt puts it, one legacy of the debates about pornography in eighteenth-century France is a concern with the circulation of women in public at all, or, as she puts it, "the passing of public women—and perhaps all women in the pornographic imagination—from man to man" (327). Although pornographic texts like *Julie philosophe* can't really be reduced to their political intention, this moral panic about women in public finds a central place in Proudhon's worry that feminist agitation will result in pornocracy. That Proudhon extrapolates his gender argument into a dystopian vision of extramarital sexuality more generally would seem to belie an anxiety that goes straight to the heart of normative sexuality.

But the relationship between pornography and democracy in eighteenth-century France is not just an important site of influence for Proudhon's concept of *pornocracy.* It also serves as an important touchstone in more contemporary debates about pornography, which seem to connect more directly, in turn, to the deployment of the term *pornocracy* in cultural studies today. As Christie McDonald has argued, discussions of pornography in eighteenth-century France have continued to inform debates about pornography in our contemporary moment. Her work considers "the ways in which certain twentieth-century arguments about sexuality and pornography look to the French Enlightenment for explanation and support" (88). McDonald argues that "the focus on sexual scandal, as it is transmitted through the media, both translates and fosters the uncertainty surrounding ethics in the sociopolitical sphere; in particular, the connection between the personal and the political for women as well as for men has been caught between an increasingly invaded private realm and a contested public morality" (88). Tracking contemporary thinkers about return to early modern France, McDonald ultimately circles back to the same question Hunt's work raises: How do women contribute to the foundation of democracy and then become excluded from it? (90). To the extent that recent scholars so easily discover the overlaps between pornography and democracy through their deployments of the term *pornocracy,* they mark continuity with this long-standing relationship between democracy and pornography, a relationship that seems to be always already modern. Scholars like Frank Krutnik and Wendy Hui Kyong Chun, for instance, do not just collapse the space between two words (democracy and pornography) in their deployments of the term *pornocracy*; they also collapse the several centuries of historical understanding, while simplifying a concept whose intervening history has been one not of condensation but of both enlargement and containment in the hands of Proudhon.

PORNOCRACY'S ANARCHIC PULSE

For Proudhon, the word *pornocracy* arguably became a tool for enlarging claims about gender roles in public that had been part of the arguments about pornography a century before. In advocating for a strict division of gendered labor and a separation of that labor into the domestic and public spheres, Proudhon would, ironically, embrace a form of social conservatism that seemed sharply at odds with his economic philosophy. He makes precisely this argument against women's suffrage (not uncommon in this historical moment) the very first time he uses the term "pornocratic":

> Change, modify, or interfere with this relation between the sexes, in whatever fashion, and you destroy marriage in its essence; from a society where justice is predominant you make a society where love is predominant; you fall back again to concubinage and infidelity; you can still have fathers and mothers, as you still have lovers, but you no longer have the family; and without the family, your political constitution will no longer be a federation of men, of families and of free cities, it will be a theocratic and pornocratic communism, the worst of tyrannies.

Later he insists that "in certain epochs, sex consciousness gets mixed up; the cowardice of men becomes an auxiliary of the woman's audacity; and we see appear these theories of enfranchisement and promiscuity, of which the last word is PORNOCRACY. At this point society is finished." The sexes, the family, the federation of men, and the free city are counterposed here against what he calls "pornocratic communism."[5] At the level of poetics, the apostrophic form of Proudhon's address here (the entire pamphlet is written in the second person) constitutes another formal paradox. He throws life into the objects of his address (feminists) whose political life he wants to stifle, while outlining a political future he would hope to extinguish before it even takes shape.

In so doing, Proudhon reveals that what he fears as much as pornocracy (or fears *through* his fear of pornocracy) is not just gender upheaval, but fantasy itself. His pamphlet concludes with the accusation, directed again at feminists, that "all your philosophy reduces to a promiscuity of notions, and that the promiscuity of notions directs you to *pure fantasy,* in *law, science, art,* and *morals;* to the arbitrary in government, to speculation in business, to shocks in the realm of justice; to prostitution and hustling in love; in one word, to PORNOCRACY." If pornocracy is, as he states, "pure fantasy," it is not just the content of pornocracy that Proudhon fears, but its standing (in his mind) as a "promiscuity of notions" and the indiscriminate circulation of thought.

This resistance to fantasy that marks Proudhon's final admonishment (in the translated selections of the pamphlet) is perhaps the most puzzling feature of his theory, but also the most promising for a queerly reparative reading. After all, he has built his entire intellectual reputation on imagining alternative forms of economic reality. Iain McKay, a recent editor of Proudhon's work, has argued that Proudhon's lasting legacy can be tied to two short statements that serve as an index to the rest of his thought: "I am an anarchist" and "Property is theft!" (1). As the "father of anarchism" and a philosopher of "mutualism," Proudhon's anticapitalist and pro-cooperative philosophies of political economy depend, fundamentally, on a "promiscuity of notions." In his *System of Contradictions in Political Economy*, Proudhon's outlines his theory of mutualism as "a law of exchange": "a system of Guarantees" that replaces old forms of civil society and imagines a "*Society no longer merely conventional, but real, which substitutes for the present piecemeal divisions of property a scientific distribution*" (107). This redistribution of property is predicated (at the class level) not only on abolishing servitude but also (at the state level) on a system of "credit for capital and protection for the state [that] subjects both capital and the state to the uses of labor; which *by the truthful honesty of its exchanges produces a real solidarity among nations*" (emphasis in original). As Proudhon imagined it, mutualism amounts to "a synthesis of the two ideas of appropriation and of communism" (108).

There is a good case to be made that Proudhon's mutualism *is*, in a strong sense, a fantasy about alternative forms of economic circulation. But the subjunctive nature of his vision—his eye to what could, would, and should be—announces itself by eschewing its own phantasmatic character. The biggest irony in the above description is Proudhon's repeated insistence that "convention" be counterpoised, not by a fantasmatic future, but by the "real": "property" divisions can be substituted with "scientific distributions" and "real solidarity" the effect of "honest exchanges." Proudhon invokes the "real," the "scientific," and the "honest" where his deepest-held desires for an alternative political economy are most salient. The affective and proleptic form of Proudhon's economic writings strikes a sharp contrast with that of his writing on pornocracy. It is clear that what Proudhon wants most for economic actors is what he would deny to women, whose publicity would carry with it the taint of pornographic sexuality and the whiff of licentiousness. Dream another economic dream, but not one that would displace gender or the family. And, whatever is worth dreaming must disavow its own dreamlike quality.

PORNOCRACY NOW

Pornocracy is no mere vestigial fantasy of an unrealized past political imaginary. It recalls its own history even as it adjusts itself to contemporary events, describing modern political regimes under such leaders as Bill Clinton, Silvio Berlusconi, and even Barack Obama, but especially Donald Trump. While pornocracy is consistent in its misattribution of political authority to sex workers and in its suggestion that political authority makes prostitutes of women, this misattribution is amplified through the term's circulation. Whether we are talking about news reports on politicians, the title of a novel by Catherine Breillat, or entire albums of music by artists including the GRS Club, The Lovely Savalas, and Enneri Blakka, who deploy *pornocracy* as a cultural diagnosis, we are just as far away from nineteenth-century anarchy as we are from the tenth-century papacy.[6] Across all these contexts, the sexist ressentiment that the term conjures up remains palpable. A sort of anthem to this ressentiment, the Arrogant Sons of Bitches' *Pornocracy* sums up quite nicely the combination of anarchism and sexism so definitive of the concept (and for what Proudhon built into his own description of the concept):

> Pornocracy, government run by whores.
> We never ask what the fuck we do this for.
> We only have one party, democracy is just a front
> They say they care about our country. All they care about is cunt.[7]

"Whores" and "cunts" become the figurative tools by which the excesses (always sexual) of patriarchal democracies can be critiqued. The lyrics muddy the distinction between rulers and harlots, deploying the figure of the "whore" as the figure of politics itself (much as Marx did when he figured all laborers, and by extension labor-as-commodity, in terms of prostitution),[8] but holding pornocratic logic firmly in place. The pronouns "we" and "they" establish pornocracy's exclusionary logic and its feats of political demonization. Who is the "we" and who the "they"? The power brokers under pornocratic conditions are still not the female harlots. Nor are those who bandy the term *pornocracy* about much invested in either embracing rule by prostitutes as a potential political good or in highlighting the constitutive contradictions of the term's circulation.

Whether we are talking about tenth-century popes or politicians today, the specter of female lovers and public policy governing female sexuality has been deployed as a trope for bankrupt political power. Clinton's and Berlusconi's affairs were well publicized, while Trump's open disdain and disregard for women and their bodies cannot be overstated. The extent of their lovers' ("harlots") influence might be debated, but it is striking that none of these men ever surrendered political office to female lovers, as the phrase "rule by harlots" would suggest. The "harlots" in question were never installed as the official agents of political rule. The same is true for the tenth-century popes. What the term's deployment flags, in effect, is a structure of fear and loathing: fear that harlots might in fact have political clout, loathing of women as potential harlots. But male political authority remains firmly intact.

Pornocracy must be understood, then, as it circulates: more as an epithet than as the actual political structure it claims to name. This epithet is hurled in multiple directions through a range of modes of address. The term names an unwanted site of political possibility in spectacularly gendered, sexist, and sexual terms, while also refusing to focalize attention on the actual political actors in question. But that is only the start of the matter. Pornocracy clearly misidentifies the rulers whose sexual indiscretions come to be borne by their female lovers. But this misidentification functions as a site of *un*recognized negativity and contradiction as the term *pornocracy* has circulated through the contemporary political world at an increasing rate. Pornocracy, in short, would seem to have a secret it prefers not to disclose. Rather than take us closer to an understanding of the disavowals it names, pornocracy, when wielded in the service of political scandal, itself marks a scene of titillation. But the remarkable consistency of usage, which encrypts the conceptual and political negativity of pornocracy, also makes that negativity available for unanticipated expansions and redeployments.

Take, for instance, an example from a news story about Obamacare that appeared on the mainstream Roman Catholic website catholicism .org, the title of which is "American Pornocracy." The website outlines a vision of pornocracy without "harlots" at all, but it retains the logic of a scandalous relationship with women. Accusing Obama of "libidinous statecraft," the authors point to Obama's support of birth control in his campaign and his defense of his daughters' right not to bear children as making "a mistake."

Sometimes the critics of the Catholic Church accuse her of being "obsessed with sex," because of her strict moral teachings. The claim is silly on its face. But the enemies of the church—like Obama—reveal their own obsession in manifold ways. From his promotion of Planned Parenthood to his kowtowing support of the Lavender Mafia: it's a prurient politics, a libidinous statecraft.

And now Obamacare will help fund all this filth. Great. Welcome to the American Pornocracy.

Pornocracy here names not a political scandal but the relatively everyday regulation of female sexuality in public. Obamacare, under the guise of funding birth control for "little girls," engages in a form of "libidinous statecraft," where *pornocracy* names the perversion of democracy itself. No one has accused Obama of sexual misconduct. Yet the term *pornocracy* nonetheless circulates as a political structure of accusation that sticks in an abstract way. Obama's daughters, along with nameless "little girls," come to stand in for the harlots here: all are fornicators in need of protection from the president, who is likewise in cahoots with Planned Parenthood and "the Lavender Mafia."

But consider, alongside this right-wing fantasy, how *pornocracy* also circulates within more liberal discourses, where it serves no less as a shorthand for the consumption of female sexuality—only here, the idea is called on to critique capitalism more generally. Chun's book *Control and Freedom: Power and Paranoia in the Age of Fiber Optics* explores the topic of pornography in the digital age. One chapter of this book, "Screening Pornography," contains a section called "Pornocracy," which presents a useful survey of the history of pornography law, commercial speech, and new media forms in the United States. But beyond the section title itself, the word *pornocracy* does not appear in the analysis at all. The term suggestively names the coming together of pornography and democracy in a capitalist state before withholding any explanation or definition of the term. Similarly, Krutnik, in an essay on the commercialization of sexual fantasy, argues that the consumer economy has facilitated "the growth of a 'pornocracy,' where magazines like *Playboy* packaged the female body as a commodity for consumption by the male gaze" (180). The definition appears in an aside, in the middle of a sentence that is otherwise representing Jeffrey Weeks's claim that "sex had for long been something you were. By the 1950's it was also something you could buy, not just in the traditional form (for men) of prostitution, but in the form of glossily marketed fantasy" (23). But Weeks does not use the term "pornocracy" at all in his own analysis. In each of these examples, the word *pornocracy* is invoked as if it had no specific historical referent or that such history was patently obvious.

It is not that Chun, Krutnik, or Weeks has been exactly negligent in failing to account fully for the history of the term they are using. It is, rather, to suggest that the circulation of the term allows it to hover over another peculiar feature of its usage. In addition to operating as a term that misnames the form of rule it claims to identify, *pornocracy* names the perversion of democracy itself.

The refusals and contradictions at the heart of pornocracy—marked by its catachrestic swerve to name what it does not avow, to collapse what it does, and to privilege some sexual forms at the expense of others—continue to haunt public life in the West. The political system conceals within itself a sexist system of sexual commodification that bears down on women and queers and that is fundamentally obfuscated by state and police crackdowns on sex work itself. Nowhere is this haunting more palpable than in queer longings and acts of worldmaking. This haunting both sustains the symbolic political power to rule (concentrating it in the hands of those bodies that conform to our narratives of respectability) and siphons that power away from those bodies Proudhon associates with the harlot, the prostitute, the sex worker. The queer has historically been allied with these figures, not in terms of identity categories, but in terms of lives lived in political depletion. The mass circulation of the term "queer" (often deployed to signify a hipper, cooler version of LGBT identity politics) sometimes conceals from view the historical solidarity of queer life with all that Proudhon groups under the umbrella of those who reign in a pornocracy. While homosexuality may currently enjoy some state recognition, it historically was aligned with promiscuity, perversion, and the exchange of sex for money.

Take the case of the recent rentboy.com scandal. In August 2015, the Department of Homeland Security and the New York City Police raided the offices of rentboy.com, a site that described itself as "the original and world's largest male escort site." Seven employees were arrested because, in the words of Acting U.S. Attorney Kelly T. Currie, "Rentboy.com attempted to present a veneer of legality, when in fact this Internet brothel made millions of dollars from the promotion of illegal prostitution."[9] But as even Currie's statement admits, "The site has disclaimers stating that the advertisements are for companionship and not sexual services." The case turns on what it means for rentboy.com precisely to operate according to the standards of business available to it under conditions of American democracy. The damning details that Currie's press release cites include the fact that the website charges a minimum monthly fee of $59.95 to advertise sexual services, that physical descriptions of the advertisers can be listed, and that from 2010 to 2015, rentboy.com had over $10 million in gross proceeds. Like so many other companies, rentboy.com simply built a (successful) business where others could transact their own business. "Money can't buy you love," the site declares, "but the rest is negotiable." The fact that there was "no legal justification" for this crackdown has ultimately led prosecutors to drop most of the charges in this case. It also raised some political eyebrows. As the *New York Times* pointed out, even if there were credible grounds to think the site's operators were breaking the law, there is "no reasonable justification for devoting significant resources, particularly from an agency charged with protecting America from terrorists, to shut down a company that provided sex workers with a safer alternative to street walking or relying on pimps" ("Homeland").

The rentboy.com scandal reproduces precisely the pornocratic logic of Proudhon's fears. As Lisa Duggan points out in her analysis of the fallout from this scandal, the state, represented by law enforcement officials, engaged in "inflammatory" acts of misreading where an advertisement came to be redescribed as an "Internet brothel" or "racket." Rentboy.com itself did not employ escorts at all. Obfuscation was the name of the legal game: terms like "Internet brothel" and "racket" circulated catachrestically, much as Proudhon circulated the term *pornocracy* to fan the flames of a paranoid fantasy. With rentboy.com, as with Proudhon, sex workers were made the scapegoats for a state (and a version of the public) that protects the privilege of moneyed, straight masculinity.

The paranoid dystopia that Proudhon forecast in the nineteenth century comes closest to its realization not on the horizon of online ads for escorts but, perversely enough, in the backlash against the crackdown itself. It was true that rentboy.com operated within a known best-practices model for the sex work industry. As Duggan points out, "This business model had been developed over many years, and it has been adopted by escorts as one of the safest ways to operate. Offering their time only in ads on the website, escorts negotiate the exact terms of exchange with clients in private. During Rentboy's 19 years of operation, this model was widely considered legal—regardless of any illegal activities of sex workers advertising as escorts." But this virtual shelter that sex workers and their clients created for themselves did not inoculate them from state-sanctioned persecution. That rentboy.com was targeted, to begin with, under the shady auspices of the Department of Homeland Security, suggested that its workers were not even free to be capitalists. The kind of pornocracy that Proudhon feared was not encapsulated in rentboy.com's business model but in public resistance to its being targeted. Before sex workers have any chance at ruling the world, sex work must not only be decriminalized, but de-moralized. High profile cases like rentboy.com are rare compared to the everyday moral policing of sex work by largely disenfranchised women, queers, and transpeople. Duggan argues that cases like rentboy.com can help to mobilize public support for decriminalization, as critics of the case disseminate the policy arguments of organizations such as Amnesty International, the Red Umbrella Project, and the Urban Institute—all of which insist that what sex workers need is not counseling but better working conditions.

Such a shift in public opinion depends, however, on a widespread remobilization of the contradictions in sexual circulation that otherwise hold firmly in place the middle-class domestic fantasy of family life as well as the logic of gendered economic dispossession. Pornocracy's history as catachresis exposes these foundational contradictions at the heart of our narratives about political rule and helps to recognize the occlusions they enact. Recuperating fantasy in the service of recasting pornocracy's phobias is essential to that enterprise. Finding and embracing the bits of cultural life cast off from dominant forms has long been a strategy for sustaining queer subcultures and counterpublics.

Along these same lines, fantasy is essential not just to dismantling the obstacle, but to imagining and expanding the grounds for pornocracy's potential for recasting our political and economic imaginary. Only then might we have a hooker for president.

Natasha Hurley is senior director of the Office of Interdisciplinary Studies and associate professor in the Department of English and Film Studies at the University of Alberta. She is the author of *Circulating Queerness: Before the Gay and Lesbian Novel* (Minnesota, 2018) and coeditor, with Steven Bruhm, of *Curiouser on the Queerness of Children* Minnesota, 2004).

Notes

1. According to Michael Warner in "Queer and Then?" Zoe Leonard "was a member of Fierce Pussy, a lesbian feminist group with roots in Act Up." The poem initially circulated anonymously, on photocopied sheets of paper during the 1992 U.S. presidential primary season.

2. "What capital does to labor, and the State to liberty, the Church does to the spirit" (1851, 271); quoted by Max Nettlau (43–44).

3. For more on papal historians' use of the term *pornocracy,* see Vaerting.

4. In this way, Proudhon's work resonates with Eve Sedgwick's later groundbreaking work on homosocial bonds *Between Men.* See also Gayle Rubin's "The Traffic in Women."

5. Similar arguments have been the common trade of right-wing commentators, particularly evangelical Christians, long after Proudhon. Pat Robertson, for instance, asserted in 1992 that "the feminist agenda is not about equal rights for women. It is about a socialist, anti-family political movement that encourages women to leave their husbands, kill their children, practice witchcraft, destroy capitalism and become lesbians." This statement appeared in a 1992 Iowa fundraising letter opposing a state equal-rights amendment and was cited in the *Washington Post* article "Equal Rights Initiative in Iowa Attacked."

6. See Catherine Breillat's *Pornocracy;* GRS Club's album *Pornocracy;* The Lovely Savalas' album *Pornocracy;* and Enneri Blakka's album *Welcome to Pornocracy.*

7. The song "Pornocracy" is on the album of the same name.

8. Marx wrote in his *Economic and Philosophic Manuscripts* of 1844 that "prostitution is only a *particular* expression of the *general* prostitution of the *laborer*" (133 n.1).

9. The complete statement from the U.S. Attorney's office is available on the U.S. Department of Justice website under the title "Largest Online Male Escort Service Raided."

Works Cited

Anonymous. 2012. "American Pornocracy." Catholicism.org, June 29. http://catholicism.org/american-pornocracy.html.

The Arrogant Sons of Bitches! 2003. *Pornocracy*. Music album.

Breillat, Catherine. 2008. *Pornocracy*. Trans. Paul Buck and Catherine Petit. Los Angeles: Semiotext(e).

Chun, Wendy Hui Kyong. 2006. *Control and Freedom: Power and Paranoia in the Age of Fiber Optics*. Cambridge, Mass.: MIT Press.

Cooper, Kenneth, and Marilee Schwartz. 1992. "Equal Rights Initiative in Iowa Attacked." *Washington Post*, August 23.

Duggan, Lisa. 2016. "What the Pathetic Case against Rentboy.com Says about Sex Work." *Nation*, January 7.

Enneri Blakka. 2011. *Welcome to Pornocracy*. Music album.

GRS Club. 2012. *Pornocracy*. Music album.

Krutnik, Frank. 1995. "The Enterprise of Seduction: Sex and Selling in Lover Come Back." *Journal of Popular Film and Television* 22, no. 4: 180–91.

Hunt, Lynn. 1993. "Pornography and the French Revolution." In *The Invention of Pornography, 1500–1800*. Ed. Lynn Hunt, 301–40. Cambridge, Mass.: MIT Press.

The Lovely Savalas. 2011. *Pornocracy*. Music album.

Marx, Karl. 1964. *Economic and Philosophic Manuscripts of 1844*. Ed. Dirk Struik. New York: International.

McDonald, Christie. 2001. "Changing Stakes: Pornography, Privacy, and the Perils of Democracy." *Yale French Studies* 100:88–115.

McKay, Iain. "Introduction." In *Property is Theft! A Pierre-Joseph Proudhon Anthology*. Ed. Iain McKay, 1–52. Edinburgh: AK Press.

Nettlau, Max. 2000. *A Short History of Anarchism*. Oakland: Freedom Press.

New York Times (editorial). 2015. "Homeland Security's Peculiar Prosecution of Rentboy." August 28.

Proudhon, Pierre-Joseph. 1851. *Les confessions d'un révolutionnaire*. Paris: Garnier.

Proudhon, Pierre-Joseph. 2011a. "What Is Property?" In *Property Is Theft! A Pierre-Joseph Proudhon Reader*. Ed. Iain McKay, 87–138. Oakland: A.K. Press.

Proudhon, Pierre-Joseph. 2011b. "The System of Economic Contradictions." In *Property Is Theft! A Pierre-Joseph Proudhon Reader*. Ed. Iain McKay, 167–256. Oakland: A.K. Press.

Sedgwick, Eve. 1997. *Novel Gazing*. Durham: Duke University Press.

U.S. Department of Justice. 2015. "Largest Online Male Escort Service Raided." August 25. http://www.justice.gov/usao-edny/pr/largest-online-male-escort-service-raided.

Vaerting, Mathilde. 1923. *The Dominant Sex: The Sociology of Sex Differentiation*. Trans. Eden and Cedar Paul. New York: George H. Doran.

Warner, Michael. 2012. "Queer and Then? The End of Queer Theory?" *Chronicle of Higher Education*, January 1. http://chronicle.com/article/QueerThen-/130161/.

"THERE'S PLENTY OF RAPISTS HERE"

"RAPE CULTURE" AND THE REPRESENTATION OF ANENE BOOYSEN'S RAPE IN THE INTERNATIONAL AND SOUTH AFRICAN PRESS

Helen Frost

On February 1, 2013, seventeen-year-old Anene Booysen was found in a construction site in the town of Bredasdorp, South Africa, where she had been gang raped and left to die.[1] Despite the shocking details of Booysen's death, her rape entered into both local and international media for its transnational connection to a similar crime that occurred two months earlier in Delhi, India. In the latter incident, a twenty-three-year-old medical student, Jyoti Singh, was gang raped on a bus in Delhi and later died in hospital. While Singh's death was a sensation in the international media, with "1,515 articles appear[ing] in the United States alone within . . . two month[s]," Booysen's death was generally only given significance through comparisons to the Delhi rape (Roychowdhury, 282). By contrasting the two cases, the international press diagnosed the South African response to Booysen's rape as inadequate when compared to the national outrage that followed Singh's death in India, while at the same time relegating these brutal versions of gendered violence to those other, "less civilized" locales. By analyzing the representation of these crimes in the international media, with a particular emphasis on Booysen's rape, I will show that the concept of *rape culture* is invested with different meanings depending on the situations described and the contexts in and from which the term is mobilized.

Despite its association with the radical feminisms of the 1970s and 1980s, talk of rape culture has regained momentum in the North American public sphere alongside such diverse controversies as Robin Thicke's song "Blurred Lines," the Steubenville rape case, and Todd Akin's infamous comments that "legitimate rape" does not result in pregnancy. While the reactions to and contexts of these crimes and controversies vary, when North Americans talk about rape culture the focus is often on structural issues: modes of representation that facilitate sexual violence, alcohol abuse in high schools and universities, and the failure of people in positions of power to take rape seriously. In contrast, the use of the label "rape culture" to describe contexts in the Global South is invariably linked to shockingly violent crimes.

In North American and European popular discourse, the treatment of women is regularly used to index modernization; for this reason, conversations about so-called rape cultures in the Global South are inevitably intertwined with global circuits of power. The treatment of the Singh and Booysen rapes in the international press reflects Gayatri Spivak's well-known claim illuminating the "collective fantasy" of colonialism: "White men are saving brown women from brown men" (48). For Spivak, the Global North reinforces its self-fashioning as the protector of global well-being by considering the "third-world woman" to be in need of protection from "her own kind" (50–52). Taking Spivak's claim as my starting point, I am interested in how the rubric of rape culture circulates and accrues different currency depending on context, with the potential of producing a disciplinary gaze that revives colonial stereotypes of brown and black men as unruly and violent, and displaces more extreme forms of gendered violence onto "less civilized" countries.

While rape culture as a concept finds its provenance in second-wave feminism, the dynamics that form our understanding of it have a much longer history. In his meditation on marriage and indictment of emergent women's movements, *Pornocracy, or Women in Modern Times,* Pierre-Joseph Proudhon describes men and women as characterized by "force" and "beauty" respectively. Proudhon's argument reflects these beliefs about female vulnerability, while it also performs a desire to police women's emancipation by restricting their sexual and intellectual "promiscuity," marked by his term *pornocracy*. Proudhon is troubled by what he sees as the intellectual equivalent of sexual promiscuity: women entering into social and intellectual spheres usually preserved for men, "salons, . . . academies, . . . bars, etc." For Proudhon, the woman who refuses to be defined purely in terms of "beauty" and enters into the realm of "force" threatens traditional conceptions of the family and of marriage; she consequently disrupts society as a whole, of which the family is the embryo. The term *pornocracy* responds to the perceived threat of gender equality and registers the desire, reflected in Proudhon's own writing, to regulate female circulation and facilitate male circulation by reinforcing male dominance. Indeed, Proudhon's fantasies of control are consonant with contemporary forms of male domination, epitomized by men's rights organizations and other such groups, which reflect anxieties spurred by women's increased freedoms.

Importantly, Proudhon's theory reminds us that fantasies of control and containment of female sexuality are seldom exclusively about sexuality; rather, as Michel Foucault has famously observed, sexuality is "an especially dense transfer point for relations of power" (103). Proudhon's obsession with protecting marriage against the changes heralded by women's emancipation also registers his concern over the "atomizing" force of "civil and commercial society" and the "social and economic malaise" of his day (Copley, 194). For this reason, the charge of *pornocracy* in Proudhon's argument responds to women entering spheres traditionally barred to them and reflects his concern that the breakdown of the unequal yet balanced "dualism" of marriage would create an unjust society defined by a "surfeit of consumption" and "the most degrading servitude." While, in Proudhon's terms, *pornocracy* refers to a social order (heralded by female emancipation) defined by "arbitrary power, economic speculation, [and] concubinage," I intend to use his term not only to describe the fantasy of containment that I see in his paradoxical articulation of gender inequality but also to establish how anxieties about pornocracy are used to validate the necessity of already-existing hierarchies in the present day.

The deployment (and co-option) of feminist discourses in the international media to describe "rape cultures" in the Global South reflects colonial imaginaries that I see as analogous to Proudhon's anxious pornocracy fantasy. The articles on Singh's and Booysen's rapes that I analyze below view men of color in a manner that is analogous to Proudhon's understanding of white women who circulate in public. Both are seen as potentially dangerous and even disruptive to an ordered society. While Proudhon accuses white women of sexual lasciviousness in order to contain their circulation in public and fortify his own privilege, for the authors of the articles discussed below, men of color are figured as rapists in order to reaffirm the importance of liberal democracy as a guarantor of gender equality. The effect of this popular articulation of "rape culture" feminism is to establish not only the boundary but also the hierarchy between "us" (the rational, Western subject) and "them" (the unruly and violent black or brown man or the passive and embattled black or brown woman).

My use of Proudhon's term draws on two concepts from critical race and postcolonial theory: Hortense Spillers's notion of the *pornotrope* and Anne McClintock's *porno-tropics*. In brief, Spillers's "pornotrope" describes meanings imposed on the black slave's fungible body, whose corporeality becomes the "source of irresistible, destructive sexuality" while it is, at the same time, reduced to "a thing, becoming *being* for the captor" (67). Spillers's notion of the pornotrope encompasses both the sexualized meanings imposed on the slave's body and its "sheer physical powerlessness" (67). The "porno" in McClintock's "porno-tropics" also refers to the nexus of desire and hyper-sexualization imposed by colonial imaginaries, but, in this case, it is used to describe the European projection of "its forbidden sexual desires and fears" onto colonial landscapes (22). In my deployment, the term *pornocracy* designates an imaginary that is used to circumscribe men of color through narratives of deficient masculinity turned violent. Here, the term is intended to echo the *porno* in *pornotrope* and *porno-tropics* to signify the colonial imaginaries evoked by Spillers and McClintock rather than the prostitution Proudhon had in mind.

As I have noted, the international press's interest in Booysen's rape was sparked by its likeness to Singh's rape: both women were gang raped, disemboweled, and left for dead.[2] By considering Booysen's case alongside the Indian case, the Western media was preoccupied with whether South Africa would also have its "Delhi moment" (Watson and Lalu, 17). Unlike the widespread demonstrations and anger at the failure of police, politicians, and senior officials to secure women's safety that followed Singh's death in India (2),[3] responses to Booysen's death in South Africa were more disparate. There were small-scale protests in Bredasdorp and Cape Town, public statements were issued from prominent political organizations and the office of the president, and the hashtag #stoprape trended on South African Twitter. Andrew Harding describes South Africa's reaction to Booysen's gang rape as "[little] more than a collective shrug" in contrast to Indians' "re-examin[ation of] their society" (2013a). By juxtaposing the two cases, the international press was able to correlate racialized masculinities with violence while simultaneously interpreting South Africa's perceived apathy about gender violence as a resistance to Western modernity.

Out of the twenty-five international articles I sourced, about a quarter explicitly defined South Africa as having a rape culture, or "a culture of sexual violence," and the remainder presented South Africa as a place where rape had "lost the power to shock," reaching "epidemic" proportions and becoming "normalized" (Smith 2013). *Toronto Star*'s Erin Cornway-Smith claimed that "in South Africa, rape is so common it barely makes the news," and even the most shocking crimes, like "rapes of elderly women and babies," receive minimal attention. Another article claims that the "history and culture of South Africa" designates it as "a deeply patriarchal society that devalues crimes against women" (Polgreen). By describing crimes that are sharply distinguished from the everyday violence often associated with rape culture in the Global North, and by representing a national public indifferent to violence against women, journalists define the problem of rape in South Africa as distinct from gender violence in other societies.

The term "rape culture" refers to "a complex of beliefs that encourages male sexual aggression and supports violence against women" (Buchwald et al.). Rape came onto the public agenda in the 1970s through the hard work of feminists who argued that it was a rampant form of violence inherent to patriarchy rather than an infrequent crime committed by strangers. Although different interpretations of the causes of sexual violence circulated at this time—considering it to be either an exertion of power distinct from sex or inherent to the structure of heterosexual sex itself—second-wave feminism's emphasis on rape as paradigmatic of male dominance placed this crime at the center of the feminist movement (MacKinnon, 646). "Rape culture" emerged as a strategic framework to describe entrenched ideas that facilitated gender violence. For feminists, rape culture is underwritten by myths that construct men as agents and women as the "objects of violence" (Marcus, 291, 393). These myths "deny or reduce perceived injury" while blaming "victims for their own victimization" (Burt, 21), and they contribute to the "social control of women" by encouraging a disproportionate fear of violent crime (Madriz, 2). In this context, "rape culture" refers to the conditions of a society that tacitly accepts rape. Such conditions, in the support they give to gender violence, potentially limit women's actions while structuring masculinity as the agency that exerts violence and domination.

In her criticism of rape's role as a central trope in American feminisms, Sabine Sielke argues that "images and figures of sexual violence have repeatedly served to establish and subsequently stabilize parameters of difference such as gender, race, ethnicity, class, and nation" (2004, 371). For Sielke, the "rhetoric of rape" is a discourse through which differences are ascribed: "Victims and violators [are] othered, set off, while the subject who assigns difference remains unmarked and unlimited in his possibilities" (373). The "rhetoric of rape," or, in this case, the rubric of rape culture, not only describes the naturalization of sexual violence against women but is haunted by the history of rape's circulation in discourse. This includes those narratives that designate racial difference through depictions of black men as sexual predators.

Through the interconnected history of colonialism and the transatlantic slave trade, "Western social thought" came to "associat[e] Blackness" with an imagined uncivilized, wild sexuality and "uses this association as one lynchpin of racial difference" (Collins, 27). While perceptions of "black hypersexuality" have occupied a "prominent place in American science, popular culture, religious traditions, and state policies" from slavery onward (63), similar tropes figuring black men as "potential rapists" and black women's bodies as sites of "unrestrained sexuality" took hold in settler colonies such as South Africa. These overdetermined images of hypersexual black men were amplified through rape narratives that indexed culturally and historically specific anxieties. As Sielke has observed, the rise of the image of the black man as "moral monster" after the abolition of slavery in the southern United States dramatized "cultural anxieties" over newly free black men and established the "dominant line within an American rhetoric of rape" that often continues to be "confirmed by feminism itself" (2002, 34). Similarly, historiography on rape in South Africa has argued that "black peril" narratives surfaced in times of crisis, where the efficacy of colonial rule and the social relations that sustained it were threatened (Scully, 338).[4] In apartheid-era South

Africa, protecting "the white body from sexual threats became synonymous with safeguarding the purity and health of the white nation" (Graham, 9). Here, anxiety over the security of white supremacy—often translated into a "medicalized discourse" of racial purity—was transferred onto white women's bodies (9). In both the American and South African examples, rape narratives that catalogued racist anxieties effectively criminalized black men, obscured the history of violence of white men against women of color, and justified the necessity of white dominance.

In contemporary discourse, these colonial imaginaries are redeployed ostensibly in the protection of mistreated women in the Global South, but with the effect of reestablishing the moral superiority of the Western subject. The international press used Booysen's and Singh's narratives to establish national, cultural, and racial difference, while the Western "subject who assign[ed] difference remain[ed] unmarked and unlimited in his possibilities" (Sielke 2004, 373). Emer O'Toole describes Western journalists' depictions of Singh's rape as "using the event to simultaneously demonize Indian society, lionise [their] own, and minimize the enormity of Western rape culture." As O'Toole suggests, the international press's description of rape in India figures brown men as dangerous while displacing concern over violent Western masculinities onto an attractive scapegoat. By focusing on the problem of certain ethnic masculinities in the representation of Singh's and Booysen's rapes, British and North American journalists were able to draw a clear line between controlled and rational Western men, on the one hand, and, on the other, racialized men in India and South Africa who were interpreted as the product of *cultures* that rape.

Gethin Chamberlain's article in the *Guardian,* entitled "If Girls Look Sexy, Boys Will Rape," epitomizes the dynamics of displacement described by O'Toole. The article's title, which comes from a series of interviews conducted with six Indian men, makes a neat equation between female desirability and uncontrollable male sexuality, thereby drawing on a familiar cultural and ideological repertoire that figures brown men as governed by their sexual urges. Chamberlain describes the interviews as revealing a "disturbing mindset" that he ascribes to Indian masculinity in general. The interviews do reveal problematic tendencies to, for instance, blame women for men's misconduct or describe male sexual desire as uncontrollable. At the same time, quoting these opinions reinforces a series of colonial stereotypes, as the following passage illustrates:

> Plenty of Indian men have joined the recent demonstrations. Plenty of Indian men are committed to the cause of women's rights. But this discussion revealed the deep moral conservatism of some young Indian males, coupled with confusion about gender roles in a society where economic modernization is outstripping social attitudes.

While Chamberlain admits that Indian men did join the protests against gender violence, it is the six men who exhibit a "moral conservatism" who are allowed to represent Indian masculinity and its discomfort with "modernization." In this light, Chamberlain uses the treatment of women to shore up his "position of cultural superiority," thereby reinforcing the legitimacy of his depiction of Indian society "as violent, aggressive, and hence primitive" (Kapur, 10–11; see also Roychowdhury, 282).

Following Booysen's rape, *Sky News* conducted a similar "study" published under the title "Shocking Attitude to Rape in South Africa." This investigation took the form of an "impromptu" survey of thirty-eight men in a township near Johannesburg. As in the *Guardian*'s article, the *Sky News* piece admits to being "unscientific" but claims to give a "snapshot of [South African] men's views on women."[5] In each case, the author relies on the assumption that these small surveys will seem credible because they reinforce familiar tropes of racialized masculinity. Just as the *Guardian* describes its interviews' content as "alarming," *Sky News* calls its interviews "extraordinary and shocking" and warns delicate readers against reading on. The responses to the survey are reprinted in full on the *Sky News* website as a series of sensationally violent stories, with no acknowledgement of the economic or sociohistorical conditions of this "South African township." Unlike Chamberlain's admission that there are at least some Indian men who reject gender violence, no similar allowance is made for South African men, who are depicted as unchecked and unrepentant rapists. The representation of African and Indian men in these two articles reproduces what one might call a pornocratic logic—not in Proudhon's sense, where the term is used to delimit dangerous female bodies and their circulation in public, but to describe how the presumed sexual deviance of black bodies is used to justify already-existing global power disparities in the name of women's freedom.

These articles not only reproduce well-worn colonial tropes of black and brown masculinity; they also invite the Western reader to imaginatively insert herself into the rape scene. In Chamberlain's article, the menace of black and brown men is amplified through the imagined body of a white woman, in this case a Western tourist: "Foreigners thinking of visiting India—particularly young women—will find these views not only repulsive, but dangerous." The *Toronto Star*'s piece, entitled "Being a Woman in South Africa Is Enough to Get You Raped, Killed," makes a similar invitation. In the article, which describes South Africa as a place "where simply being female spells premonition for attack," Catherine Porter quotes the popular statistic that 27.6 percent of South African men admit to committing rape. Porter observes, "That means if you are in an elevator with four men, one is statistically a rapist. Imagine then, squeezing onto a bus in South Africa." Both Chamberlain's and Porter's articles encourage an identification that displaces the black female body and refigures intraracial rape within the familiar colonial scene of interracial rape. In these examples, the vulnerable tourist or Western female reader becomes the vehicle for projected anxieties over race and gender, effectively reinforcing an image of Indian and South African men as "repulsive," "frightening," and as the *rightful* objects of Western fear.

What modes of erasure are produced by recasting the event of intraracial rape within familiar colonial economies of desire? While it is clear that the scenes outlined above use the white woman's body to amplify the perceived danger of racialized men, they also invite the white reader into close proximity with the victim of violence and her disordered body. A mixture of fear and desire, distance and proximity, marks the scenes described above, evoking both the specter of unruly black masculinity and sympathy for the imagined victim, in whom the Western reader is encouraged to see herself. To understand this enticement for white women to appropriate the position of victimhood, I will use the term "pornotropical imaginary." Here, I am not simply drawing on my understanding of Proudhon's deployment of the term to contain threatening women—who seem as much objects of fascination as of anxiety—in order to secure a gendered hierarchy. Instead,

I am referring to the projection of Western desires and fears onto black subjects who are treated analogously to the women in Proudhon's imaginary. In the examples above, the scene of sexual threat, as a site of both fascination and fear, encourages white women to secure themselves against dangerous black men, and it valorizes Western liberal democracy as a necessary regulatory force.

Chamberlain's and Porter's articles encourage identification, and in so doing, they evoke a scene of intimacy whereby the real violence to black and brown women is supplanted by a fantasy of eroticized danger. In her discussion of the Canadian reaction to the Rwandan genocide, Sherene Razak observes that the "pain and suffering of Black people can become sources of moral authority and pleasure, obscuring in the process our own participation in the violence that is done to them" (376). Razak's diagnosis of the role of "pleasure" and desire in Westerners' consumption of the other's suffering is significant to a *pornotropical imaginary* that allows the Western subject to shore up "moral authority" through sympathetic identification while erasing historical culpability. In her unflinching analysis of feminist academic sympathy in relation to female Holocaust survivors' testimony, Karyn Ball argues that such sympathy "entails a fantasy-prone mode of transferential identification with the other" (206). Sympathy and fantasy, for Ball, are modes of "visual symbolization" that draw on a "repertoire of images" whereby the "compassionate imaginary shares a permeable border with unconscious wishes" (209). In Chamberlain's and Porter's articles, the Western reader is invited to draw on a "repertoire of images" ranging from the virile yet dangerous man of color to the abject and powerless "third-world woman." At the same time, this reader displaces the black body in order to make black suffering intelligible. While this "transferential identification" allows for white sympathy, it does so by mobilizing an imaginary that enables the Western subject to secure her desire for "moral authority" through a pleasurable sympathetic overidentification with the plight of the "third-world woman."

That rape in South Africa is controversial can be attested in the explosive public encounter between white feminist Charlene Smith and former president Thabo Mbeki in 2001. In 1999, Smith, a journalist, wrote of her rape by a black man in her home in order to highlight South Africa's ill-equipped criminal justice and medical system.[6] Smith was particularly concerned by the difficulties she encountered procuring AZT, the anti-retroviral drug. As an antirape campaigner, Smith pointed out the venality of a system where women and girls are not only threatened by sexual violence but, under Mbeki's Aids denialism, could not easily access those drugs that might protect them from contracting the virus. Smith's tone-deaf account in the *Washington Post* of the role of tradition, religion, and "culture" in the high incidence of rape in South Africa elicited an angry response from the former president, who wrote of Smith that she was "sufficiently brave, or blinded by racist rage . . . to make the deeply offensive statement that rape is an endemic feature of African society" (cited in Graham, 3). This frequently referenced encounter reflects the difficulty of addressing sexual violence in the South African public sphere, where openly discussing rape may, indeed, be interpreted as racist.

As Shireen Hassim observes, in South African public discourse, "masculinity elides into race and race elides into coloniality rather too neatly" (2014a, 173). Hassim argues that centering conversations about rape on black masculinity deflects attention from uncomfortable conversations about the relationship between black men and black women, potentially silencing black women's experiences of violence. Hassim questions this "flattened-out" approach to racism that interprets all critiques of black masculinity as complicit in colonial logics, arguing that this ignores the "entanglements of race and gender." While the co-option of feminist perspectives in the international coverage of Booysen's rape often ignored uneven global distributions of power and histories of colonialism in favor of a limited vision of gender equality,[7] in South Africa race is often evoked in order to foreclose public acknowledgments of gender inequality. As Hassim asserts, while feminist arguments must avoid "re-inscrib[ing] a white gaze on the body of black men," they cannot circumscribe their antirape activism for fear of public censure. In Smith's case, while she unintentionally reinforced images of African masculinity and culture as less modern and more prone to violence, reflecting liberal feminism's perpetual blindness to the intersections of race and gender, her censure by Mbeki provided a powerful deterrent to feminists who might speak out against rape in more nuanced terms.

In South Africa, where a woman is more likely to be raped than to be literate, and where one in three women will be raped in her lifetime, it is unsurprising that public conversation about rape indexes broader anxieties over the state of the postapartheid nation (Moffett, 129). Despite the end of apartheid, South Africa remains a deeply unequal society affected by "poverty, . . . unemployment [and] HIV/AIDS," with 24 percent of black households compared to 1.8 percent of white households living on approximately $450 or less a month in 2011 (Statistics South Africa 2012a, 12; Beall, Gelb, and Hassim, 682). John and Jean Comaroff observe that discourse around criminality in South Africa "measure[s] a wide range of insecurities in a world of changing power relations" (2006a, 217). The South African public's "obsession" with crime and lawlessness calls into question a telos of modernization defined as the expansion of the state's capacity to "regulate everyday existence and routinely to enforce punishment" (Comaroff and Comaroff 2006b, 276). Public discussion of crime allows for contemporary South Africans to demand that the state secure order, and for certain parties this might mean securing privilege. At the same time, while Comaroff and Comaroff tacitly suggest that it is primarily the largely white economic elite that exhibits a disproportionate anxiety over crime and desire for social order, Franco Barchiesi shows that conflicting desires for "order" also characterize the precariously employed classes.

Given the scope of this essay, I cannot do justice to the complexity of Barchiesi's argument; however, his work does enrich an account of South Africa's anxieties over social disorder. Barchiesi shows that the post-1994 government's focus on providing dignified work "emancipated from shame and violations of the past" as an avenue for "democratic nation building" came to characterize the process "through which the state could selectively incorporate, co-opt, marginalize, or disqualify specific social claims" (4). By associating work with citizenship, the ANC government, and the Mbeki administration in particular, came to prioritize entrepreneurial initiative over public programs, configuring employment as the remedy to "unruly[ness]" and a way to produce modernity, discipline, and self-sufficiency (92). Although the government's discourse emphasized the market's "socially equalizing role" in rewarding industry and entrepreneurship, the forms of work available to the majority continue to be low paying and contingent (73).

According to Barchiesi, "Disenchantment with precarious employment" is transposed "into a revanchist image of order and purity" (232). The loss of the prospect of "decent" or dignified work, Barchiesi argues, results in a male working-class melancholia that translates into a desire to reestablish "ideal social orders" such as "age hierarchies" and gendered "domestic roles" (225, 232). In both the public obsession with crime described by Comaroff and Comaroff and the male working-class melancholia described by Barchiesi, the *tsotsi*—the young black urban gangster—is a figure for anxiety over social disorder, who refuses gainful employment and preys on the "productive members of society" (231).

In this light, it seems that public discourse around criminality transposes working-class men's anxieties over access to the promises of the new dispensation and the desire of a largely white economic elite to fortify its social position into concerns over social and sexual disorder and "unruly" black youths. While public representations of rape mirror these anxieties, we acquire a better understanding of the economy of rape talk in South Africa if we consider the social realities of sexual violence. The Women's Charter for Effective Equality (1994) has strongly influenced both the post-1994 constitution and the ANC government's approach to women's rights. Hassim and Meintjes observe that the heritage of the Women's Charter, with its articulated "nostalgia for the clear and unambiguous elements of the modernist, liberal, feminist project" (Manicom, 21), has been the inclusion of a few privileged women into institutional hierarchies, without amending ingrained attitudes towards gender (Meintjes, 112; Hassim 2014b, 17). Moreover, while gender and racial equality have been enshrined in the postapartheid constitution, black women remain disproportionately affected by the racialization of poverty and are more likely to be uneducated and unemployed than men (Beall, Hassim, and Todes, 683; Mills, 82).[8] The social vulnerability of black and brown women in South Africa is exacerbated by the high incidence of gender violence.

Although the Smith–Mbeki scandal highlighted the public's concern with interracial rape, sexual violence in South Africa is largely intraracial and intracommunal. Since the majority of South Africans are black, unsurprisingly most women raped in South Africa are also black (Seedat et al, 1013). During apartheid, the white supremacist government held a "monopoly on political violence," while "intimate violence," especially within black township communities, was "a kind of 'visible invisibility,' a public secret and an object of taboo" (Morris, 59). "Intimate violence" of this kind was largely ignored and rarely prosecuted unless it was interracial and the victim was a white woman. In contrast, discussions of sexual violence have proliferated in post-apartheid media, and the high incidence of rape is often "read as evidence of the new polity's failure to extend the rule of law (even into the domestic sphere)" (57). Rape narratives enter into South African public discourse as part of the broader social concern with criminality, yet the sexual valence of the crime allows it to become particularly freighted with anxiety over the moral state of the nation and the family.

As Rosalind Morris observes, "An analysis of violence and its significations is not the same as an analysis of motives or intentions" (58). In the previous section, it became clear that international articles interpreted rape in South Africa as a problem of black masculinity, effectively reinforcing global hierarchies by indexing "progress" and "modernization" through the treatment of women. The South African media was similarly concerned with narratives of progress; however, for these articles, rape became a conduit for anxiety over social and sexual disorder. In a cartoon released in the aftermath of Booysen's death, depicting her as the ghost of a girl in a school uniform, Zapiro (Jonathan Shapiro) diagnoses the public responses to her murder as "the usual lip service" and frames the rape within a broader context of political decline, signaled by the ironic question: "The constitution. How the hell can it help you?" Similarly, Ranjeni Munusamy's article "The Agony of South Africa's Daughter Anene Booysen" lists a series of political misdeeds and failures alongside Booysen's death, suggesting that "South Africa seems to be reacting to rape in the same way as other forms of exploitation. . . . We are pounded daily with the rape of the public purse and the political elite using their positions to feather their own nests." In Munusamy's statement, the nation is rendered feminine and passive in the face of gender violence, corruption, and social insecurity; it is also vulnerable to a kleptocratic state's phallic plundering. As in the international media's representation of the rape, Booysen herself is displaced, in this case allowing for the reading public to imagine itself as violated. Here, rape is used to figure society as corrupted from within by a political elite who pillages the nation for individual gain. Published in what might be considered the elite press, Munusamy's and Zapiro's responses to Booysen's rape register concerns with failed governance and disorder so as to make a plea to a neoliberal state to reestablish social stability.

Relying on normative notions of the social good, rape narratives in the South African media tend to identify poor and young unemployed men with a threat to social order, while at the same time they do little to disrupt those gender hierarchies that figure women's lives as less valuable (Morris, 60). Like the constitutional changes that formally empower women in the public sphere but do little to threaten established gender dynamics in the private sphere, these public rejections of rape are less about women's rights to autonomy over their bodies than they are concerned with a perceived threat to the coherence of the nation state from within (as political corruption) and without (in the form of the criminal youth). As columnist Rebecca Davis notes, Booysen remained "a cipher" throughout the coverage of this case, "a cautionary tale; a glimpse into the darkness at the margins and the center of our fractured society." Sarah Murphy, drawing on Mark Seltzer's conceptualization of "wound culture," argues that "the figure of the rape victim, particularly in so far as she can be represented as a 'torn and exposed individual,' has become a principal figure of a sociality that can only be constituted as a wound" (76). As the above examples have testified, rather than as a "lively 17-year-old," Booysen was identified through descriptions of her torn body, which were, in turn, used to figure the South African public as injured and "inured" to violence, as "wounded" by corruption and criminality.

In both international and local accounts, Booysen's death was used to tell distinctly colonial and postcolonial narratives of modernity and progress. In the North American and British press, the treatment of women was used as a marker of modernity. South Africa and India were *pornotroped* as *rape cultures* in order to evoke a vision of the Western subject/reader as reasonable, sympathetic, and intolerant to gender inequality. International articles—often authored by men—were written in the mode of popular (post)feminist discourse. Within this discourse, the resurgence of rape culture talk runs the risk of being dissipated and transmuted through neoliberal logics. The traces of these logics in popular feminism are evident in its focus on the individual (specifically individual choice) over structural inequalities. In the case of the examples discussed above, it also advocates for white women's preservation, protection, and even elaboration of self via *pornotropical imaginaries,* at the expense of a historical understanding of global asymmetries of power. While popular feminism may give white Western women access to modes of self-fashioning under the promise of individual choice, the black woman's body, by contrast, is not defined by choice; rather, it works as a cipher for abject and injured subjectivity.

In South Africa, where languages of "anti-racism" may be used as "rhetorical devices against the claims of the rights of women to personhood and autonomy," as scholars, we must be equally wary of perpetuating colonial logics, on the one hand, and on the other hand, of silencing the experiences of black rape survivors (Hassim 2014a, 178). In the international media, Booysen's and Singh's rape narratives slipped too easily into familiar colonial tropes, simultaneously evoking white anxieties and foreclosing the possibility of discussing intraracial rape outside of racist imaginaries. In South Africa, Booysen's mutilated body was used as a vehicle to configure the nation as a wounded site of social and economic disorder. Rather than focusing on the painful irony of postapartheid South Africa—that, although black women actively participated in the struggle for liberation, escalating violence against them from within their own communities has foreclosed their access to freedom (Samuelson, 129)—these accounts of Booysen's rape demanded that the patriarchal state reinforce order. In both cases, the treatment of sexual violence in the media reestablished notions of liberal progress at the expense of a nuanced consideration of the women these articles claim to support. Booysen's case in particular reminds us that, as feminists, we must move beyond a "rhetoric of rape," to use Sielke's phrase, one that uses rape narratives as a cipher for national anxieties or as a means to assign difference, in order to find new approaches to address intraracial rape in South Africa.

Helen Frost recently completed her doctoral research in the Department of English and Film Studies at the University of Alberta, where her dissertation focused on postapartheid rape narratives. Her research interests include the turn to affect theory, the genealogy of feminist responses to rape, and South African print culture.

Notes

1. This paper's title comes from the statement made by a South African man in Andrew Harding's "Will South Africans Ever Be Shocked by Rape?"

2. Despite their likeness, the two cases are notably differentiated by the socioeconomic status of the victims. Booysen had not completed her secondary education and worked as a cleaner. Her limited opportunities and poverty mirrored the social realities experienced by the black majority. In contrast, Singh was an aspirational figure and emblem of class mobility. As a medical student, she was represented as "a decidedly modern Indian woman" (Roychowdhury, 283). The differences between the two women's class positions and the distinct forms of identification they evoked may explain the divergent national responses to the two rapes.

3. This paper will not focus on the actual similarities and differences between rape or the public response to it in India and South Africa. Instead, I am concerned with how the Western media mobilized *perceived* differences in order to tell a particular narrative about sexual violence in South Africa.

4. The "black peril" typically refers to a period of white "social hysteria" that took hold in South Africa from 1890 to 1914 but continued to circulate in discourse beyond this period (Graham, 4).

5. By only conducting these interviews in a largely black township, the article tacitly suggests that white South Africans are exempt from these views.

6. Despite substantial reforms to South African rape law, culminating in the December 2007 *Sexual Offences Act*, the general acceptance of rape myths persists within the judicial system (Mills, 81).

7. For examples of this decontextualized coverage of Booysen's rape, see Porter; Smith; Miller; Breslaw. For a significant counterexample, see Hengeveld.

8. According to Statistics South Africa (2012b) in both 2001 and 2011, women were more likely to be unemployed than men; this disparity was particularly marked among Indian/Asian and Black African population groups (31).

Works Cited

Ball, Karyn. 2008. *Disciplining the Holocaust*. Albany: State University of New York Press.

Barchiesi, Franco. 2011. *Precarious Liberation: Workers, the State, and Contested Social Citizenship in Postapartheid South Africa*. Albany: State University of New York Press.

Beall, Jo, Stephen Gelb, and Shireen Hassim. 2005. "Fragile Stability: State and Society in Democratic South Africa." *Journal of Southern African Studies* 31, no. 4: 681–700.

Beall, Jo, Shireen Hassim, and Alison Todes. 2011. "We Are All Radical Feminists Now: Reflections on 'A Bit on the Side.'" *Transformation* 75:95–106.

Breslaw, Anna. 2013. "Brutal Western Cape Gang Rape Forces South Africa to Examine Gender Violence Epidemic." *Jezebel* 2, no. 9. http://jezebel.com/5982963/brutal-western-cape-gangrape-forces-south-africa-to-examine-gender-violence-epidemic.

Buchwald, Emile, Pamela R. Fletcher, Martha Roth. 2005. Introduction to *Transforming a Rape Culture* Rev. ed. Ed. Emile Buchwald Pamela R. Fletcher, Martha Roth, xii–xvii. Minneapolis: Milkweed Editions.

Burt, Martha R. 1980. "Cultural Myths and Supports for Rape." *Journal of Personality and Social Psychology* 38, no. 7: 217–30.

Chamberlain, Gethin. 2015. "'If Girls Look Sexy, Boys will Rape': Is This What Indian Men Really Believe?" *Guardian,* February 24. http://www.theguardian.com/world/2013/mar/24/india-rape-disturbing-attitudes-men.

Collins, Patricia Hill. 2004. *Black Sexual Politics.* New York: Routledge.

Comaroff, Jean, and John Comaroff. 2006a. "Figuring Crime: Quantifacts and the Production of the Un/Real." *Public Culture* 18, no. 1: 208–46.

Comaroff, Jean, and John Comaroff. 2006b. "Criminal Obsessions, after Foucault: Postcoloniality, Policing, and the Metaphysics of Disorder." In *Law and Disorder in the Postcolony.* Ed. Jean Comaroff and John Comaroff, 273–98. Chicago: University of Chicago Press.

Copley, Anthony. 1989. "Pierre-Joseph Proudhon: A Reassessment of His Role as a Moralist." *French History* 3, no. 2: 194–221.

Cornway-Smith, Erin. 2013. "South Africa's Gang Rape a Symbol of a Nation's Problem." *Toronto Star,* February 11. https://www.thestar.com/news/world/2013/02/11/south_africa_gang_rape_a_symbol_of_nations_problem.html.

Davis, Rebecca. 2013. "Daily Maverick's SA Person(s) of the Year 2013: Anene Booysen and Reeva Steenkamp." *Daily Maverick,* December 13. http://www.dailymaverick.co.za/article/2013-12-13-daily-mavericks-sa-persons-of-the-year2013-anene-booysen-and-reeva-steenkamp/#.VWnv7NNViko.

Foucault, Michel. 1976. *The History of Sexuality: Volume 1.* Trans. Robert Hurley. London: Penguin Books.

Graham, Lucy Valerie. 2012. *State of Peril: Race and Rape in South African Literature.* New York: Oxford University Press.

Harding, Andrew. 2013a. "Will South Africans Ever Be Shocked by Rape?" *BBC News,* January 10. http://www.bbc.com/news/world-africa-20971240.

Harding, Andrew. 2013b. "South Africa Mourns Gang Rape Victim." *Al Jazeera,* February 7. http://www.aljazeera.com/news/africa/2013/02/201328171132262482.html.

Hassim, Shireen. 2014a. "Violent Modernity: Gender, Race and Bodies in Contemporary South African Politics." *Politikon* 41, no. 2: 167–82.

Hassim, Shireen. 2014b. "Texts and Tests of Equality: The Women's Charters and the Demand for Equality in South African Political History." *Agenda* 28, no. 2: 7–18.

Hengeveld, Maria. 2013. "Race, Class, Masculinities and Violence against Women in South Africa." *Feminist Wire,* March 17. http://thefeministwire.com/2013/03/race-class-masculinities-and-violence-against-women-in-south-africa/.

Kapur, Ratna. 2014. "Brutalized Bodies and Sexy Dressing on the Indian Street." *Signs* 40, no. 1: 9–14.

MacKinnon, Catherine. 1983. "Feminism, Marxism, Method, and the State: Toward Feminist Jurisprudence." *Signs* 8, no. 4 (Summer): 635–58.

Madriz, Esther. 1997. *Nothing Bad Happens to Good Girls: Fear of Crime in Women's Lives.* Berkeley: University of California Press.

Manicom, Linzi. 2005. "Constituting 'Women' as Citizens: Ambiguities in the Making of Gendered Political Subjects in Post-apartheid South Africa." In *(Un)thinking Citizenship: Feminist Debates in Contemporary South Africa.* Ed. Amanda Gouws, 21–52. Aldershot: Ashgate.

Marcus, Sharon. 1992. "Fighting Bodies, Fighting Words: A Theory and Politics of Rape Prevention." *Feminists Theorize the Political.* Ed. Judith Butler and Joan W. Scott, 385–403. New York: Routledge.

McClintock, Ann. 1995. *Imperial Leather: Race, Gender and Sexuality in the Colonial Context.* London: Routledge.

Meintjes, Sheila. 2011. "Reflection: The Women's Struggle for Equality during South Africa's Transition to Democracy." *Transformation: Critical Perspectives on Southern Africa* 75:107–15.

Miller, Daniel. 2013. "The Gang Rape That Horrified South Africa." *Daily Mail,* February 12. http://www.dailymail.co.uk/news/article-2277543/The-gang-rape-horrified-South-Africa-Girl17-mutilated-death-dumped-building-site.html.

Mills, Shereen W. 2009–10. "Consent and Coercion in the Law of Rape in South Africa: A Feminist Transformative Approach." *Canadian Women's Studies* 28, no. 1 (Fall/Winter): 81–89.

Moffett, Helen. 2006. "'These Women They Force Us to Rape Them': Rape as Narrative of Social Control in Post-apartheid South Africa." *Journal of Southern African Studies* 32, no. 1: 129–44.

Morris, Rosalind C. 2006. "The Mute and the Unspeakable: Political Subjectivity, Violent Crime, and 'the Sexual Thing' in a South African Mining Community." In *Law and Disorder in the Postcolony.* Ed. Jean Comaroff and John Comaroff, 57–101. Chicago: University of Chicago Press.

Munusamy, Ranjeni. 2013. "The Agony of South Africa's Daughter Anene Booysen: The Agony of South Africa." *Daily Maverick,* February 8. https://www.dailymaverick.co.za/article/2013-02-08-the-agony-of-south-africas-daughter-anene-booysen-the-agony-of-south-africa/#.WzPvhtJKg2w .

Murphy, Sarah. 2007. "Traumatizing Feminism: Prevention Discourse and the Subject of Sexual Violence." In *Traumatizing Theory: The Cultural Politics of Affect in and beyond Psychoanalysis.* Ed. Karyn Ball, 67–101. New York: Other Press.

O'Toole, Emer. 2013. "Delhi Gang-Rape: Look Westward in Disgust." *Guardian,* January 1. http://www.theguardian.com/commentisfree/2013/jan/01/delhi-rape-damini.

Polgreen, Lydia. 2013. "Dropped Charges in Deadly Rape Provoke Fury in South Africa, and Pessimism." *New York Times,* June 8. https://www.nytimes.com/2013/06/09/world/africa/rape-and-murder-stirs-fury-in-south-africa.html.

Porter, Catherine. 2013. "Being a Woman in South Africa Enough to Get You Raped, Killed." *Toronto Star*, February 21, 2013. Canadian Points of View Reference Centre. EBSCOhost. login.ezproxy.library.ualberta.ca/login?url=http://search.ebscohost.com/login.aspx?direct=true&db=p3h&AN=6FP4217203017&site=eds-live&scope=site.

Razak, Sherene H. 2007. "Stealing the Pain of Others: Reflections on Canadian Humanitarian Responses." *Review of Education, Pedagogy, and Cultural Studies* 29, no. 4: 375–94.

Roychowdhury, Poulami. 2013. "'The Delhi Gang Rape': The Making of International Causes." *Feminist Studies* 39, no. 1: 282–92.

Samuelson, Meg. 2007. *Remembering the Nation, Dismembering Women? Stories of the South African Transition*. Durban: University of KwaZulu Natal Press.

Scully. Pamela. 1995. "Race, Rape and Colonial Culture: The Sexual Politics of Identity in the Nineteenth-Century Cape Colony, South Africa." *American Historical Review* 100, no. 2: 335–59.

Seedat, Mohamed, et al. 2009. "Violence and Injuries in South Africa: Prioritising an Agenda for Prevention." *Lancet* 374:1011–22.

Sielke, Sabine. 2002. *Reading Rape: The Rhetoric of Sexual Violence in American Literature and Culture, 1790–1990*. Princeton: Princeton University Press.

Sielke, Sabine. 2004. The Politics of the Strong Trope: Rape and the Feminist Debate in the United States." *Amerikastudien/American Studies* 49, no. 3: 367–84.

Smith, David. 2013. "South Africa Searches for Solutions after Teenage Girl's Gang Rape and Murder." *Guardian*, February 12. https://www.theguardian.com/world/2013/feb/13/south-africa-rape-murder.

Spillers, Hortense J. 1987. "Mama's Baby, Papa's Maybe: An American Grammar Book." *Diacritics* 11, no. 2 (Summer): 64–81.

Spivak, Gayatri Chakravorty. 2010. "Can the Subaltern Speak?" In *Can the Subaltern Speak? Reflections on the History of an Idea*. Ed. Rosalind Morris, 21–80. New York: Columbia University Press.

Statistics South Africa. 2012a. *Income and Expenditure of Households 2010/2011 Statistical Release P0100*. Pretoria: Statistics South Africa. http://www.statssa.gov.za/publications/P0100/P01002011.pdf.

Statistics South Africa. 2012b. *Gender Statistics in South Africa, 2011*. Pretoria: Statistics South Africa. http://www.statssa.gov.za/publications/Report-03-10-05/Report-03-10-052011.pdf.

Unattributed. 2013. "Shocking Attitudes to Rape in South Africa." *Sky News*, September 19. https://news.sky.com/story/shocking-attitudes-to-rape-in-south-africa-10433820.

Watson, Joy, and Vivienne Lalu. 2014. "Rupturing the Norms: The Social and Political Response to the Rape of Anene Booysen." Report produced for *Heinrich Böll Stiftung*, September 30. https://in.boell.org/sites/default/files/uploads/2014/03/rupturing_the_norms_saresponse_to_rape_anenebooysen.pdf.

Zapiro. 2013. "Gang Rape and Murder of 17-Year-Old Anene Booysen." *Mail and Guardian*, February 7. https://www.zapiro.com/cartoons/130207mg.

BOOK REVIEWS

Cultural Critique's commitment to cultural and intellectual debate and discussion is bolstered by the regular inclusion of reviews of both new and not-so-new books. Generally, books reviewed will have appeared within the past three years, although reviews of older books that are emerging or reemerging in intellectual debates are also welcome. As an academic publication, *Cultural Critique* sees itself as having a responsibility to devote space to authors whose work may not be otherwise reviewed. For *Cultural Critique*'s special issues, book reviews should share the issue's thematic focus. *Cultural Critique*'s book review editors solicit writers, books, and ideas for future contributions to this section of the journal. Please contact the book review editors at cultcrit@umn.edu or *Cultural Critique,* Department of Cultural Studies and Comparative Literature, 216 Pillsbury Drive S.E., 235 Nicholson Hall, University of Minnesota, Minneapolis, MN 55455–0229.

MELODRAMA AND ITS POLITICAL LEGACY

ORGIES OF FEELING: MELODRAMA AND THE POLITICS OF FREEDOM
BY ELISABETH R. ANKER

Koel Banerjee

Elisabeth R. Anker's *Orgies of Feeling: Melodrama and the Politics of Freedom* challenges the way the post-9/11 political discourse is popularly framed—that on "a clear and cloudless Tuesday at the dawn of the new millennium, the United States lost its innocence in a horrifying attack" (1). Instead, Anker reads the discourse of the "loss of innocence" that such a narrative is premised on, and the nation's virtue that was confirmed by this loss, through the lens of melodrama. Anker approaches melodrama not as an aesthetic mode but as a political genre that not only governs political rhetoric but more importantly creates a particular kind of citizenship and national identity, and even legitimizes the violence of state power. With contemporary U.S. politics as its principal object of inquiry, *Orgies of Feeling* maps the history, political strategies, and affective dimensions of melodrama as a political discourse. The book astutely analyzes the political firmament of the United States after 9/11, scrutinizing political speeches and media coverage, and also traces the historical conditions behind the popular civil consent that legitimized the violent state action that followed the attack. And by locating the Manichean underpinnings of melodrama outside the realm of aesthetics in the real world of politics and state power and action, her book is a valuable read for film and literary theorists who are interested in the dialectics of literary/cinematic form and their social contexts. Interdisciplinary in its scope and approach, *Orgies of Feeling* is a significant contribution to both political studies and to the study of narrative form.

Melodrama, as an aesthetic modality, comes into being in the aftermath of the French Revolution with the loss of the sacred as common denominator for imbuing everyday life with ethical significance. Peter Brooks argues that melodrama answers the longing for moral legibility in a world bereft of Church and monarch, "where the traditional imperatives of truth and ethics have been violently thrown into question, yet where the promulgation of truth and ethics, their instauration as a way of life, is of immediate, daily, political concern" (15). In a world bereft of moral absolutes, melodrama offers an ethical dimension to everyday life. To define the melodramatic modality, Anker draws on various literary and film theorists, including Linda Williams's breakdown of characteristics of melodramatic narratives in her seminal essay "Melodrama Revised." Following Williams, Anker identifies (aesthetic) melodrama as a mode that presents characters in the Manichean binary of good and evil, involves the loss of innocence of the victim-hero, and attempts to undo the loss through the dialectics of pathos and action. Anker notes that melodrama, with its emphasis on the quotidian, is identified in both literary and screen studies as the most popular form of American mass culture. The impact of melodrama is not limited to the narrative arts but is also found in religious and civic affairs, and even political rhetoric. Melodrama, Christine Gledhill argues, "acknowledges demands inadmissible in the codes of social, psychological or political discourse" (38). However, the pejorative association of melodrama with female "weepies" often came in the way of melodrama being considered a subject worthy of academic inquiry. Anker points out *Uncle Tom's Cabin* (1852) and *The Birth of a Nation* (1915) as prominent examples of American melodrama that transcend the personal as they grapple with racial issues. She also has a protracted analysis of *All That Heaven Allows* (1955), in addition to mentioning other notable women's "weepies" including *Stella Dallas* (1937) and *Mildred Pierce* (1945), as melodramatic takes on the-then contemporary social life to highlight the political dimension of what is often read as merely a lowbrow aesthetic mode.

Despite noting the dynamics of the personal and the social in these literary and cinematic melodramas, Anker makes a distinction between melodrama as an aesthetic genre and melodrama as a political genre. Crucial to this distinction is Anker's claim that the stakes of melodrama are more pervasive than mass culture. Though Anker extensively notes the political underpinnings of melodrama as an aesthetic enterprise, what Anker focuses on in this book is the more directly political use (and abuse) of melodrama, more specifically melodrama as employed by the political discourse of post-9/11 United States. However, Anker's distinction between aesthetic and political melodrama is not watertight. Anker continuously refers to various literary and cinematic instances of melodrama in order to scaffold her reading of political melodrama, both before and after 9/11. Her reading of what she terms "political melodrama," though steeped in political and social theory, also employs literary analysis, particularly rhetoric, and film theory in equal measure. With the constant back and forth between the aesthetic and political, it is hard to glean the difference between the two, especially because Anker relies so heavily on the aesthetic category while insisting that political melodrama is a separate genre. Critical theory has on countless occasions pointed out the dialectical nature of the relationship between the aesthetic and the political—for example, the debate between Bloch and Lukács on expressionism is as much about politics as aesthetics. More recently, Allen Feldman critiques realism, which has an antinomic relationship with melodrama, for giving expression to a kind of cultural anesthesia that desensitizes us to certain acts of violence, thus shedding light on the ways in which aesthetic form and the call for political action (or lack thereof) are linked. Given the long-standing intellectual investment in the intertwined relationship between the aesthetic and the political, Anker's insistence on the twain categories of melodrama as an aesthetic enterprise and political melodrama seems somewhat tenuous. In the absence of a precise definition of political melodrama, "Left Melodrama," the only chapter of her book where she does not ground her readings in literary and cinematic instances, remains, as we shall discuss later, schematic and somewhat unconvincing. This chapter, where she focuses on the political, almost at the expense of the aesthetic, lacks the nuance of the earlier chapters where her analysis of the political uses of melodrama garnered both clarity and coherence from her well-chosen examples of literary and screen melodramas.

What draws Anker to read U.S. politics after 9/11 as melodrama, prima facie an odd choice given its apparent lack of critical reception beyond film and literary studies, is that despite the mode's protean nature, melodrama creates a narrative of overcoming "unfreedom," whether domestic or on a larger scale, thus making it a very effective genre of political discourse. If the loss of innocence or virtue, with all its gendered connotations, is what motivates aesthetic melodrama, then the precondition of political melodrama is the loss of (or threat to) freedom or sovereignty. Anker, however, insists that she is "less interested in judging whether melodrama is right or wrong in its depictions political life—whether melodrama gives a true account or false one—than in discerning its multiple workings and effects, its different appeals for different sites of power and subjectivity" (7). Despite this caveat, she persuasively points out the ways in which the melodramatic modality compels an acceptance of undemocratic and rather violent forms of state-power. Cataloging similar moments of national crisis in the past, including the aftermath of Pearl Harbor and Cold War political rhetoric, Anker argues that it is the framing of these crises as a threat to national sovereignty that animates political melodrama. Melodramatic political discourse, like its aesthetic counterpart, operates within a moral economy that creates the conditions for the victim to emerge as the hero, motivated as it is by a desire for freedom. "Unfreedom," Anker's shorthand, it must be noted, is not the pyrrhic loss of a sense of American sovereignty in the aftermath of 9/11 but points to the larger conditions of the neoliberal era, including disenfranchisement, loss of agency in the face of the forces of global capital, financial instability, outsourcing of working- and middle-class jobs, and the opaque workings of the governmental agencies. Anker demonstrates how the state mobilizes melodramatic discourse to legitimize its monopoly on violence. Anker draws on Nietzsche's formulation "orgies of feeling" to explain this seemingly sudden outburst of popular opinion in favor of violent state action to reclaim this perceived loss of sovereignty. Orgies of feeling, she points out, "describe a counterintuitive attempt to ameliorate confusing feelings of powerlessness by imposing intense affects of victimization—including terror, pain, sorrow, helplessness, and shock—upon the self" (15). Anker ties this Nietzschean idea to melodrama's Brooksian structure of "confrontation of clearly identified antagonists and the expulsion of one of them" (17).

Although for its detractors, melodrama simply amplifies the mundane affairs of daily life, and hence the pejorative tag of "excess" that becomes the albatross swung around its neck; Anker is not so much interested in questions of excess but in how melodrama as a political discourse becomes the norm, especially in moments of national crisis.

Anker posits that in melodramatic orgies of feeling, the response to loss (of innocence or of sovereignty) is in the cathartic creation of an energizing subjectivity that aims to overthrow the conditions that caused this victimhood. The victim-heroes of melodramatic political discourse, unlike their aesthetic counterparts, emerge victorious and, in being thus empowered, are no longer suffering victims as melodramatic protagonists sometimes are, even at the moment of denouement. While the victim-heroes of literary and screen melodramas might or might not emerge victorious, given that such melodramas operate within the dyad of "too-late or in-the-nick-of-time," the victim-heroes of political melodramas are always victors. This premise of a guaranteed victory that political melodrama hinges on only enables people of privilege to see and present themselves as the victims (and eventual heroes) of political melodramas. In times of rampant and pervasive racist and casteist violence, the victims outnumber the victim-heroes. The socially marginalized rarely ever become the victim-heroes that political melodrama champions. The energizing subjectivity of the orgies of feeling that Anker writes about is not a universal given. The center–periphery dynamic of the world-system often determines the relative valences of acts of terror and thus sets the limits to what response to such acts are deemed appropriate.

The first chapter frames the media depictions of events immediately after 9/11 as political melodrama. This chapter, pithy and persuasive, recounts the media reportage and lays down some of the primary characteristics and conventions of the melodramatic political discourse. Anker argues that political melodramas, unlike screen and literary melodramas, which tend to be unstable as far as their generic conventions are concerned, have more solid and discernable conventions. In a manner similar to Williams's breakdown of easily identifiable features of melodramatic narratives, Anker posits that political melodramas are marked by a moral economy of good and evil. This moral economy shapes a national identity that equates the U.S. nation-state and a particular kind of citizenship as the good, and designates any threat to national and individual sovereignty as evil. It is evil, the embodiment of the Nietzsche's concept of the "venomous eye," that confers both desirability, despite the cost, and a sense of inevitability, however delayed, to the good. Political melodrama is, in this account, the most effective genre of political discourse in moments of national crisis, since the nation (and by metonymic extension, the citizen) has already proven its goodness simply by virtue of the threat posed by the venomous eye. Political action is mapped on the Manichean order of victims, heroes, and villains. In addition, this framework, comprised solely of victims-villains-heroes, that makes certain kinds of violence against the nation morally legible, renders more everyday and more rampant violence illegible. Some injuries are worthy of identification through "intensified affect" while others remain inscrutable. Given the current political moment, especially after the 2016 U.S. elections, one could even argue that political melodrama creates a false narrative of white victimization; thus, instead of making violence rarified, it makes it more rampant. Not only is the state sanctioned to carry out violent acts (including travel bans and deportation) in the name of national security, such legitimization of state violence emboldens people to often be blatantly racist and xenophobic. As Williams points out in her study of race in American popular culture, as we increasingly pretend to "live in an achieved era of equal rights for all, race has joined the category of the officially inexpressible. Mentioning it is considered in bad taste, a cynical ploy, 'playing the race card'" (2001, 300). Anker extends Williams's argument to point out that playing the race card is seen, in contexts of melodramatic framing of national tragedies, as going against national interest.

Like its aesthetic counterpart, Anker argues, political melodrama sides with the powerless. However, it creates the narrative "that makes sense of the feeling of being besieged by a dominant power, whether powerlessness that seems to come from communist infiltration of U.S. institutions, from nefarious immigrants out to steal jobs of virtuous citizens, or from the overwhelming power of capital in the counter-melodrama of left political discourse" (35–36). This dramatization of powerlessness, Anker argues, is a power strategy in that it harnesses public consent to reclaim control and thereby creates conditions for the inevitable triumph of freedom. Melodramatic orgies of feeling, motivated by a desire for freedom, can only take place if the injury is given primacy in its treatment by the melodramatic political discourse. Anker points out that the "sensation scenes" present in media coverage of the 9/11 attacks "encourages pathos in the spectator, and the 'sensation' registers aspects of seeing, feeling, and hearing to reveal the moral goodness found in both the visual scene and in the spectator who empathizes with the victims onscreen" (49–50). While the events of 9/11 brought the feeling of powerlessness of the nation and its citizens into sharp relief, the various conditions of "unfreedom" that, in an amorphous manner already festered, were given shape and a more readily identifiable enemy in the form of those who carried out the attack. Anker traces this victimhood, narrated by the popular media as a loss of sovereignty, to more pervasive and more historical conditions. The sense of powerlessness that had been festering, albeit at a more unconscious level, was amplified by conventions of political melodrama governing the image of the attacks and their coverage by the popular press. Anker persuasively claims that the Nietzschean orgies of feeling resulted from a long-term sense of powerlessness that was given form and a more discernable antagonist in the aftermath of 9/11. She points out: "Melodrama creates a politics in which state action requires national suffering" (61). The piecing together of current events in a manner that is morally and emotionally legible is not the only task that the melodramatic political discourse achieves; it presents America as that space of innocence that has been attacked and therefore must be defended.

Asserting that America is no stranger to melodrama as a dominant mode of political expression, since political discourse has categorized the world in the binaries of good and bad since the days of Eisenhower, Anker claims that the popularity of melodrama in recent times owes a lot to the genre's allegiance to the tenets of liberalism from its very inception in the aftermath of the French Revolution. While melodrama was the ubiquitous mode of American popular culture, presenting ultimately virtuous victim-heroes who were guileless in the face of evil; melodrama as a political genre framed the discourse of the Cold War era, presenting a narrative that legitimized the national security state. Anker offers a detailed archive of melodramatic political rhetoric at various moments of American history, and quite compellingly points out that postwar state power is bolstered by, and in fact draws its legitimacy in the public eye from, melodrama. Melodrama, in the way Brooks formulates it, is always political. Melodrama often aids the apparent egalitarianism of neoliberal politics by not questioning the injustices meted out by race, class, and gender-based social structures. Instead it subsumes these inequalities under the rubric of a "civic nationalism" that is defined by an abstract promise of freedom but elides the question of real lived conditions of inequality and lack of freedom. The citizenship constructed by melodrama, Anker argues, is one where "as long as you believe in the goodness of the victimized nation and trust state institutions to enable individual freedom, then this form of melodrama accepts you as a virtuous citizen. But your inclusion, and virtue, is predicated on your acceptance that your particular and racialized experiences of inequality and unfreedom are irrelevant to the construction of American goodness" (87). In depicting the nation as the true victim, thus legitimizing the state to employ all necessary means to defend it, political melodramas efface all other victims, including citizens who are victims of state-violence. This is as true now as it was in the immediate aftermath of 9/11. Heroism, in the weltanschauung espoused by a melodramatic modality, is in capitalist work ethic. In acceptance of racial and gendered inequalities, in unquestioning trust in state power, and in uninterrupted work, the worker emerges the hero of the melodramatic narrative, and even as the ideal citizen that such discourse posits.

If melodrama upholds a citizenship based on the acceptance of certain conditions of inequality and state power, how can its popularity as an aesthetic or political genre be explained? One way to explain this is by arguing that people are gullible and therefore are easily hoodwinked by popular culture or political rhetoric. This explanation, in its oversimplification, is rather inadequate in explaining how the genre has not only survived but has actually thrived. Anker has an alternative hypothesis for how melodramatic political discourse legitimizes often undemocratic forms of state power and intervention. The state, Anker argues, is always authorized. Anker, drawing on Weber and Foucault's political theories of power, argues that it is "felt legitimacy," as opposed to formal legitimacy, that, as the affective dimension of state power, mobilizes popular consent in times of crises. She points out that "the feeling the pain of national injury is equivalent to feeling the legitimacy of state power that will respond to it" (111). It is this "felt legitimacy" that ironically makes citizens not only accept but also deem desirable state surveillance, racial profiling, and even war, as the price to pay for a future of unfettered freedom. Felt legitimacy is real consent, reaffirming the conviction of citizens that only state action, however violent and antidemocratic, can undo the grievous injustice done to them by nonstate actors. However, such popular consent for intervention by the state can be sustained only for short periods of time. Anker reminds us that melodrama as a long-term political discourse to bolster public support for state power is ineffective and tenuous, as can be seen from the outraged public reaction to knowledge about the state-sponsored violence and curtailment of human rights in Guantanamo and Abu Ghraib.

The first five chapters of *Orgies of Feeling* build off of one another; and although they are somewhat repetitive, Anker manages to forcefully and convincingly make the case that melodrama imbues political discourse with an affective dimension to procure public consent for state power in the face of national crisis brought about by an easily identifiable nonstate party. Anker's claims are backed up by archival work, painstaking and in-depth analysis of political rhetoric and media coverage going way beyond the 9/11 attacks, and a historical grounding and account of the popularity of melodrama in America. Her reading of the affective landscape that melodrama, in its political avatar, creates makes her contribution valuable to not just political theory but also to melodrama scholars in the fields of literary and media studies. The final chapter of the book, "Left Melodrama," however, lacks the archival resources and the nuance of the previous chapters and is more of an afterthought than an integral part of her argument. While the question of melodrama in leftist discourse is an important one, Anker's assessment of the emancipatory and radical potential of melodrama remains somewhat wanting. It must be noted that the chapter holds importance for pointing out the radical possibilities of melodrama, which is often read as simply the resort of conservative politics. Taking her cue from Gledhill, Anker points out that given melodrama's tendency to categorize the world as victims and villains can be both reactionary and radical. The primary characteristic of melodrama of a more leftist disposition, according to Anker, is what Walter Benjamin referred to as left-wing melancholy, whereby thought itself is rendered a fetish object. While the common denominator to both mourning and melancholia is loss, according to Freud, "melancholia is in some way related to an object-loss which is withdrawn from consciousness, in contradiction to mourning, in which there is nothing about the loss that is unconscious" (245). For the mourner, it is a conscious and locatable loss; while for the melancholic, the deep feeling and sorrow for the loss becomes unconscious. In Freud's words, "In mourning it is the world which has become poor and empty; in melancholia it is the ego itself" (246). Anker argues that "left melodrama is underpinned by a refusal to acknowledge the loss of left political theory's guarantee to provide a means to revolutionary freedom, as well as the loss of intrinsic moral virtue implicitly granted to its practitioners" (205).

Anker identifies *The Communist Manifesto* as the lost object that animates left melancholy. While *The Communist Manifesto* has been previously interpreted as melodrama by Wylie Sypher and Jane Gaines; Anker's argument about the unconscious nature of such loss would benefit from more grounding. Is it the loss of the ideals of the manifesto or the realization, although unconscious, of the impossibility of such ideals in the present age? The other losses that Anker points out earlier in the book, the unconscious feeling of unfreedom that festered before finally finding an outlet and a villain in the aftermath of 9/11, how do they figure in this left-wing melancholia? The abrupt transition from the *Manifesto* to Agamben, Hardt, and Negri, bypassing the long and uneven history of materialism in the interim period, makes this chapter more schematic and even somewhat lacking in the in-depth analysis of the previous chapters. While the importance of the three thinkers she focuses on is unquestionable; Anker's rationale for focusing on these three thinkers simply for being the 'most popular critical theory in left academe' is not adequate, especially when she elides the question of Marxism and post-Marxism altogether. Neither does she address anticapitalist movements like Occupy Wall Street, thus limiting the Left to only academic discourse. Echoing Wendy Brown, Anker is committed to the concept of melancholy; however she is in certain ways identifying nostalgia as the underlying foundation of melodrama. Fredric Jameson's concept of nostalgia as the cultural logic of late capitalism could have an alternative scaffold for Anker's argument—or, perhaps even Theodor Adorno's observations on the melancholy science or the political consequences of thought in *Minima Moralia*. In sum, this chapter remains arcane, especially because it is not rooted in textual analysis (filmic or literary), unlike the previous chapters, which had better grounding in textual examples that supported and explained her argument.

Writing a history of the present is an impossible task. Anker's attempt is, however, commendable. The truth of her argument, about unfreedom and felt legitimacy, echo in the immediate present, as the

2016 U.S. elections have shown us. "Make America Great Again" is nothing but shorthand for the false narrative of white victimization. Such a narrative, melodramatic in its undertone, casts immigrants, refugees, Muslims, and African Americans as the threats to American greatness, which has to be reclaimed. The populist rhetoric of the election can be read as yet another instance of Nietzschean orgies of feeling, where the affective dimension of political melodrama is of a xenophobic nature. The loss of sovereignty is the boogeyman that haunts the public imagination enough to trigger Brexit and elect Trump. The greatest triumph of this book, then, is that it not only explains the support behind state-sanctioned warfare after 9/11 but helps us understand the ramifications of political melodrama in our present moment.

Koel Banerjee is a PhD candidate in comparative studies in discourse and society at the Department of Cultural Studies and Comparative Literature, University of Minnesota. Her doctoral dissertation, "Bollywood and the Aesthetic of Consumption," explores how an ethic of consumption underwrites the discourse on Bollywood cinema. Her research interests include Indian cinema, global melodrama, cosmopolitanism, aesthetic theory, and postcolonial theory and criticism.

Works Cited

Adorno, Theodor W., and Edmund F. N. Jephcott. 2005. *Minima Moralia: Reflections on a Damaged Life*. London: Verso.

Anker, Elisabeth Robin. 2014. *Orgies of Feeling: Melodrama and the Politics of Freedom*. Durham: Duke University Press.

Benjamin, Walter. 1974. "Left-Wing Melancholy: On Erich Kästner's New Book of Poems." *Screen* 15, no. 2: 28–32.

Brooks, Peter. 1976. *The Melodramatic Imagination: Balzac, Henry James, Melodrama, and the Mode of Excess*. New Haven, Yale University Press.

Feldman, Allen. 1994. "On Cultural Anesthesia: From Desert Storm to Rodney King." *American Ethnologist* 21, no. 2: 404–18. www.jstor.org/stable/645896.

Freud, Sigmund. 1957. "Mourning and Melancholia." In *The Standard Edition of the Complete Works of Sigmund Freud*. Vol. 14. Ed. and Trans. James Strachey, 243–58. London: Hogarth Press and the Institute of Psycho-analysis.

Gledhill, Christine. 1987. "The Melodramatic Field: An Investigation" In *Home Is Where the Heart Is: Studies in Melodrama and the Woman's Film*. Ed. Christine Geldhill, 5–39. London: British Film Institute.

Jameson, Fredric. 1991. *Postmodernism, or the Cultural Logic of Late Capitalism*. Durham: Duke University Press.

Williams, Linda. 1998. "Melodrama Revised." In *Refiguring American Film Genres: History and Theory*. Ed. Nick Browne, 42–88. Berkeley: University of California Press.

Williams, Linda. 2001. *Playing the Race Card: Melodramas of Black and White from Uncle Tom to O. J. Simpson*. Princeton: Princeton University Press.

BOOKS RECEIVED

Ahmed, Siraj. *Archaeology of Babel: The Colonial Foundation of the Humanities*. Stanford: Stanford University Press, 2018.

Balfour, Lindsay Anne. *Hospitality in a Time of Terror: Strangers at the Gate*. Lewisburg, Pa.: Bucknell University Press, 2018.

Biehl, João, and Peter Locke, eds. *Unfinished: The Anthropology of Becoming*. Durham: Duke University Press, 2017.

Carnes, Natalie. *Image and Presence: A Christological Reflection on Iconoclasm and Iconophilia*. Stanford: Stanford University Press, 2018.

Christian, Aymar Jean. *Open TV: Innovation beyond Hollywood and the Rise of Web Television*. New York: New York University Press, 2018.

Gallope, Michael. *Deep Refrains: Music, Philosophy, and the Ineffable*. Chicago: University of Chicago Press, 2017.

Green-Simms, Lindsey B. *Postcolonial Automobility: Car Culture in West Africa*. Minneapolis: University of Minnesota Press, 2017.

Hughes, Kathryn. *Victorians Undone: Tales of the Flesh in the Age of Decorum*. Baltimore: Johns Hopkins University Press, 2018.

Langford, Catherine L. *Scalia v. Scalia: Opportunistic Textualism in Constitutional Interpretation*. Tuscaloosa: University of Alabama Press, 2017.

Lause, Mark A. *The Great Cowboy Strike: Bullets, Ballots, & Class Conflicts in the American West*. New York: Verso, 2017.

Marran, Christine L. *Ecology without Culture: Aesthetics for a Toxic World*. Minneapolis: University of Minnesota Press, 2017.

McGowan, Todd. *Only a Joke Can Save Us: A Theory of Comedy*. Evanston: Northwestern University Press, 2017.

Neves, Joshua, and Bhaskar Sarkar, eds. *Asian Video Cultures: In the Penumbra of the Global*. Durham: Duke University Press, 2017.

Parker, Emily Anne, and Anne van Leeuwen, eds. *Differences: Rereading Beauvoir and Irigaray*. New York: Oxford University Press, 2018.

Robbins, Bruce. *The Beneficiary*. Durham: Duke University Press, 2017.

Singh, Julietta. *Unthinking Mastery: Dehumanism and Decolonial Entanglements*. Durham: Duke University Press, 2018.

Snorton, C. Riley. *Black on Both Sides: A Racial History of Trans Identity*. Minneapolis: University of Minnesota Press, 2017.

Snyder, Gregory J. *Skateboarding LA: Inside Professional Street Skateboarding*. New York: New York University Press, 2017.

Stage, Kelly J. *Producing Early Modern London: A Comedy of Urban Space, 1598–1616*. Lincoln: University of Nebraska Press, 2018.

Szendy, Peter. *Of Stigmatology: Punctuation as Experience*. New York: Fordham University Press, 2018.

Tautz, Brigit. *Translating the World: Toward a New History of German Literature around 1800*. University Park: Pennsylvania State University Press, 2018.

Van Deusen, Nancy E. *Embodying the Sacred: Women Mystics in Seventeenth-Century Lima*. Durham: Duke University Press, 2018.

Vardoulakis, Dimitris. *Stasis before the State: Nine Theses on Agnostic Democracy*. New York: Fordham University Press, 2018.

Zigon, Jarrett. *Disappointment: Toward a Critical Hermeneutics of Worldbuilding*. New York: Fordham University Press, 2018.

Zylinska, Joanna. *Nonhuman Photography*. Cambridge, Mass.: MIT Press, 2017.